Equality and Sex Discrimination Law

Equality and Sex Discrimination Law

Katherine O'Donovan and
Erika Szyszczak

BASIL BLACKWELL

Copyright © K. O'Donovan and E. Szyszczak 1988

First published 1988

Basil Blackwell Ltd
108 Cowley Road, Oxford, OX4 1JF, UK

Basil Blackwell Inc.
432 Park Avenue South, Suite 1503
New York, NY 10016, USA

British Library Cataloguing in Publication Data
O'Donovan, Katherine.
  Equality and sex discrimination law.

  Includes index.
  1. Sex discrimination in employment—Law and
legislation—Great Britain. 2. Sex discrimination
against women—Law and legislation—Great Britain.
I. Szyszczak, Erika. II. Title.
KD3103.W6036 1988   344.41'01133 88–11452
ISBN 0–631–14771–3   344.1041133
ISBN 0–631–15598–8 (pbk.)

Library of Congress Cataloging in Publication Data
O'Donovan, Katherine
  Equality and sex discrimination law.
  1. Great Britain. Women,. Sex discrimination
by society. Law
I. Title II. Szyszczak, Erika
344.102'878

  ISBN 0–631–14771–3
  ISBN 0–631–15598–8 Pbk

Typeset in 10 on 12 pt Times
by Downdell Ltd, Abingdon, Oxon.
Printed in Great Britain by Billing & Sons Ltd, Worcester.

To the memory of Victoria Fisher

Contents

Foreword

The fact that this book is dedicated to Victoria Fisher will need no explanation to the academic lawyers who knew her, nor to her family, friends, and past students. This dedication, however, is not simply a way of making public an appreciation of Victoria's friendship, both personal and professional, nor of celebrating a life tragically cut short. The dedication of this book, on a topic with which she was closely concerned, is an act of commitment to her ideals, her standards, and above all her dreams of a flourishing feminist legal scholarship. It is a commitment that many of her friends and colleagues share. Indeed, although her death was an extremely sad event and our grief and sense of loss enormous, perhaps the enduring reaction is one of reinvigoration, a response found not only among the women lawyers in this country and abroad with whom Victoria worked, but also among friends and colleagues in other areas of her life. In order to know why a young woman in her thirties should evoke such an exceptional response from so many people, it is necessary to know a little bit about Victoria herself.

Victoria would have been the last person to consider herself special in any way. She would have pointed to the thousand and one ways in which she was similar to the people she knew and loved. Like many of her friends she was a young university lecturer, teaching law at Leicester University. She threw herself enthusiastically into teaching, into her reading, and research. Like many of her generation she combined her paid work with a range of voluntary work in her community, which included advising on housing issues and establishing educational courses outside her university. In addition she was an active member of her trade union and a driving force behind its Women's Committee, for which she acted as convenor. During this time she worked to set up the constitution of that committee, spearheaded the campaign for widowers' pensions, and worked on the publication of the positive action pack which served as a blueprint for future activity. Her commitment, determination and sheer hard work, even when she was seriously ill, were crucial to the successful outcome of a sex discrimination case brought by Dr Huppert against the University Grants Committee.[1] This particular case led to one female academic being appointed to a 'new blood' position from which she had been excluded by the discriminatory age rules. The change in rules and the point of principle at issue should ensure a wider and easier access for women to academic posts in the future, a concern of great importance to Victoria herself.

This is not the only way in which Victoria's actions and efforts during her life continue to benefit women in practice. As a feminist Victoria's commitment to women was strong. For her, the saying, 'the personal is political', was never more true than when she complained to the Ombudsman over maladministration of her treatment for breast cancer. She was determined that no other woman should suffer the same way that she had done. While others might have felt the injustice, she did something about it. She had energy, enthusiasm, tenacity but also extremely sound judgment. In part this stemmed from the fact that she was an excellent lawyer. She subjected both sides of every argument to the most detailed scrutiny. She had a fine mind, she probed deeply and presented her arguments coherently and cogently. However it was also due to the fact that she was totally honest, to herself above all else.

This honesty was her courage and her strength. In my experience she never seemed afraid to admit her doubts or her weaknesses. One could of course say that we were friends, and that when we met to discuss work, we always met in supportive situations. One of the objects of the Women Law Teachers Group which she helped to set up, and to which Erika, Katherine and I all belong, was to provide a forum for examining our personal career problems as well as our feminist academic work. When I think of Victoria in those meetings, whether they were in friends' homes or in larger gatherings, I can always see her sitting well back in her chair and quietly expressing her difficulties as a way of expressing solidarity with all of us in that group. After the rest of us had talked for a while, sometimes at a tangent, often not wanting to expose ourselves to even that supportive gathering of feminist friends, Victoria's comments would be direct, open, and absolutely to the point. Immediately people were enabled to talk more openly, and we moved forward in whatever matter was to hand.

Victoria was the antithesis of a person who talks about herself, drawing attention inwards. She was an excellent listener and communicator. Indeed she was the expression of the facilitative type of teaching she expounded. One of her pleasures was that the chapter in the book *How to Study Law*[2] which she wrote with colleagues at Leicester University, in which she tried to give students the means to learn for themselves, had attracted favourable critical comment. It was not just the pleasure one gets from peer-group approval, a pleasure which must have been particularly sweet because she agonized about her writing. It was also that she had succeeded in what she set out to do, to pass on to a wider audience the skills she shared with her own students. I don't suppose she realized just how much the rest of us had learnt from her about feminist methodologies in teaching. Although, of course, that chapter will be immensely important to the students who read it, many more students will benefit because their teachers have learnt from Victoria how to be non-hierarchical, to encourage, guide and enable students to learn for themselves.

When she died, I think many of her family and friends, like me, were amazed to learn about her life. She was a very rounded person. She loved to travel, to see new places and meet new people, but also put much effort into creating a home with her partner Ian. Indeed she derived much pleasure from the home they created together, and the beautiful garden in which she worked in her last year. At her death we discovered a wide range of activities, people and facets of her life that we had never heard about. I think it was because she met people on their own terms. She was genuinely interested in people and tried to understand what was important to them. She concentrated on shared concerns and shared pleasures. In doing so she seemed to live primarily in the present, to give unhurriedly of her time and attentions to each of us.

When she knew she had little longer to live she determined to make the most of what time was left. She continued with plans to research into affirmative action in Australia, going for a shorter time than had been originally envisaged, but nevertheless collecting material, arranging interviews and typically assisting on a book on affirmative action. The courage of that decision, and of her determination to come home on her own when she was dying, is a source of inspiration to all of us who knew her.

We have lost our warm, supportive friend and inevitably feel regret that we can no longer share life with her. For she was great fun to be with, and for me New York will be inextricably linked with her laughter, verve and sense of wonderment at the sights, the women law academics we met, and the visions that we shared with them. The conference we attended there together – a national meeting of women law academics, practitioners, and students from all across the United States – was a four-day event of sharing experiences, learning and debating. It filled Victoria's mind with a dream of something similar in the United Kingdom for feminist lawyers. Just such a conference occurred at Easter 1986, when European Critical Legal Studies took as its theme, Feminist Perspectives on Law. Although she was very ill, and she never wrote up for publication the innovative paper she gave on motherhood, it gave Victoria tremendous satisfaction to participate in the three-day event and to meet so many women concerned with feminist legal research and scholarship. For her vision was not confined to conferences, to the formal sharing of knowledge and ideas. She realized the importance of informal contacts, and had in her writing and practical involvement tried to develop new forms to meet women's experiences and women's needs. She was committed to the development of feminist legal theory by academics, by students, by women engaged in the law outside higher education.[3] She knew the importance of working from women's own experience rather than starting from the construction of law. Her vision of feminist legal scholarship was one that not only breaks with existing knowledge and ways of seeing; it challenged the very forms by which academia and the law work. In one of her last pieces, she wrote:

> male dominance is not confined to those acts of discrimination now outlawed, but extends to domestic and sexual relations, to visual images and the very language we use. Law is only one weapon in a range of strategies which need to be developed to end women's subordination, and it should not be forgotten that this weapon is still used to entrench the status quo in some areas even while espousing change in others. The limits of law need clearer recognition.

Victoria would have welcomed this book. She contributed to it in many ways, not simply because of her practical work with discrimination in the trade union and the *Huppert* case. She was part of our discussions and thoughts for many years. She will continue to be part of our work in the years to come.

Susan Atkins

Notes

1 *Huppert* v. *UGC* is discussed in chapter 4, on p. 101.
2 Bradney, A., Fisher, V., Masson, J., Neal, A. and Newell, D. *How to Study Law* (London, Sweeter & Moscevell, 1986).
3 In recognition of this the Faculty of Law at Leicester University have established a Victoria Fisher Prize to be awarded annually to the best essay on women and law.

Preface

This is a book which exposes current legislative attempts to give women equal opportunity with men to a critical and reflective study. This legislation is now part of our current public and political rhetoric and we feel it is time for the legislation to be subjected to an appraisal which brings both legal and feminist analyses to bear upon it. Those who read the book will find a sense of disappointment at the limited success of anti-discrimination legislation. Yet it has an importance. By engaging with it in a dialectical process women can put forward their perspectives on equality. The legislation provides some recourse for individual employees seeking jobs or justice. The inadequacies and limitations of the legislation form part of the study of this book. Engagement, however frustrating, is a first step in dialogue.

The legislation and the discourse which surrounds it is couched in a bureaucratic, regulatory form. This is the language used by lawyers, courts, politicians, union officials, employers. It is foreign to many of those who wish to challenge sex discriminatory assumptions and arrangements which prevail in the United Kingdom today. Of necessity this book also uses the legislative discourse. But this must not be taken to mean that we are committed to this. The entry of women into the labour market does seem to be an acceptance of the market on its own terms. In reality women are forced to juggle with home and work, and this is reflected in a bilingualism: there is the language of care and the language of bureaucracy. Where possible we also have tried to be bilingual: to juxtapose the legal discourse and women's perspectives.

The integration of women into the labour market, and thus into existing economic, political and social organizations, is the goal of the legislation. On issues of current arrangements of domestic life the legislation is silent. It is for women to accommodate themselves to present structures. We have attempted to look at alternatives through use of the legislation and outside it. However, we recognize that while issues of equality can be discussed in several languages, those in a position of power have to be addressed in terms of the dominant discourse.

The book is intended for use on law courses which deal with sex discrimination and on women's studies courses. We hope that it will also be of practical value to those contemplating legal action, for it points out what can be expected. We have both been involved in teaching women's studies courses at undergraduate and postgraduate level and in teaching law courses. We have also given practical advice to applicants contemplating legal action and to those interested in reforming their work practices to accord with the legislation.

This book has been written over two years, during which time one of us has become a mother. Domestic commitments and separation at different academic institutions has meant that collaboration has sometimes been difficult. This accounts for differences of tone and style. We feel we are agreed on major issues discussed and that, as the book argues, differences have to be accommodated. Katherine O'Donovan has written chapters 1, 2, 3 and 8, Erika Szyszczak has written chapters 4–7.

A colleague and close friend of ours, Victoria Fisher of Leicester University, died during the time the book was being written. A sister and founder-member of the Women Law Teachers Group she was actively engaged in practical and academic work on sex discrimination. As a tribute to the tenacity and courage which inspired those who worked with her we dedicate this book to her memory. Susan Atkins of Southampton University has kindly written a dedication on behalf of all Victoria's friends.

Katherine O'Donovan
Erika Szyszczak

Chapter 1

The Quest for Equality

The coming into force in December 1975 of the Sex Discrimination Act 1975 and the Equal Pay Act 1970 was heralded as the commencement of an era of equality for women. The equality laws were preceded by a government White Paper, *Equality for Women*.[1] Ideas about equality therefore were placed firmly on the national agenda of the United Kingdom. What this chapter intends to show is that a variety of conceptions of equality may underpin the laws with little agreement on definition. These different conceptions of equality are explored here.

In political terms the idea of equality under the law is a major justification for the rule of law itself. It is evident that where formal barriers prevent certain citizens from entering educational institutions or the professions, from voting, or being public representatives, these citizens are not equal under the law. Furthermore where these barriers are *de jure* – that is, upheld by the law – then inequality is sanctioned by law. This, in turn, undermines the rule of law which fails to deliver its promise of equality. Law's legitimacy is called into question. Those subjected to legal barriers will deny the law's claims to fairness.

The removal of *de jure* barriers to women's access to the benefits and burdens of citizenship was a first stage on the road to equality, to the full participation of women in all aspects of social life. An example is the Sex Disqualification Removal Act 1919.[2] Equal status of women under the law became part of the justification for the rule of law, which it had not been previously. However it remains unclear in discussions of equality whether equal status is a formal legal category or a material condition.[3] Also unspecified is the conception of equality which underpins the anti-discrimination legislation. Ideas about equality are a matter of serious debate. We shall examine a variety of definitions and their consequences if applied through legislation and other measures. Since any formulation of a question defines the problem and the limits of its solution, the object here will be to canvass a broad spectrum of definitions.

Conceptions of Equality

The idea of equality, which is the mainspring of anti-discrimination legislation, lacks precision. In political discussion the idea of equality may be used descriptively, as a statement of fact that all persons are equal. It may also be used prescriptively, as a statement of aims that all persons should be equal. The assertion that all persons *are* equal is not self-evident; it runs into day-to-day experience of a world in which this is clearly not so. It also runs into a series of questions: equal in which respects, to whom, in what contexts? Underlying such questions is the general query: what do we mean by equality?

Equality as a statement of aims, as a prescription, appears to underlie the objects of anti-discrimination legislation. Since this is a book about equality of women with men, and since the declared aim is to investigate the British legislation on sex discrimination and equal pay, the scope of inquiry can be narrowed somewhat. So a starting point is the suggestion that the enactment of sex discrimination legislation in Britain in the 1970s was prescriptive. It represented official recognition that women and men were not equal in many areas of life. Behind this was an official belief that women and men should be treated as equals in those specific fields covered by the legislation.

Language concerning equality through anti-discrimination legislation is the language of aspiration – that all persons should be treated as equals. This is based on an idea of the fundamental equality of all human beings, of human rights. It is a relatively modern ideal. 'Liberté, egalité, fraternité' were the concepts which inspired the French revolution. It was her study of these that led Mary Wollstonecraft to raise issues about the rights of women. But given the context of women's position when she was writing, her view of equality was inevitably limited. She confined herself to advocating education for women on a par with men, as better preparation for the roles of wife and mother. Hers was an instrumental argument, in that she did not challenge structures which excluded women from participation in the public world of work and politics, but rather suggested that education would improve their performance in the domestic sphere. Only once does she suggest that there might be something more:

> A wild wish has just flown from my heart to my head, and I will not stifle it, though it may excite a horse-laugh. I do earnestly wish to see the distinction of sex confounded in society, unless where love animates the behaviour. For this distinction is, I am firmly persuaded, the foundation of the weakness of character ascribed to women.[4]

Wollstonecraft's vision of a society which makes no distinction as to sex is one version of sexual equality. This vision has been projected in modern analysis of sexual inequality by a legal philosopher.

Richard Wasserstrom points out that sex is a central organizing category in society. Unlike eye colour, which is an irrelevant category, an unimportant cultural fact, sex is crucial. 'It is evident that there are substantially different role expectations and role assignments to persons in accordance with their sexual physiology, and that the positions of the two sexes in culture are distinct.'[5] The author reviews the possibility that in the just society sex and race would be no more important than eye colour. This he terms 'the assimilationist ideal'. He poses the question whether this is the type of society to be produced by a vision of sex equality.

> On the attitudinal and conceptual level, the assimilationist ideal would require the eradication of all sex-role differentiation. It would never teach about the inevitable or essential attributes of masculinity or femininity; it would never encourage or discourage the ideas of sisterhood or brother-hood; and it would be unintelligible to talk about the virtues as well as the disabilities of being a woman or a man. Were sex like eye color, these things would make no sense.[6]

Behind this lies a theoretical debate which goes to a fundamental issue about anti-discrimination legislation and sex equality. Is the vision a society which incorporates the assimilationist ideal in which sex is no more important than eye colour? Or is the vision a society which accom-modates sexual differentiation without penalty? As Wasserstrom admits, it may be that 'pluralistic ideals founded on diversity and tolerance'[7] are a more appropriate way of handling sexual differentiation. This funda-mental question remains as yet unresolved in feminist theory.

What Wollstonecraft and Wasserstrom raise is the possibility that achievement of equality of the sexes depends on the assimilationist ideal.[8] No programme to eliminate all public distinctions based on sex has been attempted anywhere. Anti-discrimination legislation in the United Kingdom does address issues of equality, but in a more limited form. These limitations relate to matters such as the scope of the legislation, its mechanisms and remedies, and the idea of equality under-lying it. This book explores in detail issues of scope, mechanisms and remedies. An explanation of the ideas officially presented to justify the legislation will help to elucidate conceptions of equality.

The notion of equality which appears to have motivated the United Kingdom legislation on sex discrimination and equal pay is equal oppor-tunity. The White Paper which preceded the legislation declared the government's resolution 'to introduce effective measures to discourage discriminatory conduct and to promote genuine equality of opportunity for both sexes'.[9] In liberal discourse the notion of equal opportunity which was widely used in Parliament is employed to deal with perceived inequalities. Bernard Williams makes a distinction between inequality of need and inequality of merit. Need can be satisfied by simple distri-bution, whereas 'merit has a competitive sense. . . . [I]t is appropriate to speak in the case of merit, not only of a distribution of the good, but of a distribution of the opportunity of achieving the good'.[10] Competition on merit is what equal opportunity is about. To overcome the question of the relationship between need and merit liberal writers advocate minimal state provision for need, after which all compete on merit. Thus intervention because of need or inequality is a justification for state action, regulation or legislation. Thereafter the role of the state is to hold the ring for free competition.

Other writings contrast equality of opportunity with equality of outcome. For example socialist feminists argue that equal opportunity is procedural and formal whereas equality of outcome is substantive. Equal opportunity as a concept is criticized for being concerned merely to ensure that the rules of entry into competition are the same for all. Equality of outcome as a concept looks to the results of competition and then raises questions about the rules of entry. This contrast between formal equality and substantial equality makes the point that the concept of equal opportunity is limited. But it is possible to argue that the 'radical future of liberal feminism' has been overlooked.[11] The argument is that the concept of equal opportunity is more radical than its critics realize.

This argument can be explained as follows. One of liberalism's major promises is equality of opportunity. This is the central doctrine for legitimating the distribution of goods in society. It contains the idea that everyone can achieve success through personal efforts, that benefits are distributed according to merit. Merit, not need, is the standard. Fair enough – but the problem with the notion of equal opportunity is that it assumes that those who compete on merit have an equal starting point. For instance, in discussions of anti-discrimination legislation it is often assumed that once barriers to competition are removed women, who have been historically discriminated against, will show their prowess and compete equally. But this conception of equality is limited, for it abstracts persons from their unequal situations and puts them in a competition in which their prior inequality and its effects are ignored. This assumption of an equal starting point has bedevilled many writers attempting to discuss equality.

Equal opportunity contains the notion that a good or benefit will be allocated in such a way as not to exclude *a priori* any of those wishing to have it. As Williams explains:

> It requires not merely that there should be no exclusion from access on grounds other than those appropriate or rational for the good in question, but that the grounds considered appropriate for the good should themselves be such that people from all sections of society have an equal chance of satisfying them.[12]

If Williams is right then the notion of equality of opportunity is more radical than appears initially. For here we are talking not of a mechanical minimal equality, but of equality of life chances.

Williams illustrates this by his example of a society dominated by a warrior class in which hereditary status and position are derived from skill at war. Reforms are instituted to implement a new philosophy of the society, that of equal opportunity. Admission to the warrior class is by competition. It turns out, however, that the present warrior children are overwhelmingly successful in the competition, so that the reform makes no difference to the outcome. This is because better nourishment gives greater physical strength to the warrior class. Witnesses to the competition conclude that the reform is procedural rather than substantive.

The competition is based on merit, yet we are uneasy about the result. Pre-existing conditions which ante-date the competition determine the outcome. The competition appears unequal as the non-warrior children have not had the opportunity to develop the characteristic (strength) tested by the competition. Applying the same criteria or grounds for the distribution of goods, to those whose history or background is unequal, is not equal opportunity. To equal up opportunity we must recognize the effects of history, background and social conditions. If these are curable we must do something about them. Remedial action to improve environmental conditions is not a new thought. It has been the centre of much political discussion in the later twentieth century. Without such action to remedy curable environmental conditions, to even up life chances, our notion of equality of opportunity is imperfect. It is not equality of opportunity in its full sense.

Equality of opportunity in its full sense requires a fair, rational and appropriate competition for goods and benefits. This means that competitors must have an equal starting point, where possible. It goes further than lowering barriers to access to education, services and the labour market. For women to compete equally with men both sexes must start equally. The question then becomes: do women have an equal starting point with men in marketplace competition? To answer this background inequalities must be considered.

It has long been admitted by political economists that state intervention in the market may be necessary to perfect free competition. Anti-discrimination legislation is justified in this way. Although such legislation involves the restriction of preferences of some market-actors, nevertheless it opens the labour market to greater competition from women, blacks and other minorities. Yet it is also recognised in discussions of anti-discrimination legislation that legislative intervention is insufficient to perfect market competition. One proposed answer has been variously dubbed 'preferential treatment', 'positive discrimination' and 'affirmative action'. The proposal is to create an equal starting point through preferential policies in favour of racial minorities and women.[13] This answer will be considered at the conclusion of this book. For present purposes it is sufficient to show how preferential policies can arise from the full sense of equal opportunity.

Another answer to perceived limitations of equal opportunity is to propose equality of outcome or results. Where equal opportunity is procedural, outcome equality is substantial. It is evident that the creation of outcome equality would require a major social revolution. Neither capitalist nor socialist countries have attempted to equalize outcomes, although this may be a goal of socialism. Whilst liberal political theory advocates equal opportunity in an unspecified way, equality of outcome is characteristic of radical and socialist theory. Liberals object that 'equality of outcomes could be maintained only at a substantial cost to liberty'.[14] The argument is that the maintenance of strict equality would require continuous coercive interference to maintain an egalitarian distribution pattern. Anti-discrimination legislation does not attempt outcome equality. It is committed to offering equality of opportunity. The question whether this is in the narrow or the full sense is examined below. The language of the legislation under discussion is concerned with equal treatment of men and women.

Equal Treatment and Treatment as an Equal

The distinction between equal treatment and treatment as an equal was first made by Ronald Dworkin. In a somewhat elliptical passage of an article on 'reverse discrimination' he explains the distinction as follows:

> There are two different sorts of rights. . . . The first is the right to *equal treatment*, which is the right to an equal distribution of some opportunity or resource or burden. Every citizen, for example, has a right to an equal vote in a democracy; that is, the nerve of the Supreme Court's decision that one person must have one vote even if a different and more complex arrangement would better secure the collective welfare. The second is the right to *treatment* as an equal, which is the right, not to receive the same distribution of some burden or benefit, but to be treated with the same respect and concern as anyone else. If I have two children, and one is dying from a disease that is making the other uncomfortable, I do not show equal concern if I flip a coin to decide which should have the remaining dose of a drug. This example shows that the right to treatment as an equal is fundamental, and the right to equal treatment derivative. In some circumstances the right to treatment as an equal will entail a right to equal treatment, but not, by any means, in all circumstances.[15]

If this passage is taken as suggesting that people and their needs are different, then it seems to follow that rights to equality do not mean treating people in the same way. This is an argument for pluralism. It is an argument against the insistence that persons conform to a particular model in order to be equal. It is an argument against the assimilationist ideal. It raises some problems about equal opportunity in its full or partial sense.

This question of whether equality is viewed as competition between women and men starting from the same point, or as a pluralistic recognition of different qualities and needs, is fundamental to theories of sex equality. The first approach, of an equal starting point, may fulfil the criteria defined for equality of opportunity. But it does rest on the twin assumptions that women do start from the same point as men; or that if not, they can do so. The starting point is, as it were, open to all. Differences between women and men are ignored. That women might find it difficult or impossible to get to the starting point is overlooked. This version of equality can be criticized as a procrustean bed into which the sleepers must be fitted through cutting or stretching. If the model for whom the competition (or bed) is designed is male then women may find it difficult to fit. They may be forced to accept a starting point and a competition which does not suit them. Their qualities and needs may be overlooked.[16] Economic and social institutions, willing to admit women under a policy of equality, will not necessarily adapt to accommodate them. These institutions may regard their admission of women as more than sufficient to fulfil equality requirements.

If treatment as an equal implies respect for others, avoidance of stereotypes and viewing the world from another's point of view, then pluralism goes further than equal treatment. For it allows for differences in persons, their situations, their needs. It requires 'an effort at identification'[17] in the way we treat others. In this guise equality does not mean giving or receiving the same treatment, but rather giving or receiving equal concern. Each person is then taken account of in her particular environment. This may be aspirational stuff; for in terms of legislative policy pluralism may be impossible to implement.

The outlawing of preferences for one sex in certain circumstances is the goal of anti-discrimination legislation. This contains a message about equal treatment. Women are to receive the same treatment as men; they are not to be treated less favourably; they are not to be discriminated against. The Sex Discrimination and Equal Pay Acts are based on the concept of equal treatment. As has been shown above this is one, perhaps limited, definition of equality. Whether other definitions could be incorporated in legislation will be considered in the concluding chapter of this book.

One scholar would take the view that this examination of varying definitions of equality is pointless. Peter Westen states that treating people equally (alike) where they are similarly situated is the Aristotelian notion of justice. Yet there is a difficulty with the standard of measurement to be applied. 'The ideas of equality and inequality relate the consequences of applying one standard as opposed to another, but the ideas do not themselves specify particular standards of measurement.'[18] Westen argues that concepts of equality and inequality are prescriptively empty, in that they do not specify the norms of measurement. 'They are formal relationships among persons that depend on a variable prescriptive standard that must be filled in to give them actual content. That is what philosophers mean in saying that, prescriptively, the idea of equality is "formal" '.[19] This is illustrated by an example of workers A, B and C who work identical hours. C has greater seniority than A and B. A has greater skill than B and C. B is older than A and C. The question is whether they are equal for wage purposes. The answer depends on the standard that governs wages: is it according to hours, seniority, skill, or age? Thus the prescriptive rule for wages determines their equality or inequality.

Although we may not go so far as Westen in the rejection of conceptions of equality as empty, his example does illustrate the centrality of the standard against which persons are to be measured. This is taken up also by Catharine MacKinnon. She suggests that existing inequalities should be taken into account in law-making and application. Her proposal is that, in considering legal standards, a distinction should be made as to whether (a) a given standard is equally premised between women and men but unequally applied; (b) unequally premised but equally applied; or (c) equally premised and equally applied to an existing social inequality.[20] Earlier, MacKinnon had argued that the focus in equal protection law should not be on whether the sexes are similarly or dissimilarly situated; nor on 'differences'; nor on whether differences are 'arbitrary' rather than 'rational'; but upon 'inequality'. The courts should consider whether legal treatment results in systematic disadvantage because of membership of a particular group. In the area of sex discrimination the 'only question for litigation is whether the policy or practice in question integrally contributes to the maintenance of an underclass or a deprived position because of gender status'.[21]

MacKinnon's proposal attempts to get away from the similar/different approach as the model of sexual equality. This approach originates with Aristotle's Nichomachean Ethics, where equality means treating like people alike, and unlike people unalike or differently. Thus, when legal distinctions are made, the law-maker must point to some difference between persons which justifies differential treatment. In the first equal protection case to be decided in favour of women in the United States, Chief Justice Burger laid down that a classification 'must rest on some ground of difference having a fair and substantial relation to the object of the legislation, so that all persons similarly circumstanced shall be treated alike'.[22]

This case concerned the right of women to administer estates, and the Supreme Court saw no relevant difference between men and women to justify state legislation excluding women, for with respect to such activities men and women are 'similarly circumstanced'. The difficulties with the *Reed* approach and with the limitation of equal treatment to those similarly situated is that differences in the past have justified discrimination and inequality. Differential treatment has been discriminatory treatment. The use of differences as a justification for differential treatment is explored in detail in chapter 3.

It is pertinent to ask whether MacKinnon has disposed of 'the difference approach' in her focus on inequality. It seems rather that her proposal links inequality and difference. It allows in pluralist ideas of equality by admitting that not everyone starts from the same position, or is similarly circumstanced. It gets away from equal treatment which limits itself to a comparison of treatment. Pluralism goes further than equal treatment because it allows the dissimilarities between the sexes to enter in. A focus on inequality puts differential treatment to the forefront. This is a deeper approach which enables the standpoint or perspective of those, unequal in social reality, to emerge. But instead of women's difference from men being a signal for unequal treatment to follow, as it has done in the past, it would be a sign for suspicion of the existing inequality, whether it existed in law, its application, or because of extraneous factors.

What MacKinnon's scheme for inquiry into inequalities highlights is that existing approaches of equal treatment or equal standard assume that women and men can be taken to be the same. This takes no account of inequalities and differences, whether they be of social, economic or biological origin. But it is an open question whether the differences approach is entirely avoided by a focus on inequality. Feminist analysis argues that differences should not be made the justification for unequal treatment. But differences, where they exist in biology or socioeconomic structures, cannot be ignored. The problem remains that, just as courts have justified differential treatment on grounds that women and men are not similarly circumstanced, so too may they justify inequality.

In an attempt to deal with the problem of justification of inequalities Christine Littleton proposes the following framework of inquiry. The first question is whether women have greater difficulty in meeting a particular standard than men. If not, then a decision to exclude women means the standard is not being accurately applied. If there is evidence that women have greater difficulty in meeting the standard, the inquiry then moves to the question: Why? Littleton claims:

Logically there are three possible answers:

1   the handicap is natural or inherent;
2   the handicap is artificially created by the previous discriminatory denial of opportunities to develop the skills necessary to meet the standard; or
3   the handicap is illusory and appears to exist only because the standard is defined in a certain way.[23]

From this formulation one can conclude that the answer that a handicap is natural or inherent is the only justification that should be accepted by law. Answers 2 and 3 should require a positive legal remedy. However,

Littleton indicts American law and its prevailing anti-discrimination principle as unable to deal with artificial and illusory handicaps. So the net effect is that inequalities that are perceived or defined as natural can be justified in court; whereas those handicaps which are artificial or illusory, but are not so perceived or defined, are not dealt with.

The importance of MacKinnon's and Littleton's analyses is that they provide a different perspective on discrimination. There is a sense in which their analysis of inequalities combines both a pluralist approach and a broad definition of equal opportunity which takes account of background inequalities. They deny that women and men should receive equal treatment where one sex has an advantage in social reality. Their proposal involves the deconstruction of existing inequalities. The United Kingdom White Paper *Equality for Women* discussed inequalities in the status of women. There was an admission that legislation 'is a necessary pre-condition for an effective equal opportunity policy but it is not a sufficient condition. A wide range of administrative and voluntary measures will be needed to translate the ideal of equal opportunity into practical reality'.[24] The language remains that of equal opportunity and equal treatment in the narrow sense. Yet the focus on inequality is important.

Recognition of Sex Inequality

Women have long recognized, and complained of, their inequality with men. There is written evidence of this in England from at least the seventeenth century. It was one thing, however, to recognize the female predicament; analysing it and prescribing remedies was another. Early writings concentrated on women's rights within the domestic sphere, particularly on property. In the nineteenth century issues of custody of children and divorce were raised. Women's entry into public life became an issue with the suffrage campaign. It is not the purpose here to provide an historical overview of those earlier movements towards equality. Accounts are available elsewhere.[25] What is worth noting is that law was perceived as central to these reforms and campaigns.

The changes women achieved in status in the nineteenth and first half of the twentieth centuries prepared the way for the 'second wave' from the 1960s. These changes were in the direction of equal treatment with men, i.e. having the same rights over one's property, children and income. Differential treatment by the law, by persons with power, was perceived as a major source of inequality. This had long been the view of feminists. So it was hardly surprising that elimination of distinctions between the sexes was connected to the ideal of equality. Accomplishment of equal treatment required de-institutionalization of sex differences. In particular those who continued to express a preference for one sex as employees or creditors, or through pay and conditions at work, were to be penalized.

To a certain extent the current equality laws stand Mary Wollstonecraft's proposals on their heads. Her view was that women should be educated for their domestic role in life. This, she thought, would make them better wives and mothers. Contrary to this, the focus for anti-discrimination legislation is the marketplace in jobs, education, goods and services. This has led some commentators to suggest that the motivation behind the legislation is to rationalize the market by eliminating preferences for one sex. This will be further explored in the next section.

Whether equality measures are motivated by beliefs in fundamental human rights or by desires to rationalize the market, the nature of the statements made by such laws must be elucidated in a study thereof. The starting point is an aspiration of equality for all. This is followed by the realization that statements of formal equality are not enough; that inequality continues. The source of that inequality is then identified as discriminatory practices in the market place. So such discrimination is made illegal. As Roger Cotterrell explains:

> Anti-discrimination law embodies the ostensible interests of the State in going beyond and behind the equal and universal legal subject of private law to confront the sociological realities of inequalities between individuals and groups. It 'lifts the veil' off equality before the law to disclose real inequalities considered harmful to the social fabric.[26]

However the extent of the state's commitment to all forms of equality between the sexes is open to question.

If we take the aspiration of equality we find that there are many who will assert that this exists between the sexes. This is an argument that *de jure* barriers to the entry of women into educational institutions, the professions, employment, have been removed in the twentieth century. Women now have the vote and participate in political life; are equal before the law. In family law women are regarded as equal parents and partners in marriage. The trouble with this argument is that it fails to account not only for the sociological realities of inequalities, but also for the state's apparent interest in prohibiting discrimination. In the United States a similar argument has been put forward. But since the Constitution guarantees equality for all, the fact that Congress felt it necessary to enact Title VII of the Civil Rights Act 1964, containing measures of sex equality, shows that formal guarantees of equality are considered inadequate.

The realization that formal equality before the law is not enough is an admission that all is not well. What is wrong? It is suggested that sex discrimination legislation can only be understood in the context of forms of prejudice or bigotry existing in society.

Anti-discrimination law creates no special legal capacities; it creates no categories of legal persons; it has no effect on the idea of generality of applicability of legal rights and duties among legal subjects – equality before the law in its ordinary sense. Instead it seeks to *prevent* the specification, expressly or impliedly, of certain legally impermissible conditions (e.g. membership of a certain racial group) as the basis for granting or receiving benefits in defined situations. The conditions are not devised by the law but given to it by forms of prejudice existing in society. We might call them categories of bigotry. They make sense only in relation to the intentions and motivations of those against whom the law is aimed.[27]

The state, through anti-discrimination legislation, affirms its interest in the equality of citizens. It recognizes individuals as members of the polity and the wider social interest in social solidarity. It makes a legal statement prohibiting discrimination as wrong. That the statement may be limited, that the means may be ineffective, should not cause us to overlook the importance of such a statement in official discourse.

An alternative explanation for the state's interest in prohibiting discrimination on grounds of sex is that the state has an interest in regulating the market to bring about maximum efficiency and free competition.

Rationalisation of the Market

Treaty obligations within the European Economic Community imposed the requirement of equal pay for equal work for women with men on member states. Article 119 of the Treaty of Rome is the basis for the Community's programme on equal treatment which has had a major impact on the law of the United Kingdom. It seems that Article 119 was motivated by the desire to eliminate unfair competition and to rationalize the market. The Commissioner for Social Affairs in the Community explained in 1980:

The Fathers of the Treaty [of Rome] were certainly not devotees before their time of women's emancipation. This Article [119 on equal pay] was adopted purely and simply out of the fear that if women workers were underpaid, national industries would suffer a negative effect as regards their competitive position.[28]

In other words, unfair competition might be engaged in by industries in some states employing women at a lower rate than men are paid in that industry within national or EEC boundaries.

The EEC commitment to free competition in the market is expressed through anti-trust laws and the prohibition of unfair competition. Creating the conditions whereby women and men compete for employment is part of this process. Competition on equal terms involves the elimination of unjustified prejudices in favour of one sex. This can be said to be a rationalization of the market.

Max Weber identified an inherent trend towards rationalization in industrial society. In Weberian terms law is rational where 'the legally relevant facts are determined in a process of logical interpretation of meaning and as fixed legal concepts . . . in the form of strictly abstract rules'.[29] Administration of law in a rational manner requires bureaucratization, where purely technical considerations determine 'without regard to persons in accordance with calculable rules'.[30] A fully developed bureaucracy operates without bias or favour. It is genderblind. 'Its peculiar character and with it its appropriateness for capitalism is the more fully actualised the more bureaucracy "depersonalises" itself.'[31] Thus the exclusion of preferences for the male sex as employees, creditors, clients, etc. is rational in the Weberian sense. Unjustified prejudices in favour of one sex are irrational.

The intervention of the state in the labour market, and in the market for goods and services to limit the autonomy of employers and others, exemplifies Weber's thesis. When unequal treatment on grounds of sex is outlawed market actors are denied their irrational preference for persons of one sex. The perfect market is competitive. However, exceptions are made for justified preferences. Study of these exceptions, whether couched in legislative or judicial terms, reveals much about sex discrimination problems. It is of interest to note that American courts use the standard of what is rational and not arbitrary to determine when sex discrimination is permitted. In *Reed* v. *Reed* Chief Justice Burger laid down that a classification 'must be reasonable, not arbitrary, and must rest on some ground of difference having a fair and substantial relation to the object of the legislation'.[32]

Examination of the state's reasons for outlawing unjustified sex discrimination reveals a series of explanations on a variety of levels of abstraction. Some writers have looked to concepts of equality in liberal society. Others have addressed the subject in terms of human rights. A more immediate explanation has been found in British international obligations under the Treaty of Rome. Weber's theory of rationalization has been suggested as an overarching explanation.

This type of explanation helps us to understand why legislative intervention has occurred in this area. It does not explain why persons are discriminated against. This is a complex question. In this book the framework for inquiry into discriminatory practices relies on modes of analysis developed by scholars who have addressed the general problems of inequality, and of differential treatment of the sexes.

Sexism – Modes of Analysis

A wide variety of forms of analysis of sexism have been developed in the recent past. In relation to law three forms have been particularly prevalent. These are discourse analysis, sex-role stereotypes and the empirical approach. All three approaches will be used in this book.

Discourse Analysis

Discourse analysis examines the signifying practices by which females are coded and classified as women in order to be assigned their social role. Women are placed in a separate category from men. In representations and language are manifested signs of gender-appropriate behaviour. According to the semiotic view 'woman' is always the product of an ideological construction. Ideology contains inarticulated assumptions by which society operates. These assumptions permeate all aspects including the system of justice. Sexist ideology – the ideology of male dominance – may even affect those measures and institutions that are intended to ensure equality of the sexes.[33]

'Woman' as a category or a construct is analysed discursively. Analysis reveals that although such a category is universal and constant, behaviour considered appropriate varies culturally. Language is not a representation of reality but a system of signification. Even in court cases dealing with complaints of sex discrimination the judiciary's use of language may reveal assumptions and beliefs about sex roles.

Linguistic and semiotic analysis of the reported cases on equal pay and sex discrimination reveals that zoological metaphors abound in this context. Examples are 'sauce for the goose is sauce for the gander';[34] 'stork and fox';[35] 'fox and crane';[36] 'watchdog ready to bark'.[37] The author of a recent study concludes:

> One might in the context of sex discrimination focus on the readily visible sexual neutrality (in the English language) of pigeon, horse, goose and gander, stork, fox, fish and dog. One can hardly fail to observe the zoological unity of the figures, and I stress that they are specific to this cluster of cases. . . . These creatures I argue demonstrate ambivalence between nature and culture, indeed they mediate these polarised classifications.[38]

Robertshaw suggests that the association of woman with nature and man with culture emerges from his analysis. That this is so has been a major theme in feminist anthropology.[39] The language used in the analysed cases shows an ambivalence on the part of the judiciary, and uneasiness as to how to classify women. For instance is the pregnant woman a productive or reproductive worker? Yet the transformation which is the goal of the Sex Discrimination Act, which was described by the judiciary as coming 'in like a lion',[40] causes uneasiness. The insecurity of the decision-makers is expressed in their use of language.

What discourse analysis offers is the possibility of exposing ideologies associated with the categorization of persons. If the content of the construct 'woman' is changed then women will have greater freedom to be whatever they wish. 'The subjection of women, therefore, is brought about not by their "natural" inferiority but by their classification as intrinsically inferior by a male dominated culture they cannot avoid living in.'[41]

A focus on language also offers the possibility of exploring the articulation of viewpoints. Thomas Hardy's Bathsheba Everdene thought it 'difficult for a woman to define her feelings in language which is chiefly made by men to express theirs'.[42] Whilst the liberal promise of equality under the law offers a voice to all subjects, the traditional silence of women and others may result in an exclusion of their viewpoint.

Sex-role Stereotyping

Sex-role stereotyping as a form of analysis is often used in relation to sex discrimination law. One of the objects of anti-discrimination legislation in Britain is to open the labour market to competition from women. In order to do this traditional attitudes of employers about appropriate behaviour and work for women must change. When someone acts on stereotyped assumptions about the sexes, the abilities of persons to define themselves are limited. This prevents persons from being what they want to be, from achieving their human potential. The White Paper *Equality for Women* identified 'the stereotyped attitudes of both sexes about their respective roles' as a major source of discrimination.[43] Legislative measures aimed at the destruction of sex stereotypes are therefore part of the Sex Discrimination Act and its enforcement.

To analyse and counter assumptions made about the sexes is to assert individual freedom. Why should the sexual category into which one is born force one into a predetermined role? Physical characteristics should not give rise to an ascribed status. Persons should be free to make choices; they should have the option to plan and pattern their own lives. These are the ideas contained in a rejection of stereotyped assumptions.

An example of this was where an employer assumed that a married woman would give up her employment to follow her husband's career move. She was therefore denied a training opportunity. This was condemned by the Employment Appeal Tribunal as discriminatory in the following words:

> the reason for the discrimination was a generalised assumption that people of a particular sex . . . possess or lack certain characteristics, e.g. 'I like women but I will not employ them because they are unreliable'. . . . Most discrimination flows from generalised assumptions of this kind and not from simple prejudice dependent solely on the sex . . . of the complainant.[44]

Similarly, in *Hurley* v. *Mustoe* the Employment Appeal Tribunal condemned blanket assumptions about all women, based on views about, or experiences of, some. Employers must investigate each applicant or employee 'and not simply apply what some would call a rule of convenience and others a prejudice to exclude a whole class of women or married persons because some members of that class are not suitable employees'.[45]

Another example can be taken from *Shields* v. *E. Coomes (Holdings) Ltd*, where a woman and a man were employed as counterhands. The Court of Appeal took the view that their work was of a broadly similar nature. 'The one difference of any significance between them was that the man filled a protective role. He was a watchdog ready to bark and scare off intruders.'[46] The court held that this difference should not affect the rate for the job. The reasoning, which was against sex stereotypes, was as follows:

> Both the woman and the man worked alongside one another hour after hour doing precisely the same work. She should, therefore, receive the same hourly rate as he. It is rather like the difference between a barman and a barmaid. They do the same work as one another in serving drinks. Each has his or her own way of dealing with awkward customers. Each is subject to the same risk of abuse or unpleasantness. But, whichever way each adopts in dealing with awkward customers, the job of each, as a job, is of equivalent rating. . . .
>   It would be otherwise if the difference was based on any special personal qualification that he had, as, for instance, if he was a fierce and formidable figure, trained to tackle intruders. . . . But no such special personal qualification is suggested. The only difference between the two jobs is on ground of sex. He may have been a small nervous man, who could not say 'boo to a goose'. She may have been as fierce and formidable as a battle-axe.[47]

The courts dealing with complaints of sex discrimination have tried to identify those generalized assumptions which are the basis of sexual stereotypes. The value of this is that a message is sent to all persons which encourages development of aspects of personality repressed by the stereotypical exhortations and expectations of society. Entrenched stereotypical expectations are constraints on freedom and personal development. As Lorraine Code observes: 'we are looking at an intricate process in which what a person *is* affects what that person can know, and this, in turn, structures and restructures what s/he is, giving rise to altered modes of being. These, in turn, create possibilities for different modes of knowing.'[48] The gradual elimination of stereotypes will enable other possibilities to emerge. In this role or character models of persons who have taken up these possibilities are important. The models provide living instances of alternative ways of being which can be emulated.

Unfortunately some members of the judiciary reveal their own generalized assumptions about women's characteristics in giving judgment in sex discrimination cases. In *Ministry of Defence* v. *Jeremiah*

Lord Denning said: 'A woman's hair is her crowning glory, so it is said.
. . . Now Mr Jeremiah has little regard for chivalry or for the women's
hair-does.'[49] And Lord Justice Brightman referred to 'women, who are
more concerned with, and devote more time and attention to, their
personal appearances'.[50]

Empirical Analysis

Empirical analysis will be used in this book as illustrative material and as
evidence. There is no lack of empirical research for, as the authors of a
recent study state, the 'last twenty years have seen an explosion of
interest in, and writings about, women'.[51] By 1979, 61 per cent of women
of working age were in employment by comparison with 54 per cent in
1971.[52] Of the 18 per cent of the labour force who were part-time
employees in 1979, 94 per cent were women.[53] This type of analysis can
help to explain the context of equality legislation, and to estimate its
effect twelve years after coming into force.

These three approaches are not completely distinct. The critique of
sex-role stereotyping relies on the uncovering of assumptions and
ideologies. This can be done through discourse analysis. Empirical
research findings and statistics often show how outdated these assumptions are. But they also show how much further women have to go to
gain equal opportunity in any sense of the word.

Conclusion

A number of themes have emerged from this first chapter which need to
be underlined. The basic issue is how equality is defined. Distinctions
have been drawn between differing conceptions of equality, in particular
between equal opportunity in the narrow sense, and in its full sense of
equal starting point. Outcome equality has also been distinguished and
defined. One of the hard questions to be answered is whether the United
Kingdom legislation implements equality of opportunity in its full sense
by giving an equal start to all market competitors, where possible.

A second question is whether the assimilationist version of equality is
irreconcilable with the pluralist version. Within feminist theory this is an
unresolved issue. Many critics of assimilation argue that what anti-
discrimination legislation offers is an opportunity to be like a man. This
is seen as validating the way men are, rather than trying to change both
men and women; to end sex discriminatory modes of thought and action.

Some feminist writers have introduced the concept of androgyny to
resolve the debate between assimilationists and pluralists. The value
placed on the principle of androgyny is that it enables 'men and women
alike – and equally – to develop aspects of their nature repressed by the

stereotypical exhortations and expectations of society, permitting them to eschew ways of being with which they find themselves ill at ease'.[54] A third question, then, is whether equality legislation has as its goal an androgynous society.

A fourth question which arises is whether the equality under discussion is largely negative. Is it concerned with the removal of barriers to education, to the marketplace, to citizenship? Does it envisage the eradication of impediments to freedom, an end to discrimination? It is true that the removal of formal barriers based on sex must be part of any conception of equality. But there are other forms and patterns, sometimes called 'institutional discrimination', which perpetuate the status quo. Are these addressed by the equality laws?

These four questions provide a framework for this inquiry into the United Kingdom equality laws for women. Although the observations that have been made in this first chapter by no means exhaust the problem of defining equality, they may clarify some of the issues at stake in analysing anti-discrimination legislation and its success or failure. Using this framework, the next chapter presents an overview of the history of the legislation.

Notes

1   *Equality for Women*, Cmnd. 5724 (London, HMSO, 1974).
2   See Creighton, W. B., 'Whatever happened to the Sex Disqualification (Removal) Act?', 4 *Industrial Law Journal* 155 (1975).
3   Chafe, W. H., *Women and Equality* (New York, Oxford University Press, 1978).
4   Wollstonecraft, M., *A Vindication of the Rights of Women* (London, Dent, 1929) p. 63.
5   Wasserstrom, R., 'Racism, sexism and preferential treatment: an approach to the topics', 24 *University of California Los Angeles Law Review* 581 (1977) p. 587.
6   Ibid., p. 606.
7   Ibid., p. 607.
8   On assimilationist theories see Jagger, A., *Feminist Politics and Human Nature* (New Jersey, Rowman and Allanheld, 1983); Scales, A. C., 'Toward a feminist jurisprudence', 56 *Indiana Law Journal* 375 (1981); Law, S. A., 'Rethinking sex and the constitution', 132 *University of Pennsylvania Law Review* 952 (1984); Eisenstein, Z., *Feminism and Sexual Equality* (New York, Monthly Review Press, 1984).
9   *Equality for Women*, supra note 1, para. 17.
10 Williams, B., 'The idea of equality', in P. Laslett and W. G. Runciman (eds), *Philosophy, Politics and Society* (second series) (Oxford, Blackwell, 1962) p. 121.
11 Eisenstein, Z., *The Radical Future of Liberal Feminism*, (London, Longman, 1981).

12 Williams, supra note 10, p. 125.
13 The literature on preferential policies is considerable. See Nagel, T., 'Equal treatment and compensatory discrimination', 2 *Philosophy and Public Affairs* 348 (1973); Greenawalt, K., *Discrimination and Reverse Discrimination* (New York, A. A. Knopf, Borzio Books, 1982). Gertner, N., 'Baake on affirmative action for women: pedestal or cage?', 14 *Harvard Civil Liberties – Civil Rights Law Review* 173 (1979).
14 Fishkin, J. S., *Justice, Equal Opportunity and the Family* (New Haven, Yale University Press, 1983).
15 Dworkin, R., *Taking Rights Seriously* (London, Duckworth, 1978) p. 227.
16 Wolgast, E. H., *Equality and the Rights of Women* (Ithaca, Cornell University Press, 1980) Chapter 1. Rhode, D.L., "Feminist perspectives on legal ideology" in J. Mitchell and A. Oakley (eds), *What is Feminism?* (Pantheon Books, 1986).
17 Williams, supra note 10, p. 117.
18 Westen, P., 'On "confusing ideas": reply', 91 *Yale Law Journal* 1153 (1982) at p. 1159. This article was a rejoinder to criticism of Westen's previous article, 'The empty idea of equality', 95 *Harvard Law Review* 537 (1982). The criticism is contained in Burton, S. J., 'Comment on "empty ideas": logical positivist analyses of equality and rules', 91 *Yale Law Journal* 1136 (1982).
19 Westen, supra note 18, p. 1160.
20 MacKinnon, C., 'Toward feminist jurisprudence', 34 *Stanford Law Review* 703 (1982) p. 731.
21 MacKinnon, C., *Sexual Harassment of Working Women* (New Haven, Yale University Press, 1979) p. 117.
22 *Reed* v. *Reed*, 404 US 71 (1971). For a feminist discussion of difference see Eisenstein, H. and Jardine, A., *The Future of Difference* (New Brunswick, Rutgers University Press, 1985).
23 Littleton, C., 'Toward a redefinition of sexual equality', 95 *Harvard Law Review* 487 (1981) p. 500.
24 *Equality for Women*, supra note 1, para. 21.
25 Sachs, A. and Wilson, J. H., *Sexism and the Law* (Oxford, Martin Robertson, 1978); Strachey, R., *The Cause* (London, Virago, 1978).
26 Cotterrell, R., 'The impact of sex discrimination legislation', *Public Law* 469 (1981) p. 473.
27 Ibid., p. 474.
28 Vredling, H., Speech at the EEC/EOC Conference on Equality for Women, Manchester, 28–30 May 1980.
29 Weber, M., *On Law in Economy and Society* (ed. M. Rheinstein) (Cambridge, Harvard University Press, 1954) p. xiii.
30 Ibid., p. 350.
31 Ibid., p. 351.
32 *Reed* v. *Reed*, 404 US 71 (1971).
33 Ruthven, K. K., *Feminist Literary Studies: An Introduction* (Cambridge, Cambridge University Press, 1984).
34 *Peake* v. *Automotive Products Ltd,* [1977] ICR 968 at 972 (CA).
35 *Steel* v. *Union of Post Office Workers,* [1978] ICR 181 at 188.
36 *Sun Alliance and London Insurance Ltd* v. *Dudman*, [1978] ICR 551 at 556.

37   *Shields* v. *E. Coomes (Holdings) Ltd,* [1978] ICR 1159 at 1171 (CA).
38   Robertshaw, P., 'Semantic and linguistic aspects of sex discrimination decisions', in D. Carzo and B. S. Jackson (eds), *Semiotics, Law and Social Science* (Milan, Gangemi Editore, 1985) pp. 203–27 at p. 221.
39   Ortner, S. B., 'Is female to male as nature is to culture?', 1 *Feminist Studies* 5 (1972).
40   *Ministry of Defence* v. *Jeremiah,* [1980] ICR 13 at 24.
41   Ruthven, K. K., supra note 33, p. 44.
42   Hardy, T., *Far From the Madding Crowd* (Harmondsworth, Penguin Classics, 1985) p. 412.
43   *Equality for Women,* supra note 1, para. 16.
44   *Horsey* v. *Dyfed CC,* [1982] ICR 755 at 760.
45   *Hurley* v. *Mustoe,* [1981] ICR 490 at 496.
46   *Shields* v. *E. Coomes (Holdings) Ltd,* [1978] ICR 1159 at 1171.
47   Ibid., at 1171.
48   Code, L., 'Simple equality is not enough', 64 *Australasian Journal of Philosophy* 48 (1986) p. 55.
49   *Ministry of Defence* v. *Jeremiah,* [1980] ICR 13 at 22.
50   Ibid., at 29.
51   Martin, J. and Roberts, C., *Women and Employment – A Lifetime Perspective* (London, HMSO, 1984) p. 1.
52   Office of Population, Censuses and Surveys, *General Household Survey 1980* (London, HMSO, 1982) table 5:2.
53   Office of Population, Censuses and Surveys, *Labour Force Survey 1979* (London, HMSO, 1982) table 4:7.
54   Code, supra note 48, at p. 53.

Chapter 2
The Legislation

The Equal Pay and Sex Discrimination Acts came into force on 29 December 1975. Identifying the origins of this legislation is a complex matter. Women's increased participation in the labour market during the previous twenty years highlighted the discrimination against them which was a major reason for the passing of the Acts. There was compelling evidence of unequal pay and unequal conditions in employment; unequal access to the marketplace in general, and to certain sectors in particular. It is evident that without such discrimination legislation would have been unnecessary. In societies without prejudice or bigotry, without the intentions or motivations of discriminators, without institutions fixed in a particular mould, this law would make no sense. Thus, in order to understand the background to the legislation one must understand the conditions of discrimination prior to 1976. This chapter considers *de jure* and *de facto* obstacles to women's access to certain benefits and burdens enjoyed by men, using the forms of analysis discussed in chapter 1.

De Jure Obstacles

The history of women's fight for entrance into public life and the marketplace has been well documented.[1] What is significant in relation to the equality legislation of the 1970s is the centrality of law to past struggles. Law was used by women as a test of their rights to vote in national and local elections, to be elected, to be educated, to enter the professions, to be employed when married, and to be equal in marriage to their husbands. Law's initial response to these claims was denial.

To understand this denial, and its legacy today, three aspects need to be examined: the relationship between common law and legislation; judicial creativity; judicial pronouncements.

In a series of cases brought to the British courts between the 1860s and the 1930s women claimed equal treatment with men. These cases challenged restrictions on activities and rights inside and outside the home. Litigation was used in an attempt to alter society. But the outcome was a legal constitution of socially approved sex roles. In refusing equal treatment of the sexes the judiciary relied on the common law, holding that it was long established that women were without legal personality in most areas of public law, particularly if married. Where legislation had been passed extending general rights, this was interpreted in relation to common law. The judiciary did not recognize the possibility of extending rights to women through creative interpretation. Rather the opportunity was seized to pronounce on appropriate behaviour, thus constituting restrictive sex roles for women.

Chorlton v. *Lings*[2] provides an example of a case where it was open to the judiciary to recognize a right of franchise of women in national elections. Although the legislation referred only to the entitlement to vote of every 'man', the canons of statutory interpretation provided that words importing the masculine gender are deemed to include the feminine. Therefore 'man' could have been interpreted as including 'woman'. The Court of Common Pleas held, however, that women were an exception to this canon of interpretation, as the statute itself excluded those subject to legal incapacity. There was a further argument that the word 'man' in the Representation of the People Act 1867 did not include women. The provenance of the finding of legal incapacity illustrates how judicial creativity might have been exercised.

Chief Justice Bovill's view was that even if no legislative enactment had taken away women's historic entitlement to the franchise, nevertheless 'the fact of its not having been asserted or acted upon for many centuries raises a strong presumption against its having legally existed'.[3] Lawyers arguing in favour of women's franchise had presented much historical material to show women's past capacity in public life. Had the Chief Justice so wished he might have been convinced by this. Instead examples were dismissed as exceptional. The point is that the court could have allowed women's claims.

Judicial views on different roles for the sexes can be illustrated from Mr Justice Willes's concurring opinion. In his view the exclusion of women arose not 'from any underrating of the sex either in point of intellect or worth', but from 'motives of decorum and privilege of the sex'.[4] Notions of decorum and privilege are revealing. Women, it is implied, are unsuited to the arduous task of participation in the *polis*. Their role is confined to domestic life.

When legislation was passed declaring the rights of both women and men with certain property qualifications to vote in local elections, the courts denied this right to married women.[5] Chief Justice Cockburn held that although qualified single women could vote under the Act: 'A married woman's status was so entirely merged in that of her husband that she was incapable of exercising almost all public functions.'[6] Although the statute provided that words importing the masculine gender shall include females for all purposes connected with the right to vote in local elections, the court's view was that this was not intended to alter the status of married women. Despite the enactment in 1870 of the first Married Women's Property Act, which recognized the separate legal existence of married women, the view was expressed that this did not alter the common law. According to Mr Justice Hannen the Act 'was intended to protect married women in the enjoyment of the rights of property, and was not intended to extend in any way to the political rights of women; and we must not by a side wind give an extension to its effect which we can clearly see was not intended'.[7]

The subsequent history of women's struggle for participation in public life and in educational institutions shows a gradual demolition of these legal barriers. Each one had to be met in litigation and dealt with in a series of legal enactments. Yet it would have been possible, as the language of the judiciary shows, for the courts to have removed these barriers through a creative approach to interpretation of statute and precedent. But the judiciary resisted.

Nairn v. *University of St Andrews*[8] involved a claim by women graduates of Scottish universities to vote at the election of a university member of Parliament. While male graduates had this right the House of Lords denied it to females. Yet it was admitted by the Lord Chancellor that 'it may be that in the vast mass of venerable documents buried in our public repositories, some of authority, others of none, there will be found traces of women having taken some part in parliamentary elections'.[9] But again an interpretation favourable to women was denied.

The interest of these examples is that they illustrate the possible creative role of the judiciary, and therefore their importance as interpreters and enforcers of the law. The question is whether, when faced with the equality legislation, judges are willing to take an active role in implementing its spirit. Or will pre-existing legal rules govern the new legislation?

The history of women's efforts to enter medical schools and the legal profession tells a similar tale. *Jex Blake* v. *Senatus*[10] concerned the expulsion of registered women students from Edinburgh University Medical School. The Court of Sessions of Scotland upheld the exclusion of women from medical studies by the university senate. Lord Neaves gave a judgment which summarized the views of those in favour of the prohibition of women from university life. This judgment is remarkable for its proclamation in a court of law of views on sex roles. Lord Neaves's view was that women 'have not the same power of intense labour as men are endowed with', and that this inequality of the sexes would result in a reduction of standards in instruction. Furthermore women must aim at 'special acquirements and accomplishments' in 'a knowledge of household affairs and family duties' and 'those ornamental parts of education which tend so much to social refinement and domestic happiness' . . . 'while there is little doubt that, in public estimation, the want of these feminine arts and attractions in a woman would be ill supplied by such branches of knowledge as a University could supply'.[11] Thus it was in women's best interests to be excluded, despite their desire to be admitted.

This presumption that the judiciary knew best the interests of women extended to male students also. The exclusion of women would prevent 'hasty attachments, that might exercise a blighting influence on all their future life'.[12]

Attempts to enter the legal profession fared little better. A woman applied in Scotland to be admitted to examinations with a view to qualifying for practice as a law agent.[13] Since the language of the statute used the word 'person' the applicant claimed that she was entitled, as a qualified person, to sit for examination by the Society of Law Agents. The court took the view that interpretation of the word 'person' must be taken to mean 'male person'. Four members of the court looked to past usage of the word. Five stated that since women had not previously been eligible there was nothing in the statute that made them eligible.

In London a woman, Bertha Cave, attempted to join Gray's Inn as a student in 1903. On refusal by the Benchers she appealed to a special tribunal consisting of the Lord Chancellor, the Lord Chief Justice and five other judges. The tribunal's view, in refusing the appeal, was that the courts had no power to compel the Benchers to admit any person. This was a matter within the discretion of the Benchers.[14] Two conclusions can be drawn from this: firstly, there was discretion in the Inns of Court to admit women, which was later exercised in their favour; secondly, the Benchers who refused the admission of women were generally drawn from members of the judiciary. These conclusions were confirmed in a later note in the influential *Law Quarterly Review* in 1917. There it was suggested, however, that 'it is not to be expected that any Inn should admit women as members without being satisfied that the Judges will recognise their call', by giving them rights of audience.[15] A further obstacle was the attitude of the majority of the profession. Thus, despite the fact that there were no *formal* legal obstacles, women's admission became contingent on the removal of a series of informal and institutional barriers.

Bebb v. *Law Society*[16] shows that the solicitors' profession was no more sympathetic. A woman claimed to be a 'person' within the meaning of the Solicitors Act 1843 but the Court of Appeal affirmed the Law Society's view that women were not persons within the meaning of the Act. The justification for this decision was the general disability women were under at common law because of their sex. Legislation could not be taken to alter 'the inveterate practice of the centuries'[17] except explicitly.

Thus the justification by the courts returned constantly to the common law position. As Albie Sachs observes: '[t]he English common law which had so often been extolled as being the embodiment of human freedom, had in fact proved the main intellectual justification for the avowed and formal subordination of women'.[18]

At common law the notion of freedom of contract, which reached its fullest development in the nineteenth century, has been said to include freedom to discriminate. In *Allen* v. *Flood*[19] the House of Lords made clear that discrimination even 'for the most mistaken, capricious, malicious or morally reprehensible motives that can be conceived', was lawful at common law.[20] From this case it has generally been concluded that common law provides no remedy for the person who wishes to complain of discrimination on grounds of race, sex or some other ascriptive quality. Bob Hepple's view is that the notion of contractual freedom implies 'an absolute right' on the part of the employer to discriminate in the choice of his employees. He argues that, 'as racial discrimination did not arise as a crisp legal problem in the formative years of the law of contract in the nineteenth century, it cannot now be subjected to those rules'. Therefore 'when the firmly-entrenched doctrine of freedom of contract has come into conflict with the post-Second World War concept of freedom from discrimination, it is hardly surprising that the older, better-appreciated freedom has prevailed'.[21]

Thus, when race and sex discrimination were perceived as wrong, it was generally believed that legislation to make certain forms of discrimination unlawful, and to provide remedies for the victims, was the answer. Development of common law remedies was not seen as a possibility. Support for this view comes from the Ontario case of *Re Noble and Wolf*. There the court stated its view that that 'the principle of freedom of contract . . . represents a paramount public policy which is to be preferred against an alleged public policy of freedom from discrimination'. This was because it would 'constitute a radical departure from established principle to deduce any policy of the law which may be claimed to transcend the paramount public policy that one is not lightly to interfere with the freedom of contract'.[22]

Against this established view can be set 'the flexibility of the law of tort in meeting the novel demands of what the courts perceive to be public policy', and the alternative argument that the past practice of the courts 'does not justify the conclusion that, as a matter of law freedom from discrimination can never obtain judicial preference over freedom of contract'.[23] Support for this alternative view comes from a later Ontario case. In *Bhaduria* v. *the Governors of Seneca College*[24] the Court of Appeal held that a common law action may lie for discrimination. The court held unanimously that the plaintiff who can establish that she was refused employment because of her ethnic origin, and thereby suffered damages, has a common law action for discrimination against the potential employer. Although the court's reasoning relied partly on the Ontario Human Rights Code, which provides that 'it is public policy in Ontario that every person is free and equal in dignity and rights without regard to race, creed, colour, sex',[25] the common law was called upon to protect these rights. The court saw the common law as containing the fundamental right not to be discriminated against. This right was said to be not merely the creation of statute, but already embedded in the law.

On appeal, however, the Supreme Court of Canada held that such a development of common law was forestalled by the Ontario Human Rights Code.

> The view taken by the Ontario Court of Appeal is a bold one and may be commended as an attempt to advance the common law. In my opinion, however, this is foreclosed by the legislative initiative which overtook the existing common law in Ontario and established a different regime which does not exclude the Courts but rather makes them part of the enforcement machinery under the Code.[26]

The Supreme Court did not deny the possibility of a common law action for discrimination in jurisdictions without anti-discrimination legislation. This is consistent with Lord Denning's view that 'it is a cardinal principle of our law that (persons) shall not suffer any disability or prejudice by reason of their race and shall have equal freedom under the law'.[27]

Discussion of the development of common law in Ontario has suggested that 'historically freedom of contract and freedom from discrimination are competing interests which the courts have found necessary to balance in light of their perceptions of public policy'.[28] Furthermore, it is argued, the strength of freedom of contract has been gradually lessened through judicial and statutory intervention on grounds of public policy, in the twentieth century. On the other hand, freedom from discrimination has become a greater social value which is reflected in law. To sustain this view, however, one must be able to show that the common law is still capable of development by a judiciary in tune with current social values.

When anti-discrimination legislation was first introduced in Britain the prevailing view was that the common law preferred the value of freedom of contract over freedom from discrimination. That is one reason why legislation was necessary, particularly where the provision of remedies is concerned. But the same judiciary who interpret common law also interpret statutes. In the past new legislation has been interpreted as far as possible in line with the existing common law. Yet, as Hepple observes, 'judges . . . have to assume that [anti-discrimination] legislation . . . has an instrumental dimension because it obviously changes the common law'.[29] The British judicial tradition has been to eschew a recognition of the instrumental nature of legislation. This is illustrated by Lustgarten in a comparison with the American tradition:

> The deadening influence of the common law is brought into sharp focus by a comparison with American civil rights law – federal legislation creating

causes of action in federal courts. Apart from constitutional litigation, those courts concern themselves almost exclusively with interpretation of statute. They do not see that task as one of subtle linguistic analysis, nor do they locate statutes in relation to pre-existing *legal* rules. Rather they treat major statutes as blueprints of *social* policy. Hence they attempt to inform themselves fully about the social reality of the 'mischief', interpret substantive provisions broadly in the light of that understanding – not in relation to the pre-existing common law – and even create new remedies in a purposive effect to effectuate the legislative aim. The legislation created a muscular skeleton, but the courts at all levels have put on the substantial flesh.[30]

When faced with local authority policies on equal pay and a minimum wage for both sexes the House of Lords in *Roberts* v. *Hopwood*[31] held that the councillors had exceeded their powers. Lord Atkinson's view was that members of the council would fail in their duty if they 'allowed themselves to be guided in preference by some eccentric principles of socialistic philosophy, or by a feminist ambition to secure the equality of the sexes in the matter of wages in the word of labour'.[32] Because, it was said, this was done 'at the expense of the ratepayers whose money they administered', it was illegal.

The equality legislation of the late twentieth century relies on the judiciary to interpret and enforce its provisions. Yet the processes and rationalizations, which in the past denied claims to equal treatment, remain part of judicial techniques. Illustrations from history enable understanding of the mechanisms of judicial interpretation and pronouncements on behaviour which are applied in relation to anti-discrimination legislation today.

De Facto Obstacles

The demand for equal pay for work of equal value was first passed as a Trades Union Council resolution in 1888 because of fears that women workers would undercut male rates of pay. With greater participation by women in the labour market in the 1960s and 1970s political action resulted in legislative intervention in the employment market. In 1971, 54 per cent of women of working age were employed outside the home; by 1979 this had risen to 61 per cent. The employment changes are quite marked. Throughout the 1960s and 1970s there was a continuous rise in the level of economic activity among women. But because of life cycle and family responsibility patterns 'almost all the growth in employment from the 1950s onwards can be attributed to the increase in part time work'.[33] Most of these jobs are done by women.

Participation by women in the labour market led to awareness of the unequal conditions there. In the 1970s in Britain recognition of sex discrimination was placed on the political agenda and linked to the question of equal pay. Legislation to combat discrimination and to complement the Equal Pay Act 1970 was readily agreed upon. The Civil Rights legislation of the United States, passed in 1964, provided an example of a goal to be achieved.

Although there were legal obstacles to be overcome in the quest for equality, it is likely that the *de facto* obstacles are greater. As the White Paper *Equality for Women* pointed out, 'the causes of inequality are complex and rooted deeply in tradition, custom and prejudice'.[34] A variety of forms of analysis of these barriers is available. The Department of Employment produced background papers for the discussions about legislative change which gave statistical evidence of inequality.[35]

There have been a number of studies which attempt to account for inequality of the sexes. Some measures of agreement in terms of explanation has emerged from these. Two features in particular stand out. The first is that women's employment outside the home cannot be understood without reference to their domestic roles, particularly the caring role. Secondly, social and economic institutions provide the contours of barriers to marketplace activities by women. This is often termed institutional discrimination. In an attempt to combat institutional discrimination the notion of indirect discrimination was included in the Sex Discrimination Act.

The discussion in this chapter might be taken to suggest that equality between the sexes will be achieved by equal participation in paid work. This is a reflection of the equality legislation and its limited scope. This is not the position of the authors.

Immediate Background to the Legislation

As history makes clear, the common law did not ensure either equal treatment, or treatment as an equal, for women. Consequently when a number of factors came together to build up political pressure for some forms of equality for women, it was clear that legislative intervention was necessary. This has also been the case in other common law jurisdictions such as the United States, Canada, Australia and New Zealand. The factors may be identified roughly as women's political claims originating from the nineteenth century, already discussed;[36] international obligations; and internal domestic political pressures, including trade union fears of undercutting by women of the male wage.

With the advent of new international organizations in the post-war period there has been an increasing international emphasis on human rights, including ideas of equality. A focus on human rights suggests that the British equality legislation is a response to aspirational statements by international bodies. This was one source of pressure. The United

Kingdom legislation on equality of the sexes implements the spirit of international declarations on human rights. The United Nations Charter and the Universal Declaration of Human Rights prohibit sex discrimination. There are a number of subsequent United Nations Covenants in the same area to which the United Kingdom is a party, including the Convention on the Elimination of All Forms of Discrimination Against Women. The International Labour Organization has had a Convention on equal pay for work of equal value since 1951.[37] There is pressure from Europe also. For instance the European Convention on Human Rights, to which the United Kingdom is a party, outlaws discrimination on grounds of sex and provides enforcement machinery; and a great influence has come from the European Economic Community.

Before the United Kingdom became a member of the EEC in 1973, it was evident that action would have to be taken to give effect to treaty obligations in domestic law. Thus in 1970 the Equal Pay Act was passed by Parliament, to come into effect on 29 December 1975. This was followed by the Sex Discrimination Act 1975 coming into effect on the same date.[38] Article 119 of the EEC Treaty lays down the principle of equal pay for women and men. The development of equal pay legislation and case law in the United Kingdom subsequently has been strongly influenced by European Community legislation and judicial decisions.

It would be wrong to assume that there was no domestic pressure for legislation on equal pay.[39] The Trades Union Congress first passed the motion that: 'in the opinion of this Congress it is desirable, in the interests of both men and women, that in trades where women do the same work as men, they shall receive the same payment' in 1888. This was repeated by Congress on more than forty occasions in the subsequent seventy-five years. In 1963 Congress went further in favouring legislation.[40] There had been three Royal Commissions, three Government Committees, and much debate in Parliament on the issue of equal pay.[41]

The British Labour Party committed itself to equal pay in its election manifesto of 1964. However this was followed by delay, probably for economic reasons, and a number of strikes by women workers on the issue at the end of the 1960s.[42] When Barbara Castle became Minister of Employment she helped to strengthen the government's resolve. 'The position now was that there would be a move to equal pay anyhow and it was far better that we should control it and get credit for it.'[43] Furthermore, British membership of the European Economic Community, which would require legislation on equal pay, was recognized by the cabinet as an argument in favour.[44] In January 1970 the Equal Pay Bill was presented to Parliament.[45]

The second reading debate on the Bill is revealing in that it shows all parties vying for credit for the idea of legislation on equal pay. The Bill was introduced by Mrs Castle in terms of 'another historic advance in the struggle against discrimination in our society, this time against discrimination on grounds of sex'.[46] There was no opposition to the general principles contained in the Bill, although there was debate on details of form, mechanisms and enforcement. At the end of the second reading the House was not divided.

That the idea of equal pay was an idea whose time had come can be seen from the claim by the Opposition Conservative Party to an historic commitment to the idea from 1947.[47] Indeed, the Bill was criticized as being silent on the question of equality of opportunity in employment. This defect was later remedied by the Sex Discrimination Act. Together, the two Acts make up a policy on equal opportunity for women in certain areas of life.

The experience in the United States of the enactment of anti-discrimination legislation was a mixture of political response to women's pressure groups, and chance. Under the presidency of Kennedy a Commission on the Status of Women was set up, and it proposed an equal pay law.[48] This was enacted by the Federal Government in 1963 and provided a model for the British legislation. However there was no general political commitment to the Equal Rights Amendment which American feminists had first proposed in 1923, and which would have outlawed all discrimination based on sex.[49] It is said that the support given by President Kennedy to the Equal Rights Amendment in public was because of an unauthorized alteration to a speech drafted by a member of his staff.[50]

When the Civil Rights Bill first went into committee hearings in 1963 it contained no reference to discrimination on grounds of sex, but was directed at race discrimination. Yet Title VII of the Civil Rights Act 1964, dealing with employment, has been a major weapon for women in advancing equal opportunity in relation to jobs. The inclusion of sex in the anti-discrimination provisions of Title VII was the product of chance and political manoeuvring.

At the committee hearing of the Civil Rights Bill there had been no discussion of sex discrimination, but only of unequal treatment on grounds of race, colour or national origin. An attempt to include sex was defeated.[51] In the House of Representatives there was a heated debate on the Bill for two weeks, but sex discrimination was only introduced into its provisions the day before its passage. In an effort to defeat the Bill one of its opponents introduced an amendment to the section on equal opportunity in employment (Title VII) to ban sex discrimination. 'This bill is so imperfect, what harm will this little amendment do?'[52] The object was to divide the civil rights alliance and the Congressman in charge of the Bill responded by attempting to defeat the amendment. Some Representative argued that the amendment was not in the interests of women, and that government policy was to treat sex discrimination separately. However liberal women carried their colleagues and the amendment, and the whole Bill was passed.

In the Senate the Bill was taken as a whole and very little attention was paid to the question of sex discrimination, although the longest filibuster in American history took place. One study of the legislative history of the Act concludes that 'the sex provisions of Title VII can be viewed more as an accidental result of political maneuvering than as a clear expression of congressional intent to bring equal job opportunities to women'.[53] Yet there was striking evidence that the American blacks, whom the legislation was intended to benefit, shared their poor economic situation with most American women. So the Equal Employment Opportunity Commission, the administrative body set up by Title VII, became actively concerned with women's employment opportunities. Some commentators were sceptical. *The New Republic* periodical asked: 'Why should a mischievous joke perpetrated on the floor of the House of Representatives be treated by a responsible body with this kind of seriousness?'[54]

Goals of the Legislation

The goals of the United Kingdom equality legislation are to prohibit the unequal treatment of the sexes in certain well-defined areas of the economy and in education. The White Paper *Equality for Women* stated the objectives of the law: the deterrence of prejudice and behaviour which manifests that prejudice; the provision of protection from prejudice and remedies for the victims thereof; the adjustment of grievances and the release of tensions; support for those who do not wish to discriminate. Above all the law makes an unequivocal statement of public policy and official beliefs. Policies in relation to race and sex anti-discrimination laws are common. The White Paper declared that 'the Government's ultimate aim is to harmonise the powers and procedure for dealing with sex and race discrimination so as to secure genuine equality of opportunity in both fields'.[55]

Equal pay, to be effective as a measure, had to be accompanied by legislation on equality of opportunity. Although the two pieces of legislation entered into force at the same time, they were distinct measures with goals, mechanisms and enforcement procedures of their own. This has led to some difficulties for complainants of sex discrimination. The Equal Pay legislation had one clear goal: to ensure that men and women doing the same or broadly similar work, or work which has been rated equivalent, receive the same pay. In Parliament there was debate on the issue of whether the formula 'equal pay for the same work' should be used; or whether the words 'equal pay for work of equal value' were better.[56] In its definition of 'equal value' the International Labour Convention refers to 'rates of remuneration established without discrimination based on sex'. This was held up as the goal of the British legislation. In order to achieve it the Equal Pay Act contains specific measures, including the right to challenge pay on the grounds of inequality where a specific male comparator could be pointed to as doing 'like work' or work rated equivalent under a job evaluation scheme. However, where no evaluation scheme existed it was not possible to ask for evaluation to be made. In 1970 only 30 per cent of unionized jobs had such schemes.[57]

Introducing the second reading of the Sex Discrimination Bill in the House of Commons the Home Secretary, Mr Roy Jenkins, stated that the

> unequal status of women in our society is a social evil of great antiquity. Its causes are complex and rooted deeply in tradition, custom and prejudice. Its effects create individual injustice and waste the potential talents of half our population at a time when more than ever before we need to mobilise the skills and abilities of all our citizens.[58]

Most of this speech consisted of a paraphrase of the White Paper. However there were certain significant additions and admissions. The concept of indirect discrimination, which was not in the White Paper, was introduced because 'to understand the full meaning of unlawful discrimination it is essential not to confuse motive with effect'. Practices which, regardless of motives, have a discriminatory effect on persons of one sex, and cannot be shown to be justifiable, were to be outlawed. Indirect discrimination therefore covers the idea of impact. Where an ostensibly neutral practice is shown to have a disproportionate impact on women then, unless it can be justified, it is indirectly discriminatory.

The theory of disparate impact was imported to Britain from the United States under the concept of indirect discrimination. Roy Jenkins, on a visit to the USA, was impressed by a decision of the United States Supreme Court interpreting Title VII of the Civil Rights Act 1964 as prohibiting not only overt discrimination but also practices 'fair in form but discriminatory in operation'.[59] By looking beyond form, and at impact, the court broadened the concept of discrimination. The court found that Congress, in referring to denial of employment opportunities on grounds of race or sex in Title VII, had intended

> that tests or criteria for employment or promotion may not provide equality of opportunity merely in the sense of the fabled offer of milk to the stork and the fox. On the contrary, Congress has now required that the posture and condition of the job-seeker be taken into account. It has – to resort again to the fable – provided that the vessel in which the milk is proffered be one which all seekers can use.[60]

It was admitted by the Home Secretary that formal equality was not enough, and that special training would be necessary 'to help women to compete for employment opportunities on genuinely equal terms with men'. Making a distinction between 'positive' and 'affirmative' action (of which he approved) and 'reverse discrimination' (of which he did not), he stated his belief that

> We should not be so blindly loyal to the principle of formal legal equality as to ignore the actual and practical inequalities between the sexes, still less to prohibit positive action to help men and women to compete on genuinely equal terms and to overcome an undesirable historical link.[61]

The Bill received general support in Parliament, as the previous Conservative government had made a commitment to anti-sex-discrimination legislation. Discussion of the evil of discrimination led to its depiction as morally unacceptable, economically and socially harmful, and unjust to individuals. Legislation was presented as necessary 'because it affects the climate of opinion', for educative purposes, although 'social attitudes cannot be overturned by legal coercion'.[62] However, there was more opposition to a general philosophy of equal opportunity than there had been, five years previously, to the specific goals of equal pay.

Opponents of the legislation argued that 'the differentiation of sex is all-pervasive', and that 'a Bill which sets out to eliminate the effects of that differentiation except where it is total or absolute . . . is a defiance of reality'.[63] In the House of Lords this alleged difference was thought to justify unequal treatment: 'for a man to be unemployed is a threat to his masculinity, but for a woman to be unemployed is not a threat to her femininity. It will hit her purse but not her sex life.'[64] This reliance on difference, which is the traditional method of refuting women's claims to parity with men, appears to have been based on social construction of existing gender roles. No fundamental differences between women and men were referred to, perhaps because exceptions based on biological differentiation had already been incorporated in the Bill. Thus there are exceptions for 'genuine occupational qualifications'; for separate facilities (the 'lavatory clause'); for privacy.[65]

In answering the objection that men and women are different the story was recounted of a woman member of Parliament who was incensed by an advertisement for a House of Commons librarian which limited the post to male applicants. On being told by the Minister that the librarian would have to carry ladders to reach books on the upper shelves, she gave a practical demonstration in the House of her skill in ladder removal. Subsequently women were able to obtain employment in the House of Commons Library.[66] The point of this story was that beliefs about women's capabilities, which had prevented them from entering a particular employment, were proved to be false. The suggestion made by the practical demonstration is that other beliefs about the social roles of the sexes may also turn out to be false. To some extent the equality legislation has already shown this to be so.

Scope of the Legislation

In introducing the Equal Pay Bill in Parliament, the Secretary of State, Mrs Castle, explained it as follows:

> The Bill deals with three different situations. The first situation is where men and many women are doing the same or 'broadly similar' work, not only in the same establishment but in different establishments of the same employer where these are covered by common terms and conditions. The second is where they are doing jobs which are different but which have been found to be equivalent under a scheme of job evaluation. The third is where their terms and conditions of employment are laid down in collective agreements, statutory wages orders or employers' pay structures.[67]

The focus is on pay, although equal treatment in terms and conditions of employment is also covered. The three situations outlined by the Secretary of State were not so broadly covered as her speech implies. The first situation is confined to 'like' or 'broadly similar' work for the same employer. It does permit an individual woman to complain directly to an industrial tribunal and to choose a male worker in the same employment as a comparator.

The second situation presupposes that a job evaluation scheme exists, and that the complainant can ask for an evaluation to be made. Yet, as the Secretary of State admitted when she introduced the legislation, only 30 per cent of unionized jobs had such a scheme in 1970. Subsequently, the European Court of Justice has held that the rule that a woman is only to be regarded as employed on work rated as equivalent to that of any man if a job evaluation study has been carried out, is contrary to the law of the European Economic Community.[68] The Act has since been amended to allow equal-value claims with a consequent evaluation of jobs not falling within the 'broadly similar' category. However, the restriction that the complainant and comparator must work for the same employer remains.[69] One of the major criticisms of the 1970 Act was that it did not compel job evaluation, but it remains open to question whether the amendments meet the criticisms of the European Court.

The third situation discussed by Mrs Castle was discriminatory collective agreements and pay structures. Under section 3 of the 1970 Act pay structures could be referred to the Central Arbitration Committee by any party, or by the Secretary of State, for consideration. This section was repealed by the Sex Discrimination Act 1986.[70] Thus the scope of the legislation has been broadened by the introduction of 'equal value' at the behest of European law. But it has been narrowed also, for domestic political reasons, in reducing the scope of control over pay structures as a whole.

There was a deliberate decision to restrict the effect of equal treatment in terms and conditions of employment, so as to omit coverage of employers' pension schemes. The Secretary of State admitted that

> [o]n the face of it, it seems just that pensions, as part of remuneration, should be covered by the Bill, but in practice there are a number of difficulties, and as far as I can ascertain no other major country has included pensions in the scope of its provisions for equal pay.[71]

Subsequent history of the equality legislation shows that the retirement age and pensions were to prove a fertile ground for combat. The exclusion of employment terms related to retirement led to litigation before the Court of Justice of the European Communities. In *Marshall v. South West Hampshire Area Health Authority (Teaching)*[72] it was decided that the dismissal of a woman solely because she has attained the qualifying age for state pension is discrimination on grounds of sex. The point that the United Kingdom retiring age for women is sixty, whereas for men it is sixty-five, was acknowledged by the Court, but it is nevertheless contrary to the European Community Council Directive on equal treatment in relation to work to dismiss a woman solely for that reason.[73] The outcome has been an amendment of the Equal Pay Act and the Sex Discrimination Act, so that the exclusion of retirement provisions from the ambit of the Acts is no longer lawful. In general both Acts have been amended so as to make it unlawful for an employer to treat a woman differently from a comparable male employee in relation to retirement.[74]

The Sex Discrimination Act explicitly covers employment, housing education, the provision of goods and services. It specifically excludes sex discrimination by the state and in private. The White Paper, *Equality for Women*, stated that 'the status of women in relation to social security, taxation, nationality and matrimonial and family law is governed by separate legislation and will be so dealt with in the future'.[75] From this it may be concluded that the scope of the legislation is confined to the economy and the labour market. Most of the debate on the original Bill confirms this. The subject of discussion was principally employment, with some references to the educational system and the provision of goods and services. Whether the implied promise to act on other areas has been fulfilled is open to doubt.

Areas of life classified as private were originally excluded from the ambit of the legislation. This position has been modified somewhat because of a decision of the European Court of Justice. Although personal and family matters remain untouched out of 'respect for private life',[76] the exception in the 1975 Act for small employers, with less than five employees, has been condemned by the Court. This exception has been eliminated by section 1 of the Sex Discrimination Act 1986. The distinction between public and private is still maintained in the legislation by the exclusion of employment in private households.[77] The idea is that choice in personal matters is private, and that the desire for employees of a particular gender is outside the scope of the legislation.

The explicit exclusion of areas of state policy such as taxation, social security and nationality laws from the scope of the legislation, regretted by many speakers in Parliament, reinforces the distinction between public and private. Yet women's participation in the labour market is shaped by their domestic roles. It is not just a question of combining employment and family responsibilities, but also of power relations at work, assumptions that are made, and stereotypes in the ways women are perceived.[78] As the intervention of the European Court of Justice suggests, it is not possible to maintain a barrier between the public and private spheres.

The equality legislation, because of its limited scope, reinforces the dichotomy between private and public. This is particularly injurious to those women coping with a domestic and caring role in addition to their employment. But it also affects all women, in that stereotyped assumptions are made about them. The recent extensive study by Martin and Roberts of women's employment confirms that in most marriages the husband is the primary breadwinner and the wife is the primary houseworker. This division, already significant in marriage, is reinforced by the presence of children. Most of the economically inactive women in the survey of 1980 were mothers of young children. The pattern of work also varied as between men and women, but also between women with young children and other women. Nevertheless, the researchers found that women in their thirties are spending more time at work over their lifetime than women coming up to retirement. The conclusion was that the current arrangement of family life precludes women from becoming equal or joint wage-earners on the same terms as their husbands. So although the social values of the equality legislation were generally endorsed by the women surveyed, they nevertheless accepted the sexual division of labour.[79] The limited scope of the legislation ensures that it does not enter into that aspect of women's lives labelled private. Yet it is that which conditions their opportunity to be equal in those areas covered by law.

Scope is a problem. Anti-discrimination law is selective. It chooses from a maze of policies, practices, actions, official and non-official, certain aspects which are to be unlawful. This implies that it is only in these areas that discrimination occurs. Yet perhaps it is precisely in those other areas untouched by law that discrimination is deepest. As the Minister introducing the Sex Discrimination Bill explained: 'The Bill is a necessary pre-condition for an effective equal opportunity policy, but it is not a sufficient condition. A wide range of administrative and voluntary measures will be needed to translate the ideal of equal opportunity into practical reality.'[80]

Mechanisms

Freedom of contract was very much part of common law. It permitted sex or race to be used as grounds for refusing contracts or services to others. As already discussed, the object of anti-discrimination legislation was to restrict this, at least in certain areas. Law was chosen as a major weapon, 'a first step – but a major and essential step – towards true equality for women',[81] for a number of reasons. It was necessary to undo some of the effects of the doctrine of freedom of contract. There was a belief in law as an instrument of social engineering. It was thought that a public proclamation of certain values would change attitudes. And the use of law gave the government and its allies in the trade unions control over the scope and extent of change.

The methods chosen to give women equal opportunity are complex. In the case of equal pay there is a right of individual complaint to an industrial tribunal. Technically the complaint concerns a breach of contract as the Act imposes an equality clause on all contracts of employment. However, the claim is limited to cases where the claimant can compare herself to a specific man doing like work, or to an 'equal value' claim under the amendments of 1986. In both cases there must be a male comparator employed in the 'same employment', i.e. normally employed in the same establishment by the same employer. There is no possibility of basing a claim on what the employer might have paid a 'hypothetical man'.[82] However, the Secretary of State made it clear in Parliament that she intended to provide specific remedies which women could easily enforce. It may be that she balanced the limited nature of the legislation against the individual right of enforcement.[83]

Where the broader engineering of social change and equal opportunity took place through the Sex Discrimination Act the method chosen was to create a new statutory tort, and the granting of certain powers to an administrative agency created by the Act, the Equal Opportunities Commission. So far as the new statutory tort is concerned, it is up to aggrieved individuals to complain of the tort of discrimination against them. To do so they must make a formal complaint of unequal treatment to an industrial tribunal, if the complaint relates to employment. Where housing, education, goods or services are at issue, the complaint must be to a County Court.

The Equal Opportunities Commission is the body that was created by the 1975 Act to assist enforcement of the legislation. It can assist individuals in bringing complaints, act against discriminatory advertisement, seek an injunction to restrain persistent discrimination, issue non-discrimination notices and enforce them, and issue codes of practice.[84]

Most complaints of discrimination are brought by individuals.

Analysis of the claims of discrimination in employment brought to industrial tribunals shows that from 1976 to 1983 over 6,000 women and men took action. Of 1,794 complaints under the SDA, 73 per cent were by women and 27 per cent were by men. Twenty-five per cent of all complainants settled their complaints, 35 per cent withdrew them and 40 per cent proceeded to a tribunal hearing. Success at the hearing seems to have depended in part on whether applicants were legally represented. The success rate of all applicants was 27 per cent. Those with legal representation had a success rate of 39 per cent; those who represented themselves succeeded in 21 per cent of cases.[85] Over the same eight-year period 4,296 claims for equal pay were filed with industrial tribunals. Ninety-four per cent were by women and 6 per cent by men. Of these claims, half went to a hearing. The success rate at hearings was 20 per cent overall, but it is interesting to note that women's success rate was 19 per cent compared to men's at 39 per cent.[86]

These statistics suggest that some victims of discrimination are making use of the legislation to vindicate the hurt they have suffered. However there is also evidence that the complexity of the legislation acts as a deterrence to complaint, and to subsequent success. The statistics on greater success with legal representation tend to confirm this. Furthermore when the early years of the equality legislation are compared to the later years there is evidence of a fall in the number of complaints. There were 1,742 applications to industrial tribunals under the Equal Pay Act in 1976 compared to 39 in 1982. This has led some writers to suggest that too great a burden is placed on the individual complainant. There are three criticisms of the legislation involved here: that the procedural aspects are complicated, that proof is difficult, and that there is no class action comparable to that in the United States. Under a class action one complainant can represent all those affected. These criticisms point to individuation and isolation of the victim.

Questions of procedure and the burden of proof will be dealt with in detail when complaints of direct discrimination are examined in chapter 3. The lack of a class action in the United Kingdom illustrates the point about the isolation of complainants. In the United States a representative of a class, such as women, can sue on behalf of all members of the class. This creates a collective identity among all those affected by discriminatory actions. The judgment of the court affects all the members of the class, who are bound by the result. Thus the United States Supreme Court has struck down discriminatory legislation upon complaint by one widow, representing all widows.[87] This reflects an admission that all those belonging to a particular class – that is, placed in the same situation, or sharing certain characteristics – may be affected by discrimination. It is a recognition that many matters 'are conducted on a routine or bureaucratised basis and can no longer be visualised as bilateral transactions between private individuals'.[88]

It is true that an equal pay claim can be seen as affecting a wider group of people than the individual claimant. Since the claim concerns a pay structure, its success will benefit those who stand in the same place as the individual claimant. However, the repeal of section 3 of the 1970 Act, and with it the powers of the Central Arbitration Council to review a pay structure as a whole, has prevented further development of the collective approach to equal pay.[89] Whether the complaint under the United Kingdom legislation concerns equal pay or sex discrimination, the suit is set up as between individuals. The new statutory tort of unequal treatment created by the Sex Discrimination Act presupposes a discriminator and a victim, who are opposed.

Not only does a heavy burden of proof lie on the complainant, but the law views discrimination as the misguided conduct only of the respondent. As Freeman observes in relation to racial discrimination legislation in the United States: 'It is a world where, but for the conduct of these misguided ones, the system of equality of opportunity would work to provide a distribution of the good things in life without racial disparities.'[90] In other words, the individuation of the process implies that the respondent is out of step with society. It also implies that society and its institutions are concerned to ensure equality. Yet the very nature of the legislation and the process it involves for the victim leaves this open to doubt.

Anti-discrimination legislation in the United Kingdom is tightly drafted and very specific. It is for tribunals and courts to interpret the wording. The British judiciary see their task as one of subtle linguistic analysis of the wording of statutes, and not as social engineers. This may be contrasted unfavourably with the approach of the American judiciary who treat major statutes as blueprints for social policy. Furthermore the United States constitution enables statutes which are discriminatory to be struck down, whereas this cannot happen in the United Kingdom. Thus, theories of sex equality have been more clearly enunciated under American law.

The Equal Pay legislation has clear and visible targets: similar work to be paid at a similar rate. Historically this has been accepted as a principle of justice. Although the Act has been criticized as limited in scope, its specific goals and mechanisms are not particularly complex. By contrast comparisons under the Sex Discrimination Act are difficult. In order to show discrimination the applicant must compare herself (or himself) with a person drawn from the opposite sex category: then less favourable treatment on grounds of sex must be proved. There are several problems of mechanism here. Firstly, what does the legislation mean by sex? Secondly how is the comparison to be made? Thirdly, is it always possible to compare women and men?

Definitions of Sex

Comparing persons of different sex is the major mechanism for proving sex discrimination. But it is not entirely clear what is meant by 'persons of different sex' in the Sex Discrimination Act.[91] 'Woman' is defined as 'a female of any age', and 'man' as a 'a male of any age'.[92] This presupposes that femaleness or maleness is established in law. It is true that courts have given judgment on sex determination, where legislation uses a classificatory scheme based on sex. The leading case is *Corbett* v. *Corbett*,[93] where, in an action of nullity of marriage, it was held that a person's sex is determined at birth. Although the judgment in that case confined its effects to marriage, nevertheless it has been applied to criminal law and also in a sex discrimination case.

In *White* v. *British Sugar Corporation*[94] a female-to-male transsexual complained of sex discrimination when dismissed by the employer on grounds of deception as to sex. The employer had believed the complainant to be male when the offer of employment was made. Dismissal followed the discovery that the complainant had previously been classified as female. The industrial tribunal which heard the case held that the complaint of discrimination required a determination of sex. The complainant was held to be a woman, despite having the apparent sex of a man, as this was the classification at birth. The tribunal then held that the female complainant had not been treated less favourably than a man, because a man who had held himself out to be a woman would also have been dismissed. It is clear from this case that biological sex on an essentialist test is to be determined in sex discrimination legislation.

Public policy, as expressed in the equality legislation, is against discrimination between the sexes. Researchers have shown that attitudes which stereotype women and men inflexibly can lead to discrimination. This was stated in the government White Paper prior to the enactment of the legislation. It is ironic that in attempting to abrogate sexual stereotypes the means Parliament has chosen is to require all individuals to be classified sexually in an essentialist fashion. Transsexuals, homosexuals and others cannot complain under the SDA because of dismissal on grounds of sexual preference. The tribunal in the *White* case concluded: 'The laws of this country and the 1975 Act in particular envisage only two sexes, namely male and female.'[95]

Making a Comparison

Making a comparison between women and men under the Sex Discrimination Act is based on an assumption of prescriptive equality – that they should be treated equally. The complaint is an allegation that they have been treated less favourably on grounds of sex contrary to law. The Act takes the two persons to be compared as equals who can be compared.

This is made clear by section 5(3) of the Sex Discrimination Act, which requires that the persons of different sex or marital status to be compared 'must be such that the relevant circumstances in the one case are the same, or not materially different, in the other'. This presupposes that the persons under consideration can be compared, that is that they are alike in relevant respects. There is a further presupposition that the persons compared are capable of measurement.

Treating like persons alike is a fairly simple conception of justice. It is part of a long and honourable tradition. It informed Aristotle's theory of distributive justice. But the question has always been: how are we to know what is alike and what is different? It is particularly ironic that this mechanism is used for anti-sex-discrimination law, for history shows that women's claims to equality were easily denied on ground of their biological or social difference.

What is the standard for measurement of persons of opposite sexes to be compared? Ideas of equality or inequality do not specify a particular standard of measurement. Is the standard to be women's historic experience of confinement to the domestic sphere and their specific role in the reproduction of the species? Or is it to be men's greater experience of public world, and the labour market? This poses the dilemma neatly; a dilemma which will be later illustrated with reference to problems created for the legislation by women's pregnancy and child-care responsibilities.

Those compared in sex discrimination cases are mainly women and men, although the legislation also covers a comparison of married and single persons of the same sex – termed marital discrimination by the Act. The social construction of biology places women and men into separate and opposite categories. From the moment of birth to the issuing of a death certificate these categories are of immense social significance. The problems faced by transsexuals in trying to move from one category to the other illustrate the social and legal importance of gender classifications.[96] Yet anti-discrimination legislation, by making less favourable treatment on grounds of sex illegal, attempts to undo the social world. It is doubtful whether this is possible under legislation which is limited in scope, with defective mechanisms, operating on a social world in which women and men are constructed differently from the moment of birth.

Sameness and Difference

The enactment of anti-discrimination legislation represents public and official recognition of sexual inequality. Finding a suitable legislative means to deal with this remains a problem. In both the US and UK comparison and measurement of women against men has been the prevailing form. The result has been an attempt to 'screen out' those aspects of women's biology and social lives which make them different from men. In American law this has been crystallized in debates over pregnancy.

Under the SDA the lack of a male comparator has created difficulties for women complaining of sex discrimination on dismissal for pregnancy.[97] Although pregnancy is a sex-related condition the form of the SDA appears to require that such conditions which appertain to one sex only be ignored. The relevant circumstances for comparison of persons of different sex or marital status must be 'the same, or not materially different' under the Act.[98] Yet sex-related discrimination may focus precisely on those aspects of women's lives or biology which make them different from men. As Nicola Lacey observes:

> the logic of the section lies in formally equal treatment in roughly similar cases, [so] no possible argument can be raised about the specific nature of pregnancy which might merit special treatment, as acknowledged in our statutory laws on maternity leave.[99]

Behind this lies the theoretical debate, already referred to in chapter 1, which goes to a fundamental view of the purposes of anti-discrimination legislation. This debate concerns the type of society, and the type of person, that is to be the outcome of anti-discrimination principles. Is this to be a society in which the sex category to which one is assigned at birth is of no more significance than eye colour is today? Wasserstrom's ideal of the non-sexist and non-racist society is

> one in which the race of an individual would be the functional equivalent of the eye colour of individuals in our society today. In our society no basic political rights and obligations are determined on the basis of eye colour. No important institutional benefits and burdens are connected with eye colour.[100]

If such a society, termed the 'assimilationist ideal', came about, 'it would be unintelligible to talk about the virtues as well as the disabilities of being a woman or a man'.[101]

The comparative mode of proving sex discrimination is based on some idea of assimilation. Women are to be assimilated to a model predicated on maleness. But as the impeccable logic of the judiciary demonstrates, pregnancy is not part of maleness and must therefore be ignored. Qualities intrinsically related to femaleness may continue to be a barrier to equal treatment as they cannot form the basis of a complaint under the SDA, because no comparison is possible.

Criticism of the United States Supreme Court's approach to issues of equality has argued that assimilationist theory is inadequate, for it has led the judiciary to find that discrimination against pregnant women is not sex discrimination. What American feminist lawyers are looking for is some general theory of sex equality which takes account of biological difference. Thus Ann Scales argues for recognition of women's biological role in procreation and breastfeeding.[102] Sylvia Law argues that 'an assimilationist vision that ignores differences between men and women does not help us to reconcile the ideal of equality with the reality of difference'.[103] Her vision seems to be closer to a pluralist society in which persons would be respected 'free from sex-defined legal constraints'.[104] The outcome of this seems to be a search for a theory of equality which addresses in detail biological differences.

Limitations of Anti-discrimination Legislation

The British approach to anti-discrimination legislation may be contrasted with that of the United States in that the former is the specific product of legislation and the latter is largely produced by general interpretation of the Constitution. Nevertheless there are certain features in common which expose the limitations of such legislation. These can be summarized as limitations of scope, of method and of vision.

The question of biological difference has illuminated the limitations of an assimilationist approach. Not only is it evident that assimilation forces the suppression of difference, but also that a fully rounded theory of equality would take account of difference. Assimilationist theory, then, is inadequate, despite its utility in distinguishing cultural and social difference from biology. But we can go further than that and charge assimilation, and the mode of dealing with sex discrimination in the two countries, with a limited perception of women's lives.

Assimilationist theory is liberal theory. It assumes that law should not enter the private sphere of personal relations and biology – that these can be otherwise regulated. Liberals accept a dichotomy between public and private. They accept a limited role for law. Already many are disturbed by law's efforts to eliminate discrimination. So what is different about women is to be suppressed or confined to the private sphere. When women emerge into public to claim equality with men they must be able to compare themselves with men.

The notion of equal justice under law is an important promise in the Western legal order. But, as Stephanie Wildman argues, 'the continuing use of the traditional "comparison mode" of analysis – that is, comparing women to men as the starting point of equal protection review – has made the development of a real end to sex discrimination impossible'.[105] There are a number of reasons for this: reification of the categories 'woman' and 'man'; establishment of men as the normative mode; women's claims must fit existing categories.

Reification of the Categories 'Woman' and 'Man'

The paradox of sex discrimination legislation is that it requires the comparison of a woman with a man, or an unmarried person with a married person, to establish direct discrimination; and a general comparison for indirect discrimination. An assimilationist might argue that it is the prior existence of these categories that creates the problem. 'Woman' as a category or construct is produced by a society and mediated in the discourses it circulates about itself. 'Woman' in semiotic terms is not an essence but a sign. As Ruthven has observed, women's subordination is brought about by their classification as different and inferior by a male-dominated culture.[106] According to the semiotic view 'woman' is always the product of ideological construction. To accept, as sex discrimination law appears to do, that sex categories are enduring categories, that there is an essentialist view of sex, is to reinforce the very problem that the legislation is supposedly addressing. It is the deconstruction of these categories that we should be pursuing.

Establishment of Men as the Normative Model

'To the extent that being similarly situated is a prerequisite for constitutional scrutiny of differential treatment any such comparison (between women and men) will necessarily result in continued disparate treatment and discrimination.'[107] In the United States the jurisprudential model for all equal protection analysis under the Constitution is to compare members of the group discriminated against with the mainstream group. The question posed is whether the complainant is similarly situated with respect to the purpose of the law. Under the Sex Discrimination Act 1975, 'a comparison of the cases of persons of different sex or marital status under section 1(1) or 3(1) must be such that the relevant circumstances in one case are the same, or not materially different, in the other'.[108] Furthermore, in arguing for equality it has been traditional for women to claim the opportunities and resources that men have on the basis that they are the same as men. Again this means that whatever is different in women from the male norm must be suppressed. Differences here could encompass biological differences, life-cycle differences, sex-role differences – that is cultural differences in addition to biology.

So the question here is whether an equality theory can be devised which takes account of biological and cultural differences.

Women's Claims Must Fit Existing Categories

As chapter 1 has explained, it is difficult for women to define their feelings in language chiefly made by men to express theirs. This may be particularly so, where law is involved. As presently constructed, antidiscrimination legislation does not challenge institutions, language, structures that have so long excluded women. It merely asks that men move over to make a little room for the women who can conform to the male norm. To conform women must become token women, surrogate men, whose role is to confirm liberalism without challenging or changing the status quo. Furthermore, in complaining about sex discrimination the victim not only faces the individuation of the process but is also forced into a form of envy. She has to show that she has been unfavourably treated on ground of sex. But she is also a 'complainant', a dissatisfied person whose action seems to be motivated by sour grapes. This is the position the structure of the legislation forces her into, if she wishes to take action. She may 'assert her rights' and 'complain'. The very language used indicates the problems of the process.

Conclusion

In the first chapter of this book theories of equality were examined. Having considered, in this chapter, the background to the anti-discrimination legislation we may now ask: which theories have informed the law? At the outset a distinction must be made between political considerations which limited the scope of the law, and inherent limitations in law itself in tackling issues of equality.

Action by governments on behalf of victims of discrimination is political, and is therefore limited by political considerations. In the case of the United Kingdom Equal Pay Act the broader context of labour law, and the then government's relations with the trade union movement, were important factors in shaping the legislation. This was why the Secretary of State wanted to control the outcome of the move to equal pay.[109] The government's concern was not to disrupt existing pay structures unduly, and the result was a limited scope to the right to equal pay. The previous tradition of British labour law was anti-interventionist, with an emphasis on collective bargaining rather than individual rights enforceable at law.[110]

Inherent limitations in law as a method of tackling discrimination on grounds of sex or race is a separate issue from limited political commitment. Even if all governments from 1970 on had committed themselves whole-heartedly to ensuring that women received equal pay, the means to achieve this might have remained elusive. A number of questions, some of which are beyond the scope of this book, need to be asked and answered before a conclusion can be reached. It is not appropriate to discuss the impact of the legislation until the conclusion of the book. But the question of form and mechanisms have arisen in this chapter, and a view on that can be arrived at here.

Whether law, on its own, can achieve a revolution in the treatment of victims of discrimination may be a matter for scepticism. But law is the chosen instrument of change. The form in which it is couched, and the mechanisms it uses, are therefore important. The inability of anti-discrimination legislation in the United Kingdom and in the United States to process women's claims that biological difference is a source of unequal treatment has been the focus of much criticism. The question whether this is a rectifiable fault in the legislation, or whether this is an inherent limitation of law, takes us back to the theories of equality with which we started in chapter 1.

Some of the criticisms of anti-discrimination legislation and its interpretation have been followed by concrete suggestions for improvement. For example a Sex Equality Bill was introduced in Parliament in 1983 which would have dealt with certain loopholes in the law, and would have reversed the effect of some unsympathetic court decisions. However, this Bill was unable to escape the inevitable requirement of the comparison of the claimant with a male comparator.[111] Reviewing these proposals Susan Atkins has asked whether the focus should not be clearly on 'the inequality of power between men and women supported by law', instead of the present 'premise of equality between the sexes and genders'.[112]

From American feminist lawyers have come other practical suggestions. Some of these have attempted to deal with the comparative mode of the present legislation. For example Sylvia Law's proposal for the scrutiny of the impact of rules governing reproductive biology, rather than the structure or purpose of such rules, is a practical suggestion. In her view impact analysis is required by a proper concern for equality. It avoids a focus on the purpose of rules, as purpose can often be used as a justification for sex-based classification. Sexual stereotypes are also avoided, and there is no necessity for comparison between allegedly similarly situated classes of persons. Law's proposal appears to be close to an idea of outcome equality. By analysing impact, courts and rules would attempt to equalize outcomes. However, as Law herself admits, there would be a reliance on judicial discretion, which has proved unreliable in the past, as the section on history in this chapter shows.[113]

Catherine MacKinnon attempts to overcome disadvantages for women because of their differences from men with her suggestion of inequality analysis. Her proposal is that courts should take account of existing inequalities when faced with a particular issue on a legal standard.[114] To some extent this relates to Law's impact analysis; although MacKinnon's proposal involves an analysis of inequality by the judiciary before applying the standard, whereas Law's proposal involves the application of the standard first, and a subsequent analysis of its impact. Both proposals appear to rely heavily on judicial perspicacity and willingness to use discretion.[115] Both fail to take account of the history of double standards, such as protective legislation for women's employment. Both suffer from Law's criticism of MacKinnon: that the 'proposed standard may incorporate and perpetuate a false belief that a judicially enforced standard can, by itself, dismantle the deep structures that "integrally contribute" to sex-based deprivation'.[116]

Criticism of the form of anti-discrimination legislation raises broader questions about the rule of law. Two of the claimed characteristics of law are generality and neutrality. Two of the major criticisms of the equality legislation are that its ultimate project is 'the production of sameness',[117] and that it ignores women's perspectives. A conception of discrimination which views as irrational the refusal to recognize the similarity of women to men presupposes that women are similar to men. This conception of discrimination may itself give rise to unequal treatment. If women are merely given the chance to assimilate themselves to men the scope of inquiry is narrowed. The goal of assimilation demands only that women are evaluated according to criteria traditionally laid down for men. Thus both genders are encouraged to act as men do presently.[118]

This challenge to the discourse of comparative equality brings out the problems that the form of the legislation have caused for women. The comparisons required to prove unequal treatment validate the way that men are. Women's way of being, their life cycles, do not fit easily into patterns set by and for men. As Ann Freedman observes: 'assimilation into existing predominantly male social structures is an inadequate definition of equality between the sexes and one that robs equality of much of its transformative potential'.[119] The vision of society which lies behind some of this criticism is a vision of change and a new world.

Much of feminist theory is transformative, a description of a community in which difference is not merely tolerated as pluralism, but is embraced. For to 'demand only the chance to compete is to embrace the status quo in a way that tends to sanction oppressive arrangements'.[120] The inclusion of women's perspectives in public debate is seen as a first step in this transformation. What this vision expresses is dissatisfaction with current approaches to sex discrimination in American and British law.

We can conclude from this review that anti-discrimination law is limited and assimilationist. Stuck in its comparative mode the legislation is concerned to open up the labour market to new competitors, but on current terms. Certain suggestions for improvement relate to the extension of the limited scope of the legislation, and a new judicial approach to interpretation. These are possible reforms. But in so far as the criticisms relate to evils which are not susceptible to law's methods, and to a vision of a transformed society, there is no obvious role for law. Yet understanding the limitations of law, setting its comparative discourse of equality against the vision of transformation, enables a new form of analysis which could lead to the alteration of existing structures.

Notes

1 Strachey, R., *The Cause* (London, Virago, 1978); Sachs, A. and Wilson, J. H., *Sexism and the Law* (Oxford, Martin Robertson, 1978); Atkins, S. and Hoggett, B., *Women and the Law* (Oxford, Basil Blackwell, 1984); Creighton, W. B., *Working Women and the Law* (London, Mansell, 1979).

2   *Chorlton* v. *Lings*, (1868) LR 4, CP 374.

3   Ibid., at p. 385. See also Hollis, P., *Women in Public* (London, Allen & Unwin, 1979).

4   *Chorlton* v. *Lings*, op. cit., at p. 388.

5   *The Queen* v. *Harrald*, (1872) LR 7, QB 79.

6   Ibid., at p. 362.

7   Ibid., at p. 364.

8   *Nairn* v. *University of St Andrews*, [1909] AC 147.

9   Ibid., at p. 159.

10 *Jex Blake* v. *Senatus*, (1873) 11 M 784.

11 Ibid., at p. 795.

12 Ibid., at p. 796.

13 *Hall* v. *Incorporated Society of Law Agents*, (1901) reported in Sachs, A. and Wilson, J. H., *Sexism and the Law* (Oxford, Martin Robertson, 1978) p. 28.

14 20 *Law Quarterly Review* 8 (1904).

15 33 *Law Quarterly Review* 114 (1917).

16 *Bebb* v. *Law Society*, [1914] 1 ch. 286.

17 Ibid., at p. 297.

18 Sachs, A. and Wilson, J. H., *Sexism and the Law* (Oxford, Martin Robertson, 1978).

19 *Allen* v. *Flood*, [1898] AC 1.

20 Ibid., at p. 172 (per Lord Davey).

21 Hepple, B., *Race, Jobs and the Law in Britain* (Harmondsworth, Penguin, 1970) pp. 155 and 234.

22 *Re Noble and Wolf*, [1948] 4 DLR 123 at p. 139.

23 McKenna, I., 'A common law action for discrimination', 1 *Legal Studies* 296 (1981).

24 *Bhaduria* v. *the Governors of Seneca College*, [1980] 105 DLR (3d) 707.

25 RSO, 1970, c.318.

26 *Bhaduria* v. *the Governors of Seneca College*, [1980] 124 DLR (3d) 203 (per Laskin CJC).

27 Denning, A., *Freedom Under the Law* (London, Stevens, 1951) p. 51.

28 McKenna, supra note 23, p. 299.

29 Hepple, supra note 21, p. 74.

30 Lustgarten, L., 'Racial inequality and the limits of the law', 49 *Modern Law Review* 68 (1986) at p. 74.

31 *Roberts* v. *Hopwood*, [1925] AC 578.

32 Ibid., 594.

33 Martin J. and Roberts C., *Women and Employment – A Lifetime Perspective* (London, HMSO, 1984).

34 White Paper, *Equality for Women*, Cmnd. 5724 (London, HMSO, 1974).

35 Department of Employment, *Manpower Papers 9–12* (London, 1974, 1975).

36 See also Meehan, E., *Women's Rights at Work* (London, Macmillan, 1985) ch. 2.

37 International Labour Organization Convention No. 100 (1951). The Trades Union Congress called on the United Kingdom government in 1961 to ratify this Convention. In 1963 Congress called for legislation to implement the Convention.

38 The Equal Pay Act 1970 applies to the whole United Kingdom. The Sex Discrimination Act 1975 does not apply to Northern Ireland, but the Sex Discrimination (NI) Order 1976, SI No. 1042 (NI 15) is analogous.
39 Davies, P., 'The equal pay and treatment directives', paper given at the Conference on European Community Equality Law, Lincoln College, Oxford, 22–4 March 1987.
40 Hepple, B., *Equal Pay and the Industrial Tribunals* (London, Sweet & Maxwell, 1984) p. 1.
41 The Royal Commissions were:
  MacDonnell Commission on the Civil Service Cmd. 7338 (London, HMSO, 1916); Tomlin Commission on the Civil Service, Cmd. 3909 (London, HMSO, 1931); Asquith Commission on Equal Pay, Cmd. 6937 (London, HMSO, 1946).
  The Government Committees were:
  The Women's Employment Committee, Cmd. 9239 (London, HMSO, 1918); Atkin War Cabinet Committee on the Employment of Women in Industry, Cmd. 135 (London, HMSO, 1919); Anderson Committee on Pay of State Servants (London, HMSO, 1923).
42 Meehan, supra note 36, p. 38. The strike by women workers at the Ford Motor Company in 1968 was given great publicity in the national press, and is said to have had a significant impact on the government.
43 Castle, B., *The Castle Diaries 1964–70* (London, Weidenfeld & Nicolson, 1984) p. 705.
44 Ibid.
45 Parliamentary Debates, House of Commons, vol. 794, col. 1553 (28 January 1970).
46 Parliamentary Debates, House of Commons, vol. 795, col. 914 (9 February 1970).
47 Parliamentary Debates, vol. 795, col. 930 (Mr R. Carr).
48 President's Commission on the status of Women, *Report of the Committee on Private Employment*, Washington, 1963. See also Weiler, P., 'The wages of sex', 99 *Harvard Law Review* 1728 (1986).
49 See Brown, B., Emerson, T., Falk, G. and Freedman, A., 'Equal rights amendment', 80 *Yale Law Journal* 871 (1974).
50 Meehan, supra note 36, p. 61.
51 *Congressional Quarterly* (1964) p. 344.
52 *Congressional Record* vol. 110 (1964) col. 2577. This was said by the chief opponent of the Bill, Congressman Judge Howard Smith of Virginia. See also Meehan, supra note 36, p. 62.
53 Miller, R., 'Sex, discrimination and Title VII of the Civil Rights Act of 1964', 51 *Minnesota Law Review* 877 (1967) pp. 879–82.
54 *The New Republic* (4 September, 1965) p. 10.
55 White Paper, *Equality for Women,* supra note 34, para. 24.
56 The Treaty of Rome, Article 119, provides: 'Each Member State shall during the first stage ensure and subsequently maintain the application of the principle that men and women should receive equal pay for equal work.' Directives 75/117 (equal pay); 76/207 (equal opportunity); 79/7 (social security) have followed from Article 119 and from the Community Action Programme on the Promotion of Equal Opportunities for Women, 1982–5.

57 See the speech of Mrs B. Castle, supra note 46, introducing the second reading of the Equal Pay Bill in the House of Commons. Section 1(5) of the Equal Pay Act 1970 restricted the claim relating to 'work rated as equivalent to that of any men' to cases where a job evaluation study had been carried out. This was held by the European Court of Justice to be contrary to European law. See Case 61/81 *EC Commission* v. *United Kingdom*, [1982] IRLR 333.

58 Parliamentary Debates, House of Commons, vol. 889, col. 511 (1975).

59 *Griggs* v. *Duke Power Co.*, 401 US 424 (1971). See also *Dothart* v. *Rawlinson*, 433 US 321 (1977).

60 *Griggs* v. *Duke Power Co.*, 401 US 424 (1971) at p. 431.

61 Parliamentary Debates, House of Commons, vol. 889, col. 514 (1975).

62 Ibid., cols 527–8 (Mr I. Gilmour).

63 Ibid., col. 541 (Mr E. Powell).

64 Parliamentary Debates, House of Lords, vol. 362, cols 141–2 (1975).

65 Sex Discrimination Act 1975 ss.7(1); 35(1)(c) (the much derided 'lavatory clause'); s.7(2).

66 Parliamentary Debates, House of Commons, vol. 889, col. 579 (1975) (Mrs J. Knight).

67 Ibid., vol. 795, col. 917 (1970).

68 Case 61/81 *EC Commission* v. *United Kingdom,* [1982] IRLR 333.

69 Equal Pay (Amendment) Regulations 1983, SI 1983/1794 (made under the European Communities Act 1972, s.2(2)). The United Kingdom government preferred not to amend the Equal Pay Act 1970 directly.

70 Sex Discrimination Act 1986, s.9.

71 Parliamentary Debates, House of Commons, vol. 795, col. 923 (1970).

72 European Court of Justice, Case 152/84 [1986] 2 All ER 584, [1986] 2 WLR 780.

73 EC Council Directive 76/207 covers equal opportunity in training and conditions of employment. It is binding on member states of the EEC. See O'Donovan, K., 'The impact of entry into the European Economic Community on sex discrimination in British social security laws', in J. Adams (ed.), *Essays for Clive Schmitthoff* (Abingdon, Professional Books, 1983).

74 The Sex Discrimination Act 1986 ss.2 and 3 deal with discrimination as to retirement and dismissal before reaching the 'normal retiring age'. The effect has been to amend both the Sex Discrimination Act 1975 and the Equal Pay Act 1970. See also *Foster and Others* v. *British Gas PLC*, [1987] ICR 52.

75 White Paper, *Equality for Women*, supra note 34, para. 77.

76 *E.C. Commission* v. *United Kingdom,* [1984] 1 All ER 353.

77 Sex Discrimination Act 1986, s.6(3)(a).

78 O'Donovan, K., *Sexual Divisions in Law* (London, Weidenfeld & Nicolson, 1985) ch. 6.

79 Martin, J. and Roberts, C., *Women and Employment – A Lifetime Perspective* (London, HMSO, 1984) ch. 13.

80 Parliamentary Debates, House of Commons, vol. 889, col. 524 (1975) (Mr R. Jenkins)

81 Ibid., col. 525.

82 Equal Pay Act 1970, s.1(6).

83 See Davies, supra note 39.

84 Sex Discrimination Act, 1975, ss.75, 72, 62, 67–70, 56.

85 Leonard, A., 'Applications to the industrial tribunals under the Sex Discrimination and the Equal Pay Act: who they were, their claims, their success (1976–1983)', *New Law Journal* (31 January 1986) 101.

86 Ibid., part II (7 February 1986) 123.

87 *Reed* v. *Reed*, 404 US 71 (1971).

88 Chayes, A., 'The role of the judge in public law litigation', 89 *Harvard Law Review* 1281 (1976) at p. 1291.

89 Section 3 of the Equal Pay Act 1970 was repealed by the Sex Discrimination Act 1986. This repeal might be taken as an indication of limited political support for equal pay measures.

90 Freeman, A., 'Legitimizing racial discrimination through anti-discrimination law', 62 *Minnesota Law Review* 1049 (1978) at p. 1054.

91 Sex Discrimination Act, 1975, s.82(1). But see *Football Association Ltd* v. *Bennett, EOC, Towards Equality: Casebook of Decisions* (1976–81) p. 36.

92 Sex Discrimination Act, 1975, s.5(2).

93 [1971] p.83.

94 [1977] IRLR 121.

95 [1977] IRLR 121 at p. 123.

96 O'Donovan, K., *Sexual Divisions in Law* (London, Weidenfeld & Nicolson, 1985) ch. 3.

97 *Turley* v. *Allders Department Stores Ltd*, [1980] IRLR 4; *Hayes* v. *Malleable Working Men's Club*, [1985] IRLR 367.

98 Sex Discrimination Act, s. 5(3).

99 Lacey, N., 'Note: dismissal by reason of pregnancy', (1986) *Industrial Law Journal* 43 at p. 45.

100 Wasserstrom, R., 'Racism, sexism and preferential treatment: an approach to the topics', 24 *University of California Los Angeles Law Review* 524 (1977) at p. 604.

101 Ibid., at p. 606.

102 Scales, A., 'Towards a feminist jurisprudence', 56 *Indiana Law Journal* 375 (1980).

103 Law, S., 'Rethinking sex and the constitution', 132 *University of Pennsylvania Law Review* 955 (1984) at p. 966.

104 Ibid., at p. 969.

105 Wildman, S., 'The legitimation of sex discrimination: a critical response to Supreme Court jurisprudence', 63 *Oregon Law Review* 265 (1984) at p. 265.

106 Ruthven, K. K., *Feminist Literary Studies* (Cambridge, Cambridge University Press, 1984) ch. 1.

107 Wildman, supra note 105, at p. 268.

108 Sex Discrimination Act, 1975, s.5(3).

109 Castle, supra note 43.

110 Davies, supra note 39.

111 This Bill was introduced by Ms J. Richardson MP in the House of Commons in 1983. It did not receive a second reading. It combined the Equal Pay and Sex Discrimination Acts, and extended the scope of the former because the hypothetical male comparator test would have been

included. The burden of proof was reversed. A broad number of other provisions were contained in the Bill, which would have met some of the criticisms of current law.

112   Atkins, S., 'The Sex Discrimination Act 1975: the end of a decade?' Paper given to the Women Law Teachers Group Workshop, University of Birmingham, July 1985, p. 10.

113   Law, supra note 103, p. 1008.

114   MacKinnon, C., *Sexual Harassment of Working Women* (New Haven, Yale University Press, 1979) pp. 174–92.

115   See Taub, N., book review, 80 *Columbia Law Review* 1686 (1980) at p. 1691.

116   Law, supra note 103, at p. 1005.

117   Dalton, C., 'Remarks on personhood', AALS panel, 5 January 1985.

118   Littleton, C., 'Toward a redefinition of sexual equality', 95 *Harvard Law Review* 487 (1981).

119   Freedman, A., 'Sex equality, sex differences, and the Supreme Court', 92 *Yale Law Journal* 913 (1983) at p. 967.

120   Scales, supra note 102, at p. 427.

Chapter 3
Direct Discrimination

The popular idea of sex discrimination is of a person who applies for a job (or a loan) and is turned down because of being a woman. In the legislation on equality this idea is encapsulated in the term 'direct discrimination'. The 1975 Act covers five types of discrimination: direct sex discrimination, indirect sex discrimination, direct discrimination against the married, indirect discrimination against the married, and victimization. This chapter deals with direct discrimination.

Section 1(1) of the Sex Discrimination Act 1975 defines direct discrimination: 'A person discriminates against a woman in any circumstances relevant for the purposes of this Act if – (a) on the ground of her sex he treats her less favourably than he treats or would treat a man.' The Act is even-handed; men also can complain of sex discrimination. Of 1,794 applications to the industrial tribunals under the Sex Discrimination Act between 1976 and 1983, 73 per cent were by women and 27 per cent by men.[1] Direct comparison of one woman with one man, or a hypothetical man, is the mode of analysis of direct discrimination.[2] The object of the legislation is to provide a simple, straightforward mechanism for establishing that an individual has received less favourable treatment on grounds of sex than some other person. This necessarily involves comparison of the treatment of individuals belonging to different sex categories.

A fairly straightforward example is the case of *Quinn* v. *Williams Furniture Ltd.*[3] There a married woman, who asked for hire-purchase facilities at a furniture store, was told that unless her husband would act as guarantor she would not receive these facilities. She was further told that a married man did not require a guarantor. The Court of Appeal held this refusal of facilities to a married woman, which the company admitted would be granted to a man, to be unlawful discrimination.

That persons with benefits such as jobs, education, contracts or services to distribute may choose amongst the possible beneficiaries on many grounds is undeniable. What anti-discrimination legislation attempts to do is to make illegal certain grounds for choice such as sex and race. In Weberian terms law is rational where 'the legally relevant facts are determined in a process of logical interpretation of meaning and as fixed legal concepts . . . in the form of strictly abstract rules'.[4] By this Weber means a conceptual abstract approach. Administration of law in a rational manner requires bureaucratization, where purely technical considerations determine 'without regard to persons in accordance with calculable rules'.[5] A fully developed bureaucracy operates without bias or favour. 'Its peculiar character and with it its appropriateness for capitalism is the more fully actualised the more bureaucracy "depersonalises" itself'.[6] Thus the exclusion of preferences for the male sex as employees, students or debtors is rational in the Weberian sense. The intervention of the state in the labour market, and in other areas of social life, to limit autonomy exemplifies Weber's thesis. When unequal treatment on grounds of sex is outlawed market actors are denied their irrational preference for persons of one sex. In a liberal society the perfect market is competitive.

Complaint based on direct sex discrimination is one way to combat unequal treatment. This requires personal application and individual comparison of treatment which has occurred, or which continues. Because this is an individual matter the burden rests with the applicant not only to take action, but also to prove her case. She must choose the comparator, that is the actual or hypothetical male with whom she compares herself. The procedural difficulties faced by complainants will be elaborated below. These may discourage applications. It is worth noting that whilst 90 per cent of complaints are of direct sex discrimination, nevertheless the number of complaints has fallen steadily since 1976. Alan Freeman calls the American approach to discrimination 'the perpetrator perspective'. In his analysis this

> purports to be stance of society as a whole, or of a disinterested third-party gaze looking down on the problem of discrimination, and it simply does not care about results. Discrimination becomes the action of individuals, the atomistic behaviour of persons and institutions who have been abstracted out of actual society as part of a quest for villains.[7]

Direct discrimination contains this notion of something unfair caused by an individual, thus placing emphasis on the behaviour of the perpetrator. Discrimination is therefore seen as a problem of behaviour of respondents. 'It seeks to identify and catalogue perpetrators, to make sure that one has ascribed the correct evils to the correct perpetrator.'[8]

Comparison of the applicant and a person, or a hypothetical person, of the opposite sex is required. Section 5(3) of the Act requires that the comparison must be such that 'the relevant circumstances in the one case are the same, or not materially different, in the other'.[9] The complainant who alleges marital discrimination in employment must find an unmarried comparator.[10] Although it may seem simple and obvious that two individuals from opposing categories must be compared in order to prove direct sex or marital discrimination, it does not necessarily follow that this is the best way of dealing with sex discrimination. A number of assumptions are present. These are that women and men, or the married and the unmarried, can be directly compared; that all persons can be categorized according to sex; that women, whether married or not, can be fitted into slots in the employment, educational and service markets presently occupied by men.

Direct Comparison

To establish direct discrimination an applicant must show that the comparator from the other sex category has received better or more favourable treatment. Furthermore she must establish 'that the relevant circumstances in one case are the same, or not materially different in the other'.[11] This has been interpreted by the Employment Appeal Tribunal as 'principally though not exclusively talking about the personal circumstances of the applicant for employment . . . as compared with some other person'.[12] Thus where there are assumed or actual differences between the sexes no comparison is possible. Differences between the sexes may be biological or may result from social arrangements. Direct comparison means that differences, whether of biological or social origin, prevent comparison. Much of the problem of sex discrimination, then, cannot be tackled through direct comparison.

The Act espouses the 'differences' approach, which is also the approach taken in American law. Where inaccurate or preconceived distinctions are made these are termed irrational or arbitrary, and are held to be unlawful.[13] The American model which is similar finds its intellectual origins in an article by Tussman and TenBroek published in 1949. This argues that the test whether a classification is arbitrary is 'whether in defining a class, the legislature has carved the universe at a natural joint'.[14] But the separate legal classification of women and men, corresponding to a perceived traditional division, may be considered a natural joint at which to divide and make distinctions between people. The trouble with this is that, where there are differences between the sexes, this can provide a justification for differential treatment. But where the differences are of social origin, the law reinforces these, rather than combating them. As Catharine MacKinnon observes, 'while sex may be a "natural joint" at which to carve the universe, it may not be a natural point at which to subordinate one group to the other. The *social* universe is not only carved up, it is also hierarchically ordered.'[15]

The principle that like must be compared with like is rational, but it begs the question of the level of abstraction from personal characteristics at which the comparison is to be made. Are the domestic circumstances of individuals to be taken into account? Is account to be taken of women's social roles as mothers, that is as the parent with primary responsibility for children? Or are people to be regarded as individual and autonomous? The answer given to this by the courts has varied. The rejection of a mother for employment because 'it could prove difficult for you to run your home and also give full justice to the job' was not seen as direct discrimination by an industrial tribunal. Although the tribunal held that this was indirect discrimination, on grounds of marital status, it failed to appreciate that this could be regarded as direct discrimination on grounds of sex.[16] For the generalized assumption made was that a married woman has duties that single women, and men, do not have. This may be true, but if so the current form of anti-discrimination law cannot find it to be discriminatory. However, there are single women with children who may also have child-care responsibilities. And it is not unknown for single fathers to be engaged in paid employment and in raising children.

One answer to this problem of the level of abstraction of the comparison is to say that men with child-care responsibilities must be compared with women with child-care responsibilities. Thus generalized assumptions about women or men may be avoided. This is the approach which has been emphasized in certain cases. For example, in *Hurley* v. *Mustoe* the Employment Appeal Tribunal held that an employer's policy of not employing women with young children, which was not applied to men with children, was direct discrimination. It is clear from the case that the employer made two generalized assumptions. The first was that mothers have primary responsibility for children. The second was that this makes mothers unreliable employees. The Appeals Tribunal concluded:

> Finally we should make it clear what we are not deciding. First, we are not deciding whether it is, or is not, desirable for women with young children to go out to work. Strong views are held on this point. But Parliament has legislated that it is up to each mother to decide whether or not she goes out to work and employers may not discriminate against them just because they are mothers. Secondly, we are not deciding whether or not women with children as a class are less reliable employees. Parliament has legislated that they are not to be treated as a class but as individuals. No employer is bound to employ unreliable employees. Whether men or women. But he (the employer) must investigate each case, and not simply apply what some would call a rule of convenience and others a prejudice to exclude a whole class of women or married persons because some members of that class are not suitable employees.[17]

Another answer to the problem of determining whether persons are alike, or whether the relevant circumstances are similar, would be to say that personal and domestic matters should be disregarded as irrelevant. This is not the approach of the legislation, as the requirement of similar relevant circumstances shows.

The dismissal of a woman child-care officer by her employers when she announced her marriage has been held not to be direct discrimination. As the applicant was not married at the time of dismissal the tribunal also held that this could not be marital discrimination under section 3(1)(a).[18] However, the tribunal's decision must be wrong in light of *Hurley* v. *Mustoe*. The appropriate question to be asked was: would a male comparator have been dismissed on the announcement of his marriage? If the answer is no, then there is unlawful sex discrimination. If the answer is yes, the applicant's remedy must lie in employment law, but not specifically in sex discrimination law.

What this case illustrates is the difficulty tribunals have had with the complexities of the Sex Discrimination Act. Alice Leonard, in her detailed study of the performance of industrial tribunals in this area between 1980 and 1982, found that many errors were made. One explanation for this is lack of experience of tribunal members. The study established that only seven chairmen of industrial tribunals out of a total of 116 heard more than one case under the equal rights legislation.[19]

The form of the Sex Discrimination Act is such that personal and domestic matters may be used as a justification for differential treatment. The tribunal or court must make a decision as to whether these are relevant circumstances in comparison, or not. In developing a condemnation of generalized assumptions about the sexes, the Appeal Tribunal has attempted to deal with this problem. But sexual stereotypes continue to be used as justifications for employers' actions.

Sexual stereotypes assume that the sexes are different. They perpetrate perceived differences and are self-fulfilling prophecies. Stereotypes involves a denial of equality and in forcing people into sex-role straightjackets individual potential and autonomy is ignored. The courts are using anti-discrimination legislation to attack these assumptions. Thus in *Horsey* v. *Dyfed CC*, the Employment Appeal Tribunal stated that most discrimination flows from generalised assumptions

> that people of a particular sex, marital status or race possess or lack certain characteristics. . . . The purpose of the legislation is to secure equal opportunity for individuals regardless of their sex, married status, or race. This result would not be achieved if it were sufficient to escape liability to show that the reason for the discriminatory treatment was simply an assumption that women or coloured persons possessed or lacked particular characteristics and not that they were just women or coloured persons.[20]

The Appeal Tribunal held that the decision by her employers to refuse the applicant's secondment on a social work course was based on the generalized assumption that married women follow their husbands' jobs.

The Court of Appeal in *Skyrail Oceanic Ltd* v. *Coleman*[21] held that the assumption that the husband, and not the wife, is the breadwinner is discrimination on grounds of sex. The complainant in that case was employed in a business in competition with that of her husband's employer. Both employers agreed that to ensure business secrecy one of the spouses would have to be dismissed. The wife was dismissed by her employer 'as the husband was presumably the breadwinner'.

In the above cases the courts have attempted to deal with stereotypes; that is, with generalized assumptions based on sex. However, as the cases make clear, it is such assumptions, and the failure to look at the particular circumstances of each case, which make the discrimination unlawful. Thus if a discriminatory decision is justified by evidence about a particular person it will not necessarily be unlawful. Furthermore these cases suggest that if evidence of differences between the sexes can be shown (rather than assumptions about differences), then discrimination may not be unlawful. Section 5(3) may prevent comparison if such evidence of differences is shown. For comparison depends on the relevant circumstances being the same.

The Aristotelian conception of distributive justice, that like should be treated alike, is the conceptual framework of direct discrimination. From this it follows that unalike should be treated differently. In some cases differential treatment is unequal treatment. An example is unequal access to, and terms of, benefits on retirement. This affects both women and men. Women complainants have not necessarily seen the official retirement age of sixty for women as a benefit; this depends on individual circumstances. Some women whose employment has been curtailed by domestic responsibilities would like to continue after sixty. On the other hand, some male complainants envy women's earlier retirement age, which carries with it pension rights and other benefits such as travel passes, free dental treatment, reductions on various services and facilities. The state age of retirement for men is sixty-five. This has affected other matters such as redundancy, where the number of years between the age of retirement and age of redundancy has been the basis for the calculation of severance pay.[22]

Certain forms of differential treatment – although not the retirement age – are justified by their proponents as being based on biological differences. The problem for the legislator, the adjudicator or the administrator, is to decide in which respects women and men are the same, and in which respects they are different.

Sameness and Being Similarly Situated

In Weberian terms the administration of law in a rational manner requires purely technical decision-making, 'without regard to persons in accordance with calculable rules'.[23] The 'exclusion of love, hatred and every purely personal, especially irrational and incalculable feeling, from the execution of official tasks'[24] is the goal of impersonal bureaucracy.

Considering these we can see that problems arise where ascribed biological characteristics, such as the ability to bear children, intrude into the workplace.

The cases on pregnancy show the limitations of direct discrimination as a concept. As in distributive justice, the concept of direct discrimination requires that like be treated alike. There is a mandatory comparison of relevant circumstances which are 'the same' under section 5(3) of the Act. But it is difficult to assert sameness when comparing a pregnant woman and a man. Therefore pregnancy has caused considerable problems where it forms the basis of a complaint of direct discrimination.

If persons are to be compared their circumstances must be the same or similar, as required by section 5(3). Comparison is contingent on sameness. Thus pregnancy poses a problem. It would seem that there can be no direct comparison of a pregnant woman with a pregnant man; although a pregnant single woman can be directly compared to a pregnant married woman for purposes of the section on marital discrimination. When persons are compared, the requirement to prove direct discrimination on grounds of sex is that 'less favourable treatment' of one sex be shown. One answer to this problem might be to raise the level of abstraction and compare a man who has to undergo medical treatment for a specifically male condition, such as prostate gland difficulties, with a woman who is pregnant. However, some feminists object to this on the grounds that pregnancy is not an illness.

In *Reany* v. *Kanda Jean Products*[25] an industrial tribunal held that since a man could not become pregnant it was impossible to compare the pregnant female applicant with a man. Therefore the application, based on direct discrimination because of dismissal on grounds of pregnancy, failed. The lack of comparability grounded the tribunal's decision:

> In so far as the applicant complains that she is the victim of discrimination by comparison with the case of any other (hypothetical) man, the respective circumstances in each case are very materially different for obvious reasons. . . . It is physically impossible for a man in the instant case to receive preferential treatment for the reason that his case and that of the applicant is incomparable.[26]

In *Roberts* v. *BICC*[27] the refusal of an employer to pay sickness benefit to a pregnant employee was held not to be discrimination on grounds of sex. But by a literal reading of terms of employment, which excluded 'maternity or confinement' from the company's sickness benefit scheme, the tribunal held that complications in pregnancy were different from 'maternity or confinement' and that therefore the applicant should receive her pay. This decision was not based on the Sex Discrimination Act.

In *Turley* v. *Allders Department Stores Ltd*[28] the applicant alleged that she had been dismissed because of pregnancy. The issue was whether dismissal on grounds of pregnancy is less favourable treatment on grounds of sex under the direct discrimination provisions. At the Employment Appeal Tribunal it was held that the definition of discrimination in the Sex Discrimination Act precluded a finding that to dismiss a woman for pregnancy is discrimination on grounds of sex. This was explained as follows:

> You are to look at men and women, and see that they are not treated unequally simply because they are men and women. You have to compare like with like. So, in the case of a pregnant woman there is an added difficulty in the application of subsection (1) (of s.1). Suppose that to dismiss her for pregnancy is to dismiss her on the ground of her sex. In order to see if she has been treated less favourably than a man the sense of the section is that you must compare like with like, and you cannot. When she is pregnant a woman is no longer just a woman. She is a woman, as the Authorised Version of the Bible accurately puts it, with child, and there is no masculine equivalent.[29]

The tribunal suggested that the applicant's remedy lay under section 34 of the Employment Protection Act 1975, which provides that dismissal for pregnancy is unfair dismissal. The problem for the applicant, however, was that she had not worked for the qualifying period of twenty-six weeks then required for statutory protection against unfair dismissal, which has now been raised to two years.[30]

The dissenting judgment in the *Turley* case took the following approach:

> The case under the direct discrimination provision is a simple one. Pregnancy is a medical condition. It is a condition which applies only to women. It is a condition which will lead to a request for time off from work for the confinement. A man is in similar circumstances who is employed by the same employer and who in the course of the year will require time off for a hernia operation, to have his tonsils removed, or for other medical reasons. The employer must not discriminate by applying different and less favourable criteria to the pregnant woman than to the man requiring time off. That is the 'like for like' comparison, not one between women who are pregnant and men who cannot become pregnant.[31]

Whatever the merits of this opinion, it does illustrate the difficulties of the 'like for like' comparison which has bedevilled philosophers attempting to apply Aristotelian notions of distributive justice through the ages. What is the relevant element for comparison? At what level of abstraction is the comparison to be made?

A subsequent decision of the Employment Appeal Tribunal characterized *Turley*'s case is a majority decision which is purely hypothetical In *Hayes* v. *Malleable Working Men's Club*,[32] Waite J. held that *Turley* did not lay down a general principle excluding pregnancy discrimination from the ambit of the Sex Discrimination Act. 'It enshrines no principle of law of general application' and should be treated as confined to its facts. This distinction of *Turley* by the Appeal Tribunal was followed by the qualification that, if the distinction was wrong, then the Appeal Tribunal would decline to follow *Turley*. Instead they preferred the approach of the dissentient in *Turley*. This was explained as follows:

> that the proper approach is to ask whether pregnancy with its associated consequences is capable of being matched by analogous circumstances such as sickness applying to a man, and if so whether they are closely enough matched to enable a fair comparison to be made between the favourableness of treatment accorded to a man in one situation and to a man in the other.[33]

Commenting on this decision Nicola Lacey points out that

> an important dimension of the case may well become suppressed. If the Tribunal decides that a sick man would have been equally harshly treated [as the pregnant woman], by the very hypothesis of the comparison, no question can be raised about whether it was appropriate to treat a pregnant woman in the same way. Since the logic of the section lies in formally equal treatment in roughly similar cases, no possible argument can be raised about the special nature of pregnancy which might merit special treatment, as acknowledged in our statutory laws on maternity leave.[34]

Thus the stereotyped view of women as having a special biological weakness is reinforced. The sick man is in an abnormal situation. But he is the suggested comparator under the *Hayes* approach. Lacey concludes that the form of the Sex Discrimination Act 'renders it an unreliable tool for ensuring the fair treatment of pregnant women'.[35]

Other decisions highlight other difficulties of equating pregnancy and sickness. Some insurance schemes expressly disconnect the two conditions. In *Coyne* v. *Export Credits Guarantee Dept*[36] the applicant's baby was born by caesarian section. This delayed her return to work until two weeks after the expiry of her maternity leave. Her employers refused to pay sickness pay for this period as their rules were that the absence must be for an illness unconnected with pregnancy. The applicant's remedy was held to lie under the Equal Pay Act.

Pregnancy is a condition particular to women. The requirement of a male comparator for complaints of direct sex discrimination under the Sex Discrimination Act has two possible results: either there can be no remedy under the Act for the pregnant woman unfavourably treated by an employer under the Act; or the artificial comparison with a sick man must be made. Neither result is satisfactory. The first means that a condition particular to women is ignored by anti-discrimination law. Yet it is a form of sex discrimination. The second ensures the reinforcement of a damaging stereotype of the kind the Act was intended to combat.

Anti-discrimination law in the United States has also faced difficulties in determining whether the pregnant woman can be relevantly compared to a man. The Supreme Court has decided cases of discrimination on grounds of pregnancy under the equal protection clause of the Constitution and under Title VII of the Civil Rights Act 1964.[37] Let us examine firstly the equal protection approach.

Equal Protection under the United States Constitution

Differential treatment of women and men is open to constitutional scrutiny by the courts in the United States. In *Craig* v. *Boren* the Supreme Court held that sex-based classifications must serve 'important governmental objectives and [be] substantially related to the achievement of those objectives',[38] if they are not to be struck down. However, in *Geduldig* v. *Aiello*[39] it was held that where the classification at issue is between pregnant and non-pregnant persons, and not between women and men, the classification need only to be shown as serving 'rational purposes' as opposed to 'important governmental objectives'. The court found that the exclusion of disabilities arising from normal pregnancy and childbirth from disability benefits for state employees could be justified on a rational basis test. The rational basis was the cost and structure of employee contributions to the disabilities fund.

The jurisprudential model for equal protection analysis requires a comparison of the person or group complaining of discrimination with mainstream groups. This mode of equality analysis based on comparison derives from the article published in 1949 in the *California Law Review* by Tussman and TenBroek.[40] The Supreme Court has laid down that constitutional scrutiny of disparate treatment will only take place where the parties are 'similarly situated'. But as one scholar observes: 'To the extent that being similarly situated is a prerequisite for constitutional scrutiny of differential treatment, any such comparison [between women and men] will necessarily result in continued disparate treatment and discrimination'.[41]

Title VII of the Civil Rights Act 1964

The Civil Rights Act 1964, Title VII provides that it shall be an unlawful employment practice for an employer to fail or refuse to hire or to discharge any individual with respect to his compensation, terms, conditions, or privileges of employment, because of such individual's race, colour, religion, sex, or national origin. The problem for the woman who complains of pregnancy discrimination is to prove that this is discrimination on grounds of sex.

In *General Electric Co.* v. *Gilbert* the Supreme Court held that 'an exclusion of pregnancy from a disability benefit plan providing general coverage is not gender-based discrimination'.[42] The justification for the exclusion, accepted by the court, was that pregnancy is 'significantly different from the typical covered disease or disability'. In the court's view pregnancy is not a disease but is 'often a voluntarily undertaken and desired condition'.[43] Justice Brennan, in a dissenting opinion, took the view that the inclusions and exclusions in the insurance company's policy did not conform to the distinction between disability and disease on the one hand, and a voluntary condition on the other. He showed that, in the company's policy, whether or not a 'disability' was involuntary, or could be labelled a 'disease', did not strictly determine whether it was covered by the policy.[44] Title VII is also subject to a 'disparate impact' test, on which the concept of 'indirect discrimination' in the SDA is based. This is discussed in chapter 4.

The Pregnancy Discrimination Act

In 1978 Title VII of the Civil Rights Act 1964 was amended to prohibit discrimination on the basis of pregnancy. The United States Pregnancy Discrimination Act provides:

> The terms 'because of sex' or 'on the basis of sex' include, but are not limited to, because of or on the basis of pregnancy, childbirth, or related medical conditions; and women affected by pregnancy, childbirth or related medical conditions shall be treated the same for all employment-related purposes, including receipt of benefits under fringe benefit programs, as other persons not so affected but similar in their inability to work.[45]

The wording above encompasses the idea that discrimination on grounds of pregnancy is discrimination on grounds of sex. In other words it bypasses the requirement that the pregnant woman must be 'similarly situated' to a man. The Act also covers employment-related benefits for those unable to work.

Difference

The complainant of direct discrimination must show that the relevant circumstances in her case are the same as, or not materially different from, those of her male comparator. In the American terminology she must show that she is 'similarly situated'. It follows therefore that it is a defence to show that the circumstances are different. As we have already seen, pregnancy has been interpreted by the courts as a sufficiently relevant difference between women and men as to prevent a claim of direct discrimination. But difference as a defence has not been confined to pregnancy cases.

In *Peake* v. *Automotive Products Ltd*[46] the Court of Appeal held that a concession by an employer to women workers which allowed them to leave work five minutes before their male colleagues, both sexes having stopped work at the same time, was not sex discrimination because the rule was made in the interests of safety at work, was a sensible administrative arrangement, and was *de minimus*. The rationale for the concession was that the women might be jostled in the rush to leave the factory. However, in the view of the male complainant, this was direct discrimination for, on grounds of his sex, he had to stay at work for an additional two and a half working days over a year. The Appeal Tribunal held that this concession to the women workers was unlawful sex discrimination.

On appeal Lord Denning referred to the difference between women and men as justifying the five minutes grace permitted to women.

> Although the Act applies equally to men as to women, I must say it would be very wrong to my mind if this statute were thought to obliterate the differences between men and women or to do away with the difference and courtesy which we must expect mankind to give womankind. The natural differences of sex must be regarded even in the interpretation of an Act of Parliament.[47]

Concurring, Lord Justice Shaw criticized the complaint as trivial. He expressed the view that the 1975 Act was not 'designed to provide a basis for capricious and empty complaints of differentiation between the sexes. Nor was it intended to operate as a statutory abolition of every instinct of chivalry and consideration on the part of men for the opposite sex'.[48]

One comment on this decision is that the 'Court of Appeal did not appreciate the irony: a statute introduced to make unlawful gender-based classifications, which had often been rationalised by reference to chivalry or the alleged need to protect frail women, was being frustrated by precisely those factors of chivalry and paternalism'.[49] Yet the issue of sameness and difference is a thorny one. On the one hand it is undesirable that sex discrimination legislation should create a procrustean bed into which women have to fit by becoming 'the same' as men. Where certain biological differences such as pregnancy exist, the law must acknowledge these.

In the past women's differences from men, whether biological or social, whether 'natural' or constructed, have been a source of inequality. Differences meant differential treatment. Women objected to this and fought against it. Most differences, seen as relevant in the past, are dismissed as irrelevant today.

Lord Denning later reconsidered the grounds of his decision in the Peake case. In *Ministry of Defence* v. *Jeremiah*[50] women employees were not required to work in 'colour bursting shops', whereas men were required to do so by the employers. This work was dirty, protective clothing had to be worn, and thorough cleansing by showers was necessary on completion of work. The Court of Appeal held that this differential treatment was unlawful discrimination against men. Lord Denning reconsidered his views concerning safety measures and chivalry in the *Peake* case and stated:

> I think the only sound ground was that the discrimination was *de minimus*. . . . [T]he House of Lords . . . refused leave to appeal for that very reason. They thought that the decision was correct on the *de minimus* ground. In these circumstances, the other ground should no longer be relied upon.[51]

The Court of Appeal asserted that differential treatment *per se* is not unlawful sex discrimination. There must also be a detriment to the applicant, for 'mere deprivation of choice for one sex, or some other differentiation in their treatment' is not necessarily unlawful discrimination. However, as later cases show, this seems to have been a mistake. In *Gill and Coote* v. *El Vino*[52] the complaint that it was unlawful discrimination to refuse to serve women at a bar was upheld. The Court of Appeal made a declaration of breach of section 29 of the Sex Discrimination Act, which makes it unlawful to discriminate in the provision of goods and services. The court clarified that the appropriate question is whether a facility is refused as the law requires that services be provided 'in the like manner and on like terms' to women and men. If so, section 1(1)(a) then requires a comparison of the treatment of women and men. If there is differential treatment, and no good defence, unlawful discrimination has taken place. The respondent in the *El Vino* case attempted to argue that there was no detriment to women in the bar because they were served at tables. The Court of Appeal made it clear that detriment is not relevant to a case of direct discrimination. This is a confusion which arose from the *Jeremiah* case.

This clarification of the law on direct discrimination, which does not require proof of detriment, was reiterated in *Brennan* v. *Dewhurst*.[53] The Employment Appeal Tribunal held that the refusal of a job to a woman on grounds of sex was direct discrimination and an unlawful form of discrimination under the Act section 6(1)(a). The defence that detriment must be shown was rejected. Thus to directly discriminate against a person on grounds of sex is unlawful, and the complaint does not have to show detriment. The Act itself is contrary to the law.

Where both sexes have their choices restricted, although not in an identical fashion, unlawful discrimination may not exist. Although the content is different, the fact of restriction is similar. This is shown by *Schmidt* v. *Austicks Bookshop Ltd.*[54] There the applicant was dismissed for refusing to comply with the employer's rules regarding dress. Her complaint was of sex discrimination in that men were permitted to wear trousers and women were not. She wished to wear trousers to work. The

Employment Appeal Tribunal avoided the narrow interpretation of the relevant circumstances under section 5(3), which had previously been made by the industrial tribunal, and took a broader approach. The industrial tribunal's holding was that, as men did not have a choice of wearing a skirt or trousers, but had to wear trousers, just as women had to wear skirts, there was no basis of comparison as the relevant circumstances were not the same. The EAT took the line that both sexes were subjected to restrictions in their choice of clothing, 'although obviously, women and men being different, the rules in the two cases were not the same'. Therefore, their circumstances were similar and one sex was not more favourably treated than the other. 'Experience shows that under the Sex Discrimination Act 1975 a lot depends on how one phrases or formulates the matter of which complaint is made.'[55]

The contrast in the approaches of the industrial tribunal and the Employment Appeal Tribunal illustrates the point made earlier about levels of abstraction. The industrial tribunal compared skirts and trousers and found they were not comparable. Their conclusion was that the Act did not apply. The Employment Appeal Tribunal compared one restriction of choice as to clothing with another. Their conclusion was that the Act did apply, but that there was no unlawful discrimination. Whether or not the result is correct is a matter of opinion. But the approach of the Employment Appeal Tribunal, at a higher level of abstraction, is surely correct.

Sexual Harassment[56]

Sexual harassment is the term given to unwanted sexual attention, requests for sexual favours, and other conduct of a sexual nature, express or implied. It may consist of physical gestures or touching, it may be verbal, including sexual innuendoes and jokes. It has been defined by an appeal court as 'a particularly degrading and unacceptable form of treatment which it must be taken to have been the intention of Parliament to restrain'.[57] Such research as exists indicates that the principal victims are women.[58] This has been analysed as 'the exploitation of a powerful position to impose sexual demands or pressures on an unwilling but less powerful person'.[59] In employment law cases it has been recognized that 'persistent and unwanted amorous advances to a female member of [the employer's] staff' is conduct which entitles an employee to leave without notice.[60] The employee can claim constructive dismissal.

The law on unfair dismissal has provided a remedy to victims of harassment. In *Wigan Borough Council* v. *Davies*[61] the Employment Appeal Tribunal accepted as an implied term of the employment contract 'that the employer shall render reasonable support to an employee to ensure that the employee can carry out the duties of his job without harassment and disruption by fellow workers'. The harassment in this case was not sexual, but there is a line of authority suggesting that the law of unfair dismissal will cover such cases.

The protection offered by the Sex Discrimination Act 1975 is greater than that offered by unfair dismissal law, so if the complainant of sexual harassment can show less favourable treatment on grounds of sex that procedure is to be preferred. Where either the Act or unfair dismissal law forms the basis of the complaint, it is conduct in the workplace which is at issue. There sexual harassment may occur in a variety of ways. First, where sexual favours become a term of a contract of employment. Second, where sexual favours, and the acceptance or rejection of these, influence decisions on employment, such as dismissal, promotion, salary. Third, where because of sexual conduct the work environment becomes so unpleasant to the victim that she is forced to leave her job, or suffers disadvantage at work.

Porcelli v. *Strathclyde Regional Council*[62] provides an example of the third situation. The Employment Appeal Tribunal held that a failure by an employer to protect an employee against sexual harassment is unlawful discrimination on grounds of sex. At the first hearing the industrial tribunal had concluded that, although there had been a degree of sexual harassment, the male co-workers would have treated a man they disliked just as unpleasantly as they treated the applicant. This led the tribunal to the conclusion that the applicant had not been treated less favourably than a man. Part of the conduct complained of consisted of jokes, innuendoes, remarks and gestures of a sexual nature. The EAT's view was that the aspects of the male conduct which had 'sexual overtones could have no relevance in their conduct towards a man'.[63] The applicant was subjected to a detriment in being forced to seek a transfer from the school at which she worked. Detriment is covered by section 6 of the Sex Discrimination Act setting out the forms of discrimination rendered unlawful. Section 6(2)(b) makes it unlawful for an employer to discriminate against a woman 'by dismissing her, or subjecting her to any other detriment'. However, it is doubtful whether detriment requires proof of something as drastic as a job transfer. Just being in a hostile environment of sexual innuendo and behaviour, such as that experienced by the plaintiff, may be enough.[64]

On further appeal to the Court of Sessions (Scotland) the Lord President, Lord Emslie, pointed out that the issue was one of treatment, and not of 'the motive or objective of the person responsible for it'. Therefore the employers' motives were irrelevant, since the applicant's co-workers had based their treatment of her on her sex. Although the co-workers would have behaved badly to a man whom they disliked, in their treatment of the applicant sex was used as a 'particular kind of weapon'. The nature of the treatment complained of must be identified in cases under the Sex Discrimination Act. If it contains elements of a sexual character which would not be directed against a man, then a case has been made out.[65]

The issue of difference again creates difficulties. Section 6 of the Act defines the circumstances in which it is unlawful to discriminate on ground of sex. But in order to prove discrimination the applicant must show that she has been treated less favourably than a man has been, or would have been treated. She must also prove that the unfavourable treatment is because she is a woman. What if the employer argues that she was dismissed because she refused to have a relationship with him, and not because she was a woman? He could add that he would similarly dismiss a male employee who refused. It would seem then that the discrimination was not on the ground of sex.[66]

The courts in the United States have developed a 'but-for' test to show that sexual harassment is sex discrimination. In *Barnes* v. *Costle*[67] the US Court of Appeals held that the dismissal of a female employee for refusing sexual advances amounted to sex discrimination. The test was explained as follows:

> But for her womanhood . . . her participation in sexual activity would never have been solicited. To say, then, that she was victimised in her employment simply because she declined the invitation is to ignore the asserted fact that she was invited only because she was a woman.[68]

It was also the case the 'no male employee was susceptible to such an approach'.[69] This might be thought to imply that only women can be victims of sexual harassment, but that was not the court's meaning. It is the harassment of employees of one sex only that is unlawful. Thus the court clarified that '[i]n the case of the bisexual superior, the insistence upon sexual favours would not constitute gender discrimination because it would apply to male and female employees alike'.[70]

Sex discrimination law cannot offer protection where employees are harassed on sexual grounds but not because of their sex. Again, the comparison of one sex with the other is essential. Where the employer subjects both women and men to unwelcome sexual demands their remedy will lie elsewhere. It is only where different criteria are applied to women and men that sex discrimination law is applicable.

In the development of the law on sexual harassment the American courts initially took the view that there must be demonstrated employment repercussions before unlawful discrimination could be said to have occurred. In *Smith* v. *Rust Engineering*[71] the plaintiff lost her case because she failed to show a relationship between the unwanted sexual advances and her terms and conditions of employment. In this case the perpetrator of the sexual attention was a co-worker. But in *Fisher* v. *Flynn*,[72] where the conduct complained of came from a superior, nevertheless the plaintiff university teacher lost her case. The court did not apply an analysis of power relations to the action. Rather the court held that the plaintiff had not shown

> a sufficient nexus between her refusal to accede to romantic overtures and her termination [of employment]. She has not alleged that the department chairman had the authority to terminate her employment or effectively recommend the same. . . . [T]he romantic overtures were but an unsatisfactory encounter with no employment repercussions and consequently not actionable'.[73]

The distinction between unwanted sexual attention itself, and employment consequences which follow the rejection thereof, was maintained by the United States courts until 1981. This distinction was neatly summed up by the Colorado District Court in *Heelan* v. *Johns-Manville Corp.* as follows: 'Under the facts of this case, the frequent sexual advances by a supervisor do not form the basis of the Title VII violation that we find to exist. Significantly, termination of the plaintiff's employment when the advances were rejected is what makes the conduct legally objectionable.'[74] As Michael Rubenstein points out, the trouble with this approach is 'that it leaves the woman against whom *no* retaliation has been taken with no recourse against the harassment'.[75]

The United States Equal Employment Opportunity Commission dealt with this point in its guidelines on sexual harassment at work, issued in November 1980. The guidelines state the view that harassment is unlawful where it creates an intimidating, hostile or offensive work environment. This, indeed, was the view taken by the Employment Appeal Tribunal in the British case of *Porcelli*.[76] The EEOC guidelines are as follows:

> Unwelcome sexual advances, requests for sexual favours, and other verbal or physical conduct constitute sexual harassment when (1) submission to such conduct is made either explicitly or implicitly a term or condition of an individuals's employment, (2) submission to or rejection of such conduct by an individual is used as the basis for employment decisions affecting such individual, or (3) such conduct has the purpose or effect of unreasonably interfering with an individual's work performance or creating an intimidating, hostile or offensive working environment.[77]

The United States Supreme Court has endorsed these guidelines and firmly condemned both 'quid pro quo' and 'hostile environment' forms of sexual harassment which are covered by Title VII as unlawful discrimination. In *Meritor Savings Bank, FSB* v. *Vinson*[78] the court rejected the employer's assertion that economic discrimination or reprisals must be shown to establish sexual harassment, and unanimously held that it is enough for the plaintiff to show that she was obliged to suffer unwelcome sexual advances where 'such conduct has the purpose or effect of unreasonably interfering with an individual's work performance or creating an intimidating, hostile, or offensive working environment'.[79] However,

on the issue of whether the employer is strictly liable for the actions of
supervisors or co-workers in sexual harassment, a distinction has been
drawn between economic reprisal and hostile environment cases. In the
quid pro quo situation there is strict liability, but where the environment
is hostile the standard is less stringent.

The endorsement by the Supreme Court of unlawful sexual harassment as including a hostile work environment is important. For otherwise, as the court in *Bundy* v. *Jackson* has pointed out, the employer
could

> implicitly and effectively make the employee's endurance of sexual intimid-
> ation a 'condition' of her employment. The woman then faces a 'cruel
> trilemma'. She can endure the harassment. She can attempt to oppose it,
> with little hope of success, either legal or practical, but with every prospect
> of making the job even less tolerable for her. Or she can leave her job, with
> little hope of legal relief and the likely prospect of another job where she
> will face harassment anew. [80]

In Britain the law on sexual harassment is yet to be developed. In order
to succeed on a complaint under the Sex Discrimination Act the applicant
must show that on grounds of her sex she was treated less favourably by
her employer in relation to her terms and conditions of employment than
a similarly situated man was treated or would have been treated. The Act
sets out specifically the forms of discrimination which are unlawful.
Under section 6(2)(a) and (b) it is unlawful to discriminate against a
woman in relation to promotion, transfer, training, or 'any other
benefits, facilities or services, or by refusing or deliberately omitting to
afford her access to them'; or 'by dismissing her or subjecting her to any
other detriment'. Quid pro quo harassment is covered the word 'detriment', and in *Porcelli* v. *Strathclyde Regional Council* the Employment
Appeals Tribunal held that the unpleasant work environment which
forced the applicant to ask for a job transfer was a detriment. But Lord
Emslie in the Court of Sessions interpreted detriment as 'disadvantage'
citing Brandon J. in the *Jeremiah* case in support. [81] This was later
approved by the Court of Appeal in *De Souza* v. *Automobile Association*
where the court held for detriment there must be a finding that a reasonable worker would or might feel disadvantaged in the circumstance or
conditions in which she or he had to work. [82] Disadvantage as a concept
has a broader sense than economic reprisals. It could include a hostile
work environment which has been shown to cause psychological damage
and stress. [83]

A narrow interpretation of the requirement of detriment may cause
problems to the victim of sexual harassment who does not wish to leave
her job. The American cases establish that the work environment is part
of the terms and conditions of the employment contract. This should also
be the position in Britain. A hostile work environment, undercutting a

woman's autonomy by sexualizing her role, is a disadvantage in itself. The courts should not insist that the woman resigns or asks for a transfer before she has a remedy. Unfavourable working conditions are detrimental in themselves.

Sexual Preference[84]

Is discrimination against a person, because of preference for sexual partners of the same sex, discrimination on grounds of sex? It seems that discrimination against someone on grounds of lesbianism or homosexuality is not covered by the Sex Discrimination Act. Less favourable treatment on the grounds of sexual preference is distinguishable from less favourable treatment on the grounds of sex. Furthermore, even if a comparison is made between women and men, the respondent can defend himself by arguing that all persons with a sexual preference for their own sex category would be so treated. However, if it can be shown that the respondent treats male homosexuals neutrally but lesbians less favourably on grounds of sexual preference, then there is evidence of sex discrimination. This approach found favour with a United States District Court in *Valdes* v. *Lumbermen's Mutual Casualty Co.*[85] The court recognized that a *prima facie* case was made out by a woman who alleged that her employers refused to promote lesbians but were willing to promote homosexual males. But such a claim is based on less favourable treatment on grounds of sex and not on grounds of sexual preference.

In a series of cases the courts of the United States have rejected claims based on discrimination on grounds of sexual preference.[86] It has been held that the equality legislation did not contemplate discrimination against homosexuals.[87] The ingenious argument that there is less favourable treatment on grounds of sex where a male is dismissed for his attachment to Mr X whereas Ms Y (also attached to Mr X) is not, has been rejected by the courts. In *DeSantis* v. *Pacific Telephone and Telegraph Co. Inc.* the United States Court of Appeal rejected the idea that this argument demonstrates different employment criteria for homosexuals. The court criticized 'appellants' efforts to "bootstrap" Title VII protection for homosexuals . . . [w]e note that whether dealing with men or women the employer is using the same criterion: it will not hire or promote a person who prefers sexual partners of the same sex. Thus this policy does not involve different decisional criteria for the sexes'.[88]

The approach taken by the American courts in cases of sexual preference has its British counterpart in a case involving a transsexual. In *White* v. *British Sugar Corporation*, where the transsexual applicant was dismissed, the employers justified their action by saying that all transsexuals, male-to-female and female-to-male, would be treated alike.[89] The applicant was a female-to-male transsexual who was dismissed on the discovery of transsexualism. The tribunal held that there was no discrimination. The question was held to be whether the employer had treated

> the applicant on the ground of her sex less favourably than they would have treated a man. If the applicant had been a man and he had held himself out to the respondents as a female and had been employed as such and used the female toilet facilities and the like and then it had been discovered that he was a man, the Tribunal had no hesitation in deciding that in the circumstances the respondents would have dismissed him. According in the present case there was no discrimination on the grounds of the applicant's sex. [90]

In the United States transsexuals have not convinced the courts that discrimination on grounds of transsexualism is discrimination on grounds of sex. It has been held that dismissal from employment because of a change of sex is not covered by the legislation. [91] The absence of legislative history indicating a broader reference of the term 'sex' in the language of Title VII has been used to close down claims by transsexuals. [92] In *Sommers* v. *Budget Marketing Inc.* [93] it was held that the plain meaning should be ascribed to the word sex in Title VII and that 'the legislative history does not show any intention to include transsexualism in Title VII'.

The problems faced by homosexuals and transsexuals in bringing their complaints under the Sex Discrimination Act illustrate, again, the limitations of the Act. The requirement of comparison of treatment across the sexes, combined with the further requirement that the relevant circumstances must be similar, operates to shut out many complaints. It may be that some of these applications would be better dealt with under laws on unfair dismissal, or other employment laws. But there is a connection between sexual stereotypes which the Act attempts to combat and sexual choices and preferences which it ignores.

Defences

Direct discrimination cases pose difficulties for the complainant in that the burden of proof is on her to show that she was unlawfully discriminated against on grounds of her sex. It is open to the respondent to defend himself, and the possibilities are there. As Michael Rubenstein points out: 'The one certitude in a sex discrimination case is that the employer is not going to stand up in court and say that the ground for his action was that the complainant was a woman.' [94] This raises two questions: first, the problem of proving that the treatment received was on grounds of sex; second, to what extent is the motive of the respondent relevant?

The applicant may succeed in proving that she has received less favourable treatment than her male comparator, but the assertion that this was on grounds of her sex can be contested in a number of ways. The respondent may put forward explanations for his actions couched in gender-neutral terms. The burden of proof rests on the applicant, despite the White Paper, *Equality for Women*, which stated:

> Complaints which are not settled by conciliation nor withdrawn will be heard by the tribunals. The complainant will have to show at the outset that the respondent has acted to the complaint's detriment in circumstances suggesting that such detrimental action has been taken on grounds of sex or marriage. It will then be for the respondent to prove that the complainant has not been less favourably treated than other persons on those grounds.[95]

In other words, the burden of proof to show that the action taken is not on grounds of sex or marriage was to be placed on the respondent.

In the Parliamentary debates on the Sex Discrimination Bill several speakers raised the point that the policy of the White Paper had not been followed. It was argued that the burden of proof on the woman complaining of discrimination was unfair. Ms Jo Richardson, in the House of Commons, pointed out that the respondent is 'likely to be a substantial organisation with large resources', whereas the complainant is likely to be 'a solitary figure . . . nervous about legal proceedings'. Thus if 'she has to bear the whole onus of proof, it is unlikely that she will ever have the courage to bring the case, and, therefore, the heart of the Bill will, perhaps, be rendered useless'.[96]

Baroness Fisher also raised this point in the Lords:

> As I read the Bill, it is now for the complainant to establish that discrimination was the reason for the act complained of; so the burden will be on the woman to prove that there is a case to answer. . . .
>
> [T]he employer, or the distributor of goods and/or services, or – the educational establishment being what it is – those people . . . will be able to afford to employ the right kind of people to put a case against her.[97]

Recent research bears out the point that individual complainants are at a disadvantage because of a lack of expert advice and assistance.[98] It is not just a question of greater resources but also of legal technicalities. The respondent, if heard by the tribunal, can contest the assertion that the action complained of was on grounds of sex or marriage.[99] He may put forward explanations for his actions couched in gender-neutral terms. Thus height or strength may be said to be the criteria for particular forms of employment. However the courts have occasionally come to the aid of complainants by holding that once a *prima facie* case of discrimination has been made out, and there is evidence of preference for one sex over the other, the burden of proof shifts. The Equal Opportunities Commission has stated that the burden of proof is crucial to the outcome of many cases under the Act. Lacking clear proof, complainants often have to rely on equivocal evidence that the less favourable treatment was on grounds of sex. The point is that less favourable treatment *per se* is not unlawful, so although the applicant may be able to fulfil that aspect of proof in her claim, she may not be able to show that her sex was the cause. The Commission considers that the task of discharging the burden of proof 'will remain a daunting prospect for unaided applications and likely to discourage the courts and tribunals from drawing the inferences from the primary facts of a case which are so frequently essential'.[100] Accordingly, the Commission proposes that 'once the applicant proves less favourable treatment in circumstances consistent with grounds of sex or victimisation', the burden of proof should shift on to the respondent to prove non-sexual or non-victimization grounds for the less favourable treatment of the applicant.[101]

Moberly v. *Commonwealth Hall* is an example of a case where the courts have helped applicants. There Kilner Brown J. in the Employment Appeal Tribunal stated that he 'would take the view that where there has been established an act of discrimination, and where it has been established that one party to the act of discrimination is male and the other is female, prima facie that raises a case which calls for an answer'.[102] The Northern Irish Court of Appeal in the *Wallace* case has taken the view that, where it is established that the complainant had qualifications, experience, and had demonstrated commitment superior to the male appointee, and where she is unsuccessful, there is evidence of discrimination of grounds of sex.[103] In such cases it is for the respondent to prove that the asserted reasons for the action are genuine and not related to sex. If he fails to do so then the case for less favourable treatment on grounds of sex has been made out. It is this approach that the Equal Opportunities Commission wishes to make uniform.

What if the criteria are applied to one sex only? The American courts call a criterion or factor applied to one sex which is not applied to the other sex the 'sex-plus' question. The idea is that the criterion is gender plus an additional factor, as explained in *Phillips* v. *Martin-Marietta Corporation*.[104] Where a sex-plus standard is applied the effect is to discriminate against a sub-class within the gender group as a whole. Thus the rejection of a woman job applicant on the grounds that she had children does not initially appear as sex discrimination. Not all women have children; therefore the standard does not affect women as a group. However, if this standard is not applied to men then, in American law at least, the sex-plus standard is recognized as sex discrimination.

In *Hurley* v. *Mustoe*[105] the respondent had a policy against employing women with young children, but had no such policy in relation to men. The Employment Appeal Tribunal was not troubled by the fact that women without children were employed. It made a finding of direct discrimination under section 1. Although the decision was not articulated in terms of the sex-plus criterion, the reasoning in the case appears to be in line with similar American decisions where this has been articulated. For example in *Phillips* v. *Martin-Marietta Corp.* [106] where the sex-plus standard was first identified, this was a case in which a policy of not employing married women with children was held to be unlawful.

Horsey v. *Dyfed County Council* [107] provides a similar example. There a woman was refused a job opportunity because the employer made certain assumptions based on the fact that she was married. These were that, if necessary, she would give up her job to follow her husband if he were transferred. The Employment Appeal Tribunal saw this as a case of generalized assumptions about people of a particular sex. But it may also be interpreted as a case in which sex-plus marriage as a standard was held to be discriminatory.

The motive of the respondent in treating the applicant less favourably on grounds of sex or marriage than he would treat a man is not relevant to proving a case of unlawful discrimination. In *Grieg* v. *Community Industry and Ahern* [108] the argument that the employer's motives were good, in refusing to allow the complainant to start work, was rejected. The Employment Appeal Tribunal held that the applicant had been treated less favourably than a man because, as the only woman in the team, she was refused permission to start work. Despite the respondent's claim that his motives were protective, the claim of direct discrimination contrary to section 6(1)(c) of the Act was upheld.

During the debates on the Sex Discrimination Bill in Parliament language was used making a distinction between 'intentional' and 'unintentional' discrimination. For example, the Under-Secretary of State for Employment referred to 'a second concept of discrimination – the concept of the effects test. If a person imposes an unjustifiable test, which has the effect, whether it was intended or not, of excluding women, that practice or habit of behaviour should also amount to discrimination.' [109] The context makes clear that this 'innocent', 'unmeaning', 'unintended' discrimination is to be covered by the concept of indirect discrimination and by the section of the Act on discriminatory practices (s.37). However, the inference might be drawn that direct discrimination is concerned with intentional discrimination.

There is no requirement, as such, to prove an intention to discriminate. But the requirement that the complainant makes out a case that the action complained of is on grounds of sex or victimization or marriage, amounts to roughly the same. This is why the decisions in the *Moberly* [110] and *Wallace* [111] cases are important. However, the issue of burden of proof remains a major problem so long as all courts and tribunals do not follow this approach. In an attempt to overcome the problem of conflicting approaches the Employment Appeal Tribunal laid down certain guidelines in *Khanna* v. *Ministry of Defence*. There the Employment

Appeal Tribunal explained that, as direct evidence of discrimination is seldom going to be available, 'the affirmative evidence of discrimination will normally consist of inferences to be drawn from the primary facts'. If these indicate some kind of discrimination then the employer must give an explanation. Failing 'clear and specific explanation being given by the employer to the satisfaction of the industrial tribunal, an inference of unlawful discrimination from the primary facts will mean the complaint succeeds'.[112]

Other matters which may be raised in defence are contained in the Act itself. Because of tight and specific drafting many exceptions had to be written into the legislation. It is evident that these limit scope and can be used as defences.

Exceptions Specified in the Sex Discrimination Act

Specific exceptions are made in the legislation for particular cases such as the police, prison officers, ministers of religion, midwives and mine-workers. At first glance it might seem that these exceptions undercut the effect of the legislation, but closer inspection reveals that some, at least, relate to the difficult issue of sameness and difference.

In the case of the police there is to be no differential treatment of women and men except 'as to requirements relating to height, uniform or equipment, or allowances in lieu of uniform or equipment; or so far as special treatment is accorded to women in connection with pregnancy and childbirth; or in relation to pensions to or in respect of special constables or police cadets' (section 17(2)).

Issues of height, clothing and pregnancy frequently occur in relation to sex discrimination. For prison officers a differential standard of height is also permitted (section 18(1)). This makes sense, for if the policy of the legislation is to outlaw sex discrimination, then height requirements applied equally to women and men, such as that all applicants must be six feet tall, would clearly be unfair to women. Tables of average heights of the sexes demonstrate that women are, on average, shorter than men.

The exceptions for ministers of religion and midwives fall into categories of compliance with doctrines of religion and avoidance of offence to members of the congregation, or to women in childbirth. The limitation on women's work in the mines where the duties 'ordinarily require the employee to spend a significant proportion of his time below ground' (section 21(1)), appears to be for the protection of women workers. However, this may be open to question, as the history of women's work in the mines shows.[113]

In the field of education exceptions are made for single-sex establishments, for transition from single-sex to coeducational establishment, and for physical training (ss.26 and 27). This is probably sensible because there is mounting empirical evidence to suggest that girls do better at single-sex schools. Yet, for social engineers, this evidence raises questions about the efficacy of anti-discrimination legislation in changing attitudes. A major reason why girls do better in single-sex schools is because they receive more individual attention.[114] Physical training (s.28) raises issues of different physical abilities and privacy which will be considered later in this chapter.

Exceptions for the letting of small premises can be explained by the provision requiring that, to qualify for the exception, the landlord or a close relative must be living on the premises, and sharing accommodation with the tenants. Issues of embarrassment in close proximity then arise.

Why political parties and voluntary bodies and charities are excluded is unclear. In *Hugh-Jones* v. *St John's College, Cambridge*[115] the exception for charities contained in section 43(2) of the Sex Discrimination Act was applied. Women were excluded from membership of the college by the college statutes enacted several centuries previously. A woman who was told that she would not get a research fellowship complained of sex discrimination. The Employment Appeal Tribunal held that there was no unlawful discrimination because of the exception for charities, the college being a charitable foundation. Furthermore, section 51(1) makes an exception for instruments and Acts passed prior to the Sex Discrimination Act, and the college statutes also fell under that exception.

Genuine Occupational Qualifications

The problem of differences can be illuminated by considering the exceptions where sex is taken to be a 'genuine occupational qualification'. Discrimination in the employment field is permitted where 'the essential nature of the job calls for a man for reasons of physiology (excluding physical strength or stamina) or, in dramatic performances or other entertainment, for reasons of authenticity, so that the essential nature of the job would be materially different if carried out by a woman'.[116] In *Thorn* v. *Meggitt Engineering Ltd*[117] the industrial tribunal ignored the exclusion of physical strength and stamina contained in the Act, and found that a requirement of strength and a minimum height of five foot eight inches was justifiable. This decision seems to have been in error as the tribunal applied provisions on justifiability in indirect discrimination to a complaint of direct discrimination. The requirements in terms of proof, and the defences open to the respondent under the two concepts of direct and indirect discrimination, are quite separate. However, this is an early case and the tribunals have appeared to understand the complications of the law better in later cases.

It seems however that, despite the provisions of the law, physical strength and stamina may be accepted by the judiciary as a reason for differential treatment of the sexes. This conclusion can be drawn from the decision of the Court of Appeal in *Noble* v. *David Gold & Sons Ltd.* There, the company had divided the workforce in book packing, and the male workers were assigned heavier tasks. Redundancies occurred within the workforce and the management decided that these were to take place in the light work section. Six of the women made redundant complained of sex discrimination. The Court of Appeal held that the division of work between women and men was based on practical experience and physical capacities. Lord Denning's view was: 'There is no sex discrimination at all. It is a natural division which comes about because of the different physical qualities of the two sexes.'[118] Since the redundancies came about in the light work section, it was fair and reasonable to dismiss the women.

The problem with this, as seems to be recognized by section 7(2)(a) of the Sex Discrimination Act, is that 'different physical qualities', or 'a natural division', or physical strength or stamina, may be a code for discrimination on grounds of sex. So although physiology is the reason given, or the standard applied, there may be no opportunity for women employees or job applicants to prove their ability to carry boxes or ladders. The stereotypes of all men as more able than any women to carry heavy loads are precisely what was condemned by the Court of Appeal in other cases.

There may lurk behind the provisions on genuine occupational qualifications, and the way in which these have been interpreted, the view expressed by Lord Monson in the second reading debate on the Act, in the House of Lords: 'there are certain occupations which men feel, and I think a great many women, perhaps rationally or irrationally, are unfeminine and unsuited for women'.[119] There is evidence to show that industrial practice is to look to strength as a reason for excluding women from certain work, despite the law. A study of engineering reports that a belief in women's lack of physical strength is used to justify differential treatment in employment.[120] A refusal to employ women in the offshore oil industry is explained by the words 'too heavy for women . . . things which women simply cannot do'.[121] An investigation into equal opportunities on the railways reveals that strength is imposed as a criterion for certain jobs. Furthermore, becoming a manager may be barred to women because it is felt that to retain authority a manager must prove ability to do all jobs.[122] Yet frozen points on railway lines can be dealt with by technology rather than physical strength.

However in *Roadburg* v. *Lothian Regional Council*[123] the employer's decision that a certain social work post was reserved for a man was held to be direct discrimination by the industrial tribunal. The argument that drunkenness and threatening behaviour of male clients created a need for a man was not accepted. It might be plausible to suggest that strength and stamina are necessary qualifications to deal with difficult male clients, but the industrial tribunal rejected such an implied suggestion, which is in any case unlawful.

Sex is also a genuine occupational qualification where there is a need to preserve decency or privacy because of physical contact, or undress, or use of sanitary facilities (s.7(2)(b)). Again this brings to the fore the issue of sexual difference and unwanted sexual attention. Personal matters of hygiene may come under this heading, as in the case where the job description for a supervisor included taking care of women's sanitary towels. In *Timex Corporation* v. *Hodgson*,[124] it was accepted that, under such circumstances, the nature of the work was such that it could only be performed by a woman.

When the Sex Discrimination Act was enacted several writers expressed the view that the exception for genuine occupational qualifications could be used to exclude women from jobs they were qualified to hold. The courts have attempted to prevent this exception from acting as a proxy for discrimination on grounds of sex. Thus in *Wylie* v. *Dee and Co.*,[125] the refusal to hire a woman tailor because she would have to take inside leg measurements of male customers was not accepted. Being male was not taken as essential to the work. As the tribunal pointed out, there are other methods of taking leg measurements. For instance the customer could provide his trousers for measurement by the tailor. The line between excuse and justification is hard to draw. Sex was justified as a job requirement in *Sisley* v. *Britannia Security Systems Ltd.*[126] The Employment Appeal Tribunal held that, where the employees rested on beds provided by the employer between shifts, and took off their uniforms to prevent creasing, limiting employees to members of one sex only was justified. Since being in a state of undress, and using sanitary facilies, was reasonably incidental to the work, employees might reasonably object to the presence of members of the other sex on grounds of decency and privacy.

Other cases in which sex may be a genuine qualification for work under the Sex Discrimination Act also use notions of privacy, embarrassment, reasonable objection, sanitary facilities, sleeping accommodation and undress. The problems that are raised by the presence of the two sexes sharing work, accommodation, or facilities can be reduced to two aspects. There is the aspect of personal preference, feelings of embarrassment, desire for privacy, which may be invaded by the unwanted presence of members of the other sex. Thus sex may be lawfully specified for a job in a private home where there is physical or social contact with, or because of knowledge of intimate details of, a person living there (section 7(2)(ba)).[127]

The second aspect is the practical. This covers problems of providing separate accommodation, or sanitary facilities, for the employee, or because of the nature of the establishment, such as a hospital or prison. Also covered are personal services promoting the welfare of individuals, jobs limited to men because of employment law restrictions on the employment of women, duties in countries whose laws or customs are inimical to the employment of women, or where the job is for a married couple. [128]

The emphasis in the Act on the physical, the biological, and on privacy is significant, for this shows the limitations of formal rationality when applied to the sexes. It remains an open question as to whether these exceptions will continue or whether the inevitable process of rationality will overcome the recognition of physical and biological difference. The importance attributed to difference cannot be attributed to women or men as a class, for the courts have emphasized the individual basis of treatment. [129]

Private Clubs and Exceptions for Private Households

There are certain areas covered by the label 'private' or 'privacy' into which the legislation does not enter. This is expressed either by limiting coverage to 'the public' or by making exceptions for 'the private'. The section of the Act dealing with the provision of goods, facilities and services (section 29) is limited 'to the public or a section of the public'. As a consequence, despite the reception by the Equal Opportunities Commission of nearly 2,000 complaints about discrimination in private clubs since 1976, the Act offers no redress. Most complaints appear to be about two categories of membership, with women having restricted privileges. [130]

The Equal Opportunities Commission has attempted to encourage changes within clubs by voluntary means but, ten years after the inception of the legislation, declares its awareness 'of no significant progress towards equality of status for women members of mixed private clubs resulting from such attempts; on the contrary, there is much evidence of repealed failure'. Therefore the Commission proposes to bring all private clubs which have had persons of both sexes in membership in the recent past within the provisions of the Act. The time-clause is designed to prevent clubs from voting to discontinue their female membership. [131]

It has already been argued that one of the major forces in the process of rationalization is the European Economic Community. Thus the European Court of Justice cut down the scope of the exception in s.6(3) of the Sex Discrimination Act 1975 for private households and firms with less than six employees. This provision has now been repealed by the Sex Discrimination Act 1986. The court stated:

It must be recognised that the provision of the 1975 Act in question is intended, in so far as it refers to employment in a private household, to reconcile the principle of equality of treatment with the principle of respect for private life which is also fundamental.[132]

The court, whilst asserting that there is an area of private life into which law does not enter, criticized the generality of the exclusion as going beyond what is permitted by Community law.[133] The 1975 Act has been amended by a section covering private homes. This permits an employer to choose the sex of an employee for a job which involves living or working in a private home where there is physical or social contact with, or knowledge of the intimate life of, someone living there who might object to the sex of the employee.[134] In other words, for such private employment personal preference for a woman or man as employee can be exercised.

Other Exceptions

General exceptions for sport, insurance or communal accommodation are contained in the Act. In *Football Association* v. *Bennett*,[135] a girl of eleven applied for registration as a member of her local football team. The team, and the league of which the team was part, were willing to accept the girl but the Football Association refused to register her because of her sex. The Court of Appeal considered s.44 of the Act which permits single-sex sporting competitions 'where the physical strength, stamina or physique of the average woman puts her at a disadvantage to the average man'.

The Court of Appeal held that 'woman' in the Act is defined as a female of any age, so the fact that the applicant was aged eleven did not affect the situation. Sir David Cairns said: 'The words "average woman" do not envisage any arithmetical average at all, but means something like "the ordinary woman" of the sort of age and sort of physical characteristic who would be likely to engage in that sport.' This may be contrasted with the Australian Sex Discrimination Act 1984 which, whilst permitting single-sex sporting competitions, also allows mixed sporting activities for children under the age of twelve. It does seem to be contrary to the spirit of the legislation that stereotyping in physical abilities and skills should take place amongst pre-pubescent children.

The Equal Opportunities Commission reports a case of a football team from an English primary school which was disqualified by the Football Association in 1985 after reaching the semi-final of their County Schools League, on the ground that two of its members were girls. Deploring this decision as contrary to the promotion of equality of opportunity the Commission recommends an amendment to the Act, excluding from its scope the participation in sporting competitions of children of primary school age.[136] Thus, bodies such as the Football Association could not rely on the exception for sport contained in section 44 to exclude, on grounds of sex, younger children from participating in competitions for which they are qualified.

Differential treatment of the sexes for purposes of insurance is permitted by section 45 of the Act. There is a test of whether the differential treatment relied on 'actuarial or other data on which it was reasonable to rely', and whether the differential treatment 'was reasonable having regard to the data and any other relevant factors'.[137] There has been one County Court case so far in which section 45 has been used to justify differential treatment. There the judge found it reasonable for an insurance company to justify its practice of charging women 50 per cent more than men for Permanent Health Insurance.[138]

The Equal Opportunities Commission proposes the repeal of section 45 for a number of reasons. First the Commission is critical of the way in which actuarial data which go back to the 1950s, and were produced for a purpose significantly different from that of assessing health risks for permanent health insurance, were used in the case. Second the Commission is critical of the way in which the section was interpreted in court. Third the Commission sees the grouping of the sexes into two classes for purposes of insurance as contrary to the spirit of the Act, and which may lend support 'to modes of thinking and practice which the SDA was intended to proscribe'.[139] The general tenor of the Act, and its more authoritative judicial interpretations, is to outlaw generalities related to sex. Individuals are to be treated in accordance with their particular characteristics, and not in accordance with sex classification.[140]

Certain public appointments, whilst not specified as exceptions, have been placed outside the Act. For example, in *Knight* v. *Attorney General*[141] it was held that appointment by the Crown as a Justice of the Peace was not covered by the Sex Discrimination Act as there is no employment involved and therefore no breach of section 6, where a woman was refused appointment. Other public appointments, such as rent officers, have also been omitted from the coverage of the legislation. In *Department of Environment* v. *Fox*[142] the Employment Appeal Tribunal held that it had no jurisdiction over appointments as rent officers as these are not covered by the Act. Neither section 1 of the Act, nor section 85(2) which deals with the extension of the Act to cover employment by the Crown, applied to the type of employment involved in being a rent officer. It would, of course, be possible to deal with such cases by amended legislation.

More serious failures of legislation, in terms of scope and omissions, relate to state action. In chapter 2 the deliberate intention of the authors of the legislation and of Parliament to omit coverage of matters of taxation, social security, nationality and family law was discussed. This was a policy which was justified in Parliament with a promise of separate legislation. It can also be explained through reflection on what equality legislation can be expected to achieve. Although such deliberate policy limitations to the legislation by its creators may give rise to scepticism about their commitment to its ideals, nevertheless there was open discussion on these issues. Less attention and justification has been given to other deliberate exclusions from the legislation of details affecting state policy.

Any legislation existing before the coming into force of the Sex Discrimination Act is untouched by anti-discriminatory policies (section 51). Furthermore subordinate legislation passed subsequently on the authority of an earlier Act is exempt from the provisions of the anti-discrimination legislation. In practice this means that discrimination unlawful under one piece of legislation can be justified by earlier legislation. This had led to adverse decisions by the European Court of Justice.[143] As the Sex Discrimination Act has been in force for over ten years the time may now be ripe for government departments to review legislation and remove remaining discriminatory provisions.

The duty on the state to refrain from discrimination on grounds of sex is further limited by a provision in the Act which restricts the application of this duty to acts which are the sort of acts 'done by a private person'.[144] Thus where a legal issue arose concerning the provision of goods, facilities or services to the public under section 29, the House of Lords held that certain types of government acts, which could not be done by private persons, were not covered by the Act, which applies only to marketplace activities. The case concerned immigration policy which discriminated against married women by not accepting them as 'heads of households' on a par with married men. Lord Fraser of Tullybelton expressed the view that the immigration scheme in which the husband is assumed to be the head of the household, without particular inquiry in each case, is discriminatory against women. However 'not all sex discrimination is unlawful'.[145] In particular, section 29 is limited to the direct provision of services or facilities such as medical services or library facilities, and does not cover a case where there is no direct provision of services to the public.

Judicial Interpretation

Most commentators on the Act stress the difficulties posed for complainants and court by the conceptual structure of the law. The Equal Opportunities Commission, and several studies, emphasize the complexities of the legislation.[146] As Roger Cotterrell observes:

> [D]iscrimination against a woman 'on the ground of her sex' (SDA s.1(1)(s)) has somehow to be distinguished from all other possible discriminations which focus on her personality or abilities. In direct discrimination, act and intention are telescoped together in a particularly complex way because the concepts which the law must use are moulded by the prejudices which it is aimed against.[147]

It is easier for the judiciary to focus on objective indications of discrimination than on the forms of prejudice existing in a society which produced the equality legislation. For example the refusal to extend to married women the credit facilities extended to married men is a clear instance of discrimination.[148] The tribunals and courts can cope where the complainant's better relevant qualifications provide an objective basis;[149] or where a *prima facie* case is made out enabling the burden of proof to be shifted from the applicant to the respondent;[150] the courts have also aided the applicant in drawing out evidence to support her claim by making the hearing 'partake of something at all events of an inquiry into what has gone on'.[151] The development of the condemnation of generalized assumptions based on sex, rather than the particular qualities of an individual, is important.

There is, however, other evidence to suggest that some judges and tribunal members do not altogether understand or sympathize with the legislation. Thus cases of direct discrimination have been reduced to judicial remarks that 'a woman's hair is her crowning glory'.[152] A woman's complaint of dismissal on marriage was referred to as 'trivial and banal even when topped up with much legalistic froth';[153] and the woman was told by a judge of the Court of Appeal that 'when she had dried her tears, she would have had to look for new employment and count herself lucky to find it'.[154]

It is not surprising that certain complaints appear trivial to the Court of Appeal. But applicants are not responsible for the structure and form of the legislation. Individual complaint is the mode chosen by the draughtsmen and by Parliament. Furthermore the thrust of decisions has been individualization, for 'Parliament has legislated that (women) are not to be treated as a class but as individuals'.[155] Taken in particular and isolated context complaints may indeed appear 'trivial and banal'. Taken as a whole the complaints reveal a rather different picture. A woman subjected to an interview by a man who indicates by his demeanour that he has no intention of employing a woman;[156] a woman subjected to a series of hostile questions about women's abilities,[157] or about her family plans;[158] women dismissed from their jobs on marriage,[159] or refused training because they are married,[160] or because it is assumed that their children prevent them from working;[161] a qualified and experienced woman teacher not interviewed for promotion;[162] women dismissed because they are pregnant;[163] women downgraded to women's work[164] or refused permission to start work;[165] women refused a drink at a bar and required to sit down;[166] girl pupils denied access to a higher class on grounds of sex rather than merit;[167] the picture is one of struggles to overcome prejudice. The necessity for the legislation has been demonstrated, even if it is not fully successful.

In certain cases the tribunals and courts have taken an unnecessarily narrow view of the legislation. An example is *Oliver* v. *Malnick*

(No. 2)[168] where it was held that the complaint should have been under the Equal Pay Act and not the Sex Discrimination Act. The complainant had accepted a job at a salary of £4,000 a year. She later discovered that a male comparator was paid at a higher rate. The tribunal's view was that those sections of the latter Act, dealing with terms of employment, are concerned with prospective future employment, such as job applications. Therefore, if after accepting a job a woman discovers that a male comparator is better-paid, she must use the Equal Pay Act. However, a broader interpretation of section 6 of the Sex Discrimination Act is possible. This could have helped the applicant within the spirit of the legislation.

Alice Leonard suggests that tribunals are not so much hostile to the legislation as confused by it. In her study of the performance of tribunals over two years from 1980 to 1982 she discovered misunderstandings and misapplications of the legislation. Examples are the importation of a question of intention where an act of discrimination had occurred, and was conceded to have done so. On the basis that the discrimination was not intended the application was dismissed. This is clearly incorrect as the legislation does not require proof of intention.[169] Another major error which was found in 58 out of 129 cases, was the failure to consider whether the applicant was treated less favourably than a male comparator. Where an applicant claimed that her employment conditions were less favourable than those of male comparators in similar positions in the company the tribunal dismissed her claim. The tribunal wrote:

> the applicant considered that she ought to have a company car. In the past she has been getting her driving expenses . . . [S]he had been given to understand by the company chairman that he did not agree that women should have a company car at all. It seems to us to be of little importance whether her car was a company car provided for her or whether, alternatively, she ran her own car and was given a mileage allowance.[170]

Four explanations for misunderstanding of the law by tribunals are offered by Leonard. On the basis of observation of hearings and review of decisions she concludes that lack of expertise, confusion with unfair dismissal cases, lack of evidence by applicants, and inaction by the tribunals themselves are the main causes.[171] Lack of expertise arises from lack of familiarity. Out of 492 panel positions used for hearing sex discrimination and equal pay cases between 1980 and 1982, 379 were occupied by members who heard only *one* case in that period. Forty-nine people heard two cases. Only five members heard three cases, and no member heard more.[172]

Industrial tribunal panels are much more likely to sit on unfair dismissal cases than on equal treatment cases. This means that they tend to judge the employer's actions in accordance with 'reasonableness', which is the standard for whether a dismissal is fair. However in equality cases the standard is that of equally favourable treatment. Bob Hepple's view is that the 'enormous interplay between unfair dismissal and discrimination jurisdictions makes the tribunals inclined to respect a wide band of "reasonable" managerial decisions'.[173] Leonard points out that, at tribunal level, the distinction between the standard for unfair dismissal claims and unequal treatment claims may be confused. This is supported by cases where the Employment Appeal Tribunal had to order new hearings. These were sex discrimination cases where the tribunals had failed to distinguish principles and evidence applicable in unfair dismissal cases but inappropriate in discrimination cases.[174]

Lack of evidence by applicants, and failure to present their case convincingly, appears to be a major problem. In technical terms, failure to provide documentary evidence, witnesses, relevant statistics and comparative evidence, and to cross-examine effectively, add up to lack of success at tribunal hearings.[175] This relates to the burden of proof currently placed on applicants. The complexities of the legislation also create difficulties for applicants. However, tribunals could assist applicants in the presentation of cases, instead of making difficulties about the evidence as sometimes happens. Tribunals are apparently reluctant to question the parties seriously and to test their evidence. It seems that this can be accounted for by a view that proceedings are adversarial, that objectivity would be sacrificed by greater participation, and by a lack of expertise.[176] Yet when tribunals were first introduced into the judicial system their vaunted qualities were informality, assistance to applicants and lack of procedural difficulties.[177]

The higher courts do not always appear to understand the goals of the legislation. Lack of sympathy and the trivialization of complaints have already been discussed. Atkins and Hoggett suggest that the judiciary have conceptual problems with the structure of the legislation. Discrimination cases have to be accommodated within a traditional civil law setting, but the legislation does not fit easily into an existing legal category. Some aspects of discrimination are analogous to crime. Equal pay cases are based on contract but sex discrimination seems to lie uneasily between negligence and defamation.[178] The courts are influenced not so much by personal prejudice as by their notions of individual justice. 'Concentration on intentional conduct has focused on the individuals concerned, without reference to social standards. Indeed, concentration on the merits of individuals has led the judges to fail to appreciate the social importance of the law they are applying.'[179]

Criticisms of the equality legislation, and of the way in which it is interpreted and administered, can lead to proposals for improvement. The Equal Opportunities Commission, conscious of its role as monitor of the legislation, has taken seriously critical research studies. Proposals for change are under discussion. If implemented these will improve the legislation itself and its implementation. However, a deeper question remains. Is the basic structure of the legislation 'a good one' as asserted by the Commission?[180] This is what is considered in the conclusion.

Conclusion

In this chapter two fundamental problems of equality legislation have been identified. These are its individualistic nature and its comparative mode. These problems are not susceptible of easy resolution by legislative amendment and improved implementation. Nor have they been avoided in other jurisdictions which have introduced equality legislation. Equality of treatment under the law is a question of individual rights. Only those who are similarly situated can claim equal treatment. Thus the issue remains one of comparison – who is the same as whom? Escaping from this 'alike treated the same', 'unalike treated differently' dilemma is a conceptual problem. As examples in this chapter concerning anatomy, biology, pregnancy and privacy confirm, we are locked into a comparative mode of thought. The presentation of issues in terms of rights has its defects.[181]

This is not intended as an assertion that equality legislation is pointless. On the contrary, despite difficulties and failures the legislation has had a profound effect on the content and language of political rights in Britain. It has altered consciousness. In terms of a dialectical process the equality legislation can be considered successful. It has 'encouraged the articulation of feminist vision and furthered the process of political assertion'.[182] The arguments and discussions, the questions and issues, have created the conditions for the development of deeper analysis. Even if we cannot yet see the way away from individual comparison, we have dispelled some obscurities.

Notes

1 Leonard, A., *The First Eight Years* (Manchester, EOC, 1986) p. 9. This is a report on applicants to the industrial tribunals, 1976–83, under the Sex Discrimination and Equal Pay Acts. Some of the findings have been published by the author in 136 *New Law Journal* pp. 99–102 and pp. 123–5 (1986).

2 By contrast the equal pay legislation limits applications to cases where an actual comparator is named, who works for the same employer as the applicant. The Equal Opportunities Commission consultative document, *Legislating for Change* (1986, para. 2.7) proposes that a hypothetical comparator be introduced into equal pay claims.

3 [1981] ICR 328 (CA).

4 Weber, M., *Law, Economy and Society* (Cambridge, Mass., Harvard University Press, 1954). Introduction by M. Rheinstein, p. xlix.

5 Ibid., p. 350.

6 Ibid., p. 351.

7   Freeman, A. D., 'Legitimizing racial discrimination through antidiscrimination law: a critical review of Supreme Court doctrine', 62 *Minnesota Law Review* 1049 (1978).

8   Freeman, A. D., 'Antidiscrimination law: a critical review', in D. Kairys (ed.), *The Politics of Law* (New York, Pantheon, 1982) pp. 96–116 at p. 99.

9   In this chapter references to 'the Act', are references to the Sex Discrimination Act 1975. The provisions of section 5(3) are as follows:

> 5(3) A comparison of the cases of persons of different sex or marital status under section 1(1) or 3(1) must be such that the relevant circumstances in the one case are the same, or not materially different, in the other.

Anti-sex discrimination law in the United States has developed the concept that plaintiffs must be 'similarly situated' to those to whom they compare themselves. See Scales, A. C., 'The emergence of feminist jurisprudence', 95 *Yale Law Journal* 1373 (1986).

10   Section 3(1) of the Sex Discrimination Act provides: 'A person discriminates against a married person of either sex in any circumstances relevant for the purposes of any provision of Part II if –
(a)   on the ground of his or her marital status he treats that person less favourably than he treats or would treat in unmarried person of the same sex.'
Part II of the Act deals with discrimination in the employment field.

11   Section 5(3) of the Act; note 9, supra. In this chapter references to complainants under the Act will be as if complainants are female. Women form the majority of complainants. See Alice Leonard's finding that women form 73 per cent of applicants, note 1, supra.

12   *Grieg* v. *Community Industry and Ahern*, [1979] ICR 356 at p. 361 (EAT).

13   In *Reed* v. *Reed*, 404 US 71 (1971) the United States Supreme Court held that women had an equal right with men to administer estates, as they are 'similarly situated' in such matters. There is no demonstrable difference to justify differential treatment.

14   Tussman, T., and TenBroek, J., 'The equal protection of the laws', 37 *California Law Review* 341 (1949) p. 346.

15   MacKinnon, C., *Sexual Harassment of Working Women* (New Haven, Yale University Press, 1979) p. 109.

16   *Thorndyke* v. *Bell Fruit Ltd*, [1979] IRLR 1.

17   *Hurley* v. *Mustoe*, [1981] ICR 490 at p. 496 (EAT). See also [1983] ICR 422 (EAT) on the question of damages.

18   *Bick* v. *Royal West of England Residential School of the Deaf*, [1976] IRLR 326.

19   Leonard, A., *Judging Inequality* (London, The Cobden Trust, 1987) p. 71. The Equal Opportunities Commission consultative document *Legislating for Change* (1986, paras 4.2.11 to 4.2.15) contains a discussion of these findings. The Commission proposes to dispense with the jurisdiction of the County Court over cases relating to education or the provision of goods, facilities and services, and to transfer all individual cases under the equality legislation to industrial tribunals presided over by chairmen who have received special training and including by members with appropriate experience.

20   [1982] ICR 755 at p. 760 (EAT).

21 [1981] ICR 864 (CA).
22 *Roberts* v. *Tate and Lyle*; *Barber* v. *Guardian Royal Exchange Assurance Group*, [1983] ICR 521. See Shrubsall, V., 'Sex discrimination: retirement and pensions', 48 *Modern Law Review* 373 (1985).
23 Weber, M., supra note 4, p. 350.
24 Ibid., p. 351.
25 [1978] IRLR 427.
26 Ibid., at p. 428.
27 [1976] IRLR 404.
28 [1980] ICR 66.
29 Ibid., at p. 70.
30 The Equal Opportunities Commission consultative document, *Legislating for Change* (1986, para. 6.12) discusses the apparent inequity of a two-year service qualifying condition for claims of unfair dismissal, if dismissal for pregnancy is treated separately under equality legislation and no service condition is required. It might then seem that pregnancy as a reason for dismissal was privileged. However the Commission argues that since 'the onset of motherhood is known to be one of the causes of the disadvantages experienced by working women, the special protection of the equality legislation is justified'. The Commission also seems to favour a special provision in the Employment Protection (Consolidation) Act 1978 with no qualifying period from dismissal for pregnancy.
31 supra note 28; at p. 71.
32 [1985] ICR 703. This case was heard by the EAT together with *Maughan* v. *NE London Magistrates Court Committee*. The *Maughan* case, when reheard by an industrial tribunal, resulted in a finding that dismissal for pregnancy is contrary to the Sex Discrimination Act.
33 Ibid. at p. 708.
34 Lacey, N., 'Note: dismissal by reason of pregnancy', 15 *Industrial Law Journal* 43 (1986) at p. 45.
35 Ibid. See also the EOC consultative document, *Legislating for Change* (1986, para. 6.11) which refers to two cases where industrial tribunals have found discrimination contrary to the SDA on the dismissal of a pregnant woman.
36 [1981] IRLR 51.
37 See Scales A. C., 'Towards a feminist jurisprudence', 56 *Indiana Law Journal* 375 (1980–1); Erickson, N. S., 'Pregnancy discrimination: an analytical approach', 7 *Women's Rights Law Reporter* 11 (1981); Law, S. A., 'Rethinking sex and the constitution', 132 *University of Pennsylvania Law Review* 955 (1984); Frug, M. J., 'Securing job equality for women: labour market hostility to working mothers', 59 *Boston University Law Review* 55 (1979).
38 429 US 190 (1976) at p. 197.
39 417 US 484 (1973).
40 Tussman and TenBroek, supra note 14.
41 Wildman, S., 'The legitimation of sex discrimination: a critical response to Supreme Court jurisprudence', 63 *Oregon Law Review* 265 (1984) at p. 268.
42 429 US (1976) 125 at p. 136. See also Finley, L., 'Transcending equality theory', 86 *Columbia Law Review* 1118 (1986).
43 Ibid.

44   Ibid., at p. 151.
45   Pub. L. No. 95–555, para. 1, 92 stat. 2076. Siegal, R. B., 'Employment equality under the Pregnancy Discrimination Act of 1978', 94 *Yale Law Journal* 929 (1985).
46   [1977] ICR 968.
47   Ibid., at p. 973.
48   Ibid., at p. 975.
49   Pannick, D., *Sex Discrimination Law* (Oxford, Clarendon Press, 1985) at p. 29.
50   [1980] ICR 13; [1980] QB 87 (CA)
51   Ibid., at p. 25.
52   [1983] 1 All ER 398.
53   [1984] ICR 52.
54   [1978] ICR 85.
55   Ibid., at p. 88.
56   There is a broad literature on sexual harassment. See MacKinnon, C. A., *Sexual Harassment of Working Women* (New Haven, Yale University Press, 1979); Clarke, L., 'Sexual harassment and the Sex Discrimination Act', 132 *New Law Journal* 1116 (1982); Pannick D., 'Sexual harassment and the Sex Discrimination Act', [1982] *Public Law* 42. See also the EOC Information Leaflet, No. 16: *Sexual Harassment* (1987).
57   Lord Emslie, L. P., in the Scottish Court of Sessions, [1986] ICR 564 at p. 569.
58   Rubenstein, M., 'The law of sexual harassment at work', 12 *Industrial Law Journal* (1983) 1 at p. 2.
59   Note 'Sexual harassment claims of abusive work environment', 97 *Harvard Law Review* 1451 (1984).
60   Lawton, L. J., in *Western Excavating (EE) Ltd* v. *Sharp*, [1978] QB 761.
61   [1979] IRLR 127.
62   [1985] ICR 177 (EAT). [1986] ICR 564 (Scot. Ct. of Sessions).
63   The Employment Appeal Tribunal judgment [1985] ICR 177 at p. 182.
64   *Meritor Savings Bank, FSB* v. *Vinson* 106, Supreme Court 2399 (1986).
65   [1986] ICR 564. See also the judgment of Lord Brand.
66   See Clarke, L., 'Sexual harassment and the Sex Discrimination Act 1975', 132 *New Law Journal* 1116 (1982).
67   561 F 2d 983 (1977).
68   Ibid.
69   Ibid., at 990.
70   Ibid.
71   DC Ala. (1978) 20 FEP Cases 1172.
72   CA 1 (1979) 19 FEP Cases (1979).
73   Ibid.
74   [1978] 20 FEP Cases 251.
75   Rubenstein M., op. cit. note 58 at p. 5.
76   [1985] ICR 177 (EAT).
77   See Rubenstein, op. cit. note 58 at p. 5.
78   106 Supreme Court 2399 (1986).
79   Ibid., at 2405, quoting EEOC guidelines.
80   *Bundy* v. *Jackson*, CADC. (1981) 24 FEP Cases 1155.

81 Supra note 65. The issue of 'detriment' as required by s.6(2)(b) of the Act appears to have been resolved in *Ministry of Defence* v. *Jeremiah*, [1980] ICR. See also Carty, H., Note, 49 *Modern Law Review* 653 (1986).

82 *De Souza* v. *Automobile Association*, [1986] ICR 514.

83 Taub, N., 'Keeping women in their place: stereotyping *per se* as a form of employment discrimination', 21 *Boston College Law Review* 345 (1980) p. 361; 'Comment: sexual harassment – hostile work environment', 100 *Harvard Law Review* 276 (1986).

84 There is discussion on the question whether discrimination on grounds of sexual preference is discrimination on grounds of sex in the following: Pannick, D., 'Homosexuals, transsexuals and the Sex Discrimination Act', [1983] *Public Law* 279; Wein, S. A. and Remmers, C. L., 'Employment protection and gender dysphoria: legal definitions of unequal treatment on the basis of sex and disability', 30 *Hastings Law Journal* 1075 (1979).

85 26 FEP Cases 252 (1980).

86 *Macauley* v. *Massachusetts Commission Against Discrimination*, 21 FEP Cases 927 (1979).

87 *Gay Law Students Association* v. *Pacific Telephone and Telegraph Company*, 19 FEP Cases 1419 (1979).

88 608 F. 2d. 325 (1978) at p. 331.

89 [1977] IRLR 121.

90 Ibid., at p. 123.

91 *Grossman* v. *Bernards Township Board of Education*, 11 FEP Cases 1196 (1975); affirmed 538 F. 2d. 319 (1976); cert. denied 429 US 897 (1976); *Voyles* v. *Davies Medical Center*, 403 F. Supp. 456 (1975); affirmed 570 F. 2d. 354 (1978). *Vlane* v. *Eastern Airlines*, 35 FEP Cases 1348 (1984).

92 *Holloway* v. *Arthur Andersen & Company*, 556 F. 2d. 659 (1977).

93 27 FEP Cases 1217 (1982).

94 Supra note 58 at p. 10.

95 Cmnd. 5724 (London, HMSO, 1974) para. 86.

96 Parliamentary Debates, House of Commons, vol. 893, cols 1467–8 (London, HMSO, 1975).

97 Parliamentary Debates, House of Lords, vol. 362 cols 154–5 (London, HMSO, 1975). The Equal Opportunities Commission proposes a shift in the burden of proof from the applicant to the respondent, once a *prima facie* case of sex discrimination has been made out. It would then be for the respondent to prove non-sexual or non-victimization grounds for the less favourable treatment (*Legislating for Change*, 1986, para. 4.2.26).

98 Leonard, A., *Pyrrhic Victories* (EOC, London, HMSO, 1987).

99 In *Humphreys* v. *Board of Managers of St George's Church of England Primary School*, [1978] ICR 546, the Employment Appeal Tribunal stated that the burden of proof was on the applicant, but that normally the respondent should be heard. In *Oxford* v. *DHSS*, [1977] IRLR 225 the EAT held that the burden rests on the complainant.

100 EOC, *Legislating for Change* (1986), para. 4.2.25. See also Bindman, G., 'Proving discrimination: is the burden too heavy?', *Law Society Gazette* (17 December 1980); Pannick, D., 'The burden of proof in discrimination cases', *New Law Journal* (27 August 1981).

101 Ibid., para. 4.2.26.

102 [1977] IRLR 176 at p. 178.

103   *Wallace* v. *South Eastern Education and Library Board*, [1980] IRLR 193.
104   400 US 542 (1971).
105   [1981] ICR 490.
106   400 US 542 (1971).
107   [1982] ICR 755 (EAT).
108   [1979] ICR 356 (EAT). See also *Creagh* v. *Speedway Sign Service Ltd*, Appeal No. EAT 312/83, 7 February 1984.
109   Parliamentary Debates, House of Commons, vol. 893, col. 1430 (London, HMSO, 1975).
110   [1977] IRLR 176.
111   [1980] IRLR 193.
112   [1981] ICR 653, per Browne-Wilkinson J. at p. 658.
113   John, A., *By the Sweat of their Brow: Women Workers at Victorian Coal Mines* (London, Croom Helm, 1980).
114   Spender, D. and Sarah, E. (eds), *Learning to Lose* (London, Women's Press, 1981).
115   [1979] ICR 848.
116   SDA, section 7(2)(a). The EOC wishes to replace the word 'physiology' by the word 'anatomy'. This is because anatomy is a more appropriate term for physical sexual characteristics as an integral part of a job. EOC, *Legislating for Change* (1986) para. 3.3.4.
117   [1976] IRLR 241.
118   [1980] ICR 543, at p. 549.
119   Parliamentary Debates, House of Lords, vol. 362, col. 148 (London, HMSO, 1975).
120   Bennett, Y. and Carter, D., *Day Release for Girls* (Manchester, EOC, 1985) p. 66.
121   Moore, R. and Wybrow, P., *Women in the North Sea Oil Industry* (Manchester, EOC, 1984) p. 35.
122   Robins, D., *Wanted: Railman – Report on an Investigation into Equal Opportunities for Women in British Rail*, EOC Research Series (London, HMSO 1986).
123   [1976] IRLR 283.
124   [1981] IRLR 530.
125   [1978] IRLR 101.
126   [1983] ICR 628.
127   Section 7(2)(ba), inserted in the SDA 1975 by the Sex Discrimination Act 1986, s.1(2). See Collins, H., 'The decline of privacy in private law', 14 *Journal of Law and Society* 91 (1987).
128   SDA 1975 s.7(2)(c)(d)(e)(f)(g). The EOC proposes that s.7(2)(d), referring to the essential character of establishments such as hospitals and prisons, be repealed. The Commission has also proposed the repeal of ss.(7)(2)(f) and 7(2)(h). These two exceptions deal with restrictions on the employment of women because of protective legislation, and with the employment of married persons as a couple.
129   *Hurley* v. *Mustoe*, [1981] ICR 490 (EAT). See also SDA s. 35.
130   Equal Opportunities Commission, *Legislating for Change* (1986) para. 3.2.2.
131   Ibid., para. 3.2.4.

132   *Commission of European Community* v. *United Kingdom,* [1984] 1 All ER
      353 at p. 363.
133   Equal Treatment Directive 76/207. *Official Journal of the EEC,* 1976, Law
      39, p. 40.
134   Sex Discrimination Act 1986, s.1(2) inserting s.7(2)(ba) into the Sex
      Discrimination Act 1975.
135   Equal Opportunities Commission, *Towards Equality (1976–1981),* p. 36
      (CA). See also Pannick, D., *Sex Discrimination in Sport* (EOC, 1983).
136   Equal 'Opportunities Commission, *Legislating for Change* (1986) para.
      3.3.8.
137   Sex Discrimination Act 1975, s.45.
138   Equal Opportunities Commission, *Legislating for Change* (1986) para.
      3.3.11. The case is *Pinder* v. *Friends Provident,* (1985, unreported).
139   Ibid., para. 3.3.12.
140   See further *Los Angeles Department of Water and Power* v. *Manhart,* 435
      US 702 (1978). Bernstein, M. and Williams, L., 'Title VII and the problem
      of sex classifications in pension programs', 74 *Columbia Law Review* 1203
      (1974). Sydlaske, J., 'Comment: gender classifications in the insurance
      industry', 75 *Columbia Law Review* 1381 (1975); Brilmayer, L., Hekeler,
      R., Laycock, D. and Sullivan, T., 'Sex discrimination in employer-
      sponsored insurance plans', 47 *University of Chicago Law Review* 505
      (1980); Pannick, D., *Sex Discrimination Law* (Oxford, Clarendon Press,
      1985) pp. 189–96.
141   [1979] ICR 194.
142   [1979] ICR 736.
143   *R.* v. *Secretary of State for Education, ex parte Schaffter,* [1987] IRLR 53.
144   Sex Discrimination Act 1975, s.85(1).
145   *Amin* v. *Entry Clearance Officer, Bombay,* [1983] 2 All ER 864 (HL) at
      p. 871. Lord Scarman (dissenting) took the view that section 85(1) of the
      SDA means that the Act applies to the public acts of government as it does
      to private persons. Furthermore, section 29(1) is wide enough to cover the
      immigration scheme which 'is properly described as offering a facility to
      some members of the public' (at p. 879).
146   See e.g. Snell, M., Glucklich, P. and Povall, M. *Equal Pay and Oppor-
      tunities,* Department of Employment Research Paper No. 20, 1981;
      Leonard, supra note 1; Coussins, J., 'Equality for women: have the laws
      worked', *Marxism Today,* January 1980, p. 6.
147   [1981] *Public Law* 473.
148   *Quinn* v. *Williams Furniture Ltd,* [1981] ICR 328 (CA).
149   *Conway* v. *Queen's University of Belfast,* [1981] IRLR 137.
150   *Wallace* v. *South Eastern Education and Library Board,* [1980] IRLR 193;
      Moberly v. *Commonwealth Hall,* [1977] IRLR 176.
151   *Humphreys* v. *Board of Managers of St George's Church of England
      Primary School,* [1978] ICR 546.
152   *Ministry of Defence* v. *Jeremiah,* [1980] ICR 13 (CA) per Lord Denning at
      p. 22.
153   *Skyrail Oceanic Ltd* v. *Coleman,* [1981] ICR 864 (CA), per Shaw L.J. at
      p. 872.

154 Ibid., at p. 873.
155 *Hurley* v. *Mustoe*, [1981] ICR 490 (EAT), per Browne-Wilkinson, J, at p. 496.
156 *Brennan* v. *Dewhurst*, [1984] ICR 52.
157 *Saunders* v. *Richmond Borough Council*, [1977] IRLR 362 (EAT).
158 *Gates* v. *Wirral Borough Council*, EOC Information Leaflet No. 1 (1985).
159 *Maclean* v. *Paris Travel Service Ltd*, [1976] IRLR 202 (IT); *Bick* v. *Royal West of England Residential School for the Deaf*, [1976] IRLR 326; *North East Midlands Co-operative Society* v. *Allen*, [1977] IRLR 212 (EAT);
160 *Horsey* v. *Dyfed County Council*, [1982] ICR 755 (EAT).
161 *Hurley* v. *Mustoe*, [1981] ICR 490 (EAT).
162 *Hay* v. *Lothian Regional Council*, EOC Information Leaflet No. 6 (1985); *Miller* v. *Strathclyde Regional Council*, EOC Information Leaflet No. 15 (1986).
163 *Turley* v. *Allders Department Stores*, [1980] ICR 66.
164 *Gubala* v. *Crompton Parkinson Ltd*, [1977] IRLR 10 (IT).
165 *Grieg* v. *Community Industry and Ahern*, [1979] ICR 356 (EAT).
166 *Debell, Sevket and Teh* v. *The London Borough of Bromley*, EOC Information Leaflet No. 7 (1985).
167 *Gill and Coote* v. *El Vino*, [1983] 1 All ER 398.
168 [1984] ICR 458 (IT).
169 Leonard, A., supra note 19, p. 31.
170 Ibid., p. 35.
171 Ibid., ch. 3. See also Earnshaw, J., *Sex Discrimination and Dismissal*, UMIST, Department of Management Sciences, Occasional Paper No. 8505 (1985).
172 See EOC, *Legislating for Change* (1986) para. 4.2.9. See also Dickens, L., Jones, M., Weekes, B. and Hart, M., *Dismissed: A Study of Unfair Dismissal and the Industrial Tribunal System* (Oxford, Basil Blackwell, 1985) p. 62.
173 Hepple, B. A., 'Judging equal rights', (1983) *Current Legal Problems* 71 at 83.
174 Leonard, supra note 19, p. 74. Examples are *Creagh* v. *Speedway Sign Service Ltd*, Appeal No. EAT 312/83, 7 February 1984, and *Hassan* v. *Harlow District Council and J. Ward*, Appeal No. EAT 161/84, 28 December 1984.
175 Leonard, supra note 19, pp. 78–85. Dickens et al., supra note 172, p. 190.
176 Leonard, supra note 19, pp. 85–98. For example some tribunals rejected written evidence, or unsworn written evidence. Applicants were surprised that this was so. See also EOC, *Legislating for Change* (1986) paras 3.1.6 and 4.2.11–4.2.15.
177 Report of the Committee on Administrative Tribunals (the Franks Committee, Cmd. 218 (London, HMSO, 1957).
178 Atkins, S. and Hoggett, B., *Women and the Law* (Oxford, Blackwell, 1984) pp. 33–8.
179 Ibid., p. 35.
180 EOC, *Legislating for Change* (1986) para. 1.2.
181 See 'A critique of rights', 62 *Texas Law Review* 1363 (1984); Olsen, F., 'Statutory rape: a feminist critique of rights analysis', 63 *Texas Law Review*

387 (1984); Westen, P., 'The rueful rhetoric of "rights" ', 33 *University of California Los Angeles Law Review* 977 (1986).
182 Schneider, E., 'The dialectic of rights and politics: perspectives from the women's movement', 61 *New York University Law Review* 587 (1986) at p. 650.

Chapter 4
Indirect Discrimination

In contrast to direct discrimination, indirect discrimination is a more detailed legal concept. In theory at least, the concept is designed to have a wider impact than direct discrimination since it recognizes the importance of differences between the sexes. It is intended to deal with the effects of seemingly neutral conditions which have a disproportionate impact upon one sex. To put it another way, requirements or conditions which in reality mask an intentional preference for one sex.[1]

The boundary between indirect and direct discrimination is often blurred, for hardly ever will an employer admit direct discrimination, but will use some other pretext to justify a discriminatory action.[2] However, we can point to some situations where indirect discrimination may occur. Instances of such discrimination are acknowledged as being fairly uniform throughout the European Community as well as North America, not only in the application of legislative measures but also in collective agreements and established customs and practices throughout industry. In relation to access to employment this may be in the way jobs are described and advertised. For example, neutral wording in advertisements may be accompanied by texts or job descriptions or pictures indicating a sex bias. Recruitment or selection criteria may be based on factors such as height, mobility, physical strength or educational requirements which are not essential to the job, and with which a larger proportion of women cannot comply. Similarly protective legislation may be invoked as a means of excluding women from certain kinds of work when the requirements are not essential to the job. Other informal mechanisms may apply – such as 'word-of-mouth' recruitment or extending overtime hours in male employment rather than recruiting more part-time workers, or taking into account marital status or intention to have children when recruiting female applicants.

Once in employment many of the practices carried out at the recruitment stage are perpetuated in relation to working conditions, promotion procedures and the criteria used for promotion. Again informal methods may disguise preconceived stereotyped notions of women as workers. Work schedules, training sessions and refresher courses may be organized at times of day difficult for workers with family responsibilities, especially if they are organized some distance from the work-place. There may be different opportunities for parental and family leave.

In relation to termination of employment, indirect discrimination may occur in dismissals linked to a worker's pregnancy (although this may be implemented in the guise of other reasons such as attendance records) or family commitments may be taken into account, presumed head-of-household status or factors which favour a male attachment to labour market profile such as on-the-job service, educational qualifications, selection of part-timers or those with least service first for redundancy.

The Development of the Legal Concept

In a claim of indirect discrimination intention is irrelevant. It is the *effects* of the action which are important. As Christopher McCrudden[3] points out, the concept moves beyond the individual nature of the claim and provides a basis for intervening against the present effects of past and other forms of institutional discrimination. In an indirect discrimination claim the focus of attention is switched from direct comparison of individuals to a wider perspective of looking at women as a class, or to paraphrase the words of an American judge, a focus on the 'posture and condition' of women as a group as compared with men as a group. Thus a complaint of indirect discrimination requires the legal process to look at the general characteristics of women which prevent them from complying with what are seemingly neutral conditions or requirements. In particular such features as their child-bearing biological role, their socially ascribed child-rearing, family caring and domestic role, as well as other aspects such as social stereotyping in education and training, must be considered. It is precisely these characteristics which women feel have been ignored in the past, and which significantly affect their participation in the labour market. These factors are relevant to the concept of indirect discrimination because these characteristics may turn a 'neutral' employment condition into a gender-based standard.

Described in this way indirect discrimination appears to offer a more sophisticated response to redressing gender inequalities. At the heart of indirect discrimination is a focus upon the *effects* of a particular discriminatory practice on an identifiable group within society. The concept also admits that pluralistic demands should be met by setting an equality of opportunity standard. There is, however, a divergence between this ideal and the way it has been translated into a legal reality.

The legal starting point for the concept was the unanimous American Supreme Court decision in a racial discrimination case, *Griggs* v. *Duke Power Co.*[4] This case acknowledges that the Civil Rights Act 1964 gave little assistance in bringing those groups in American society who were not in fact equal to the white male majority up to an equal starting point. While affirmative (positive) action programmes were perceived at both the practical and theoretical level as one way of addressing this problem, the judicial response was more immediate in its articulation of the legal concept of 'disproportionate adverse impact'.[5]

The intellectual underpinning of the concept is found in American case-law. The decision in *Griggs* v. *Duke Power Co.* adopted a two-step method of analysis. First the complainant had to show that the employer's challenged employment practice had an adverse impact upon his or her group in comparison with other groups, and then the burden moved to the employer to justify the practice by showing that the practice had 'a manifest relationship to the employment in question'. This is summarized in the famous words of Burger, CJ:

> Congress has now required that the posture and condition of the job-seeker be taken into account. . . . The Act proscribes not only overt discrimination, but also practices that are fair in form, but discriminatory in operation . . . good intent or absence of discriminatory intent does not redeem employment procedures or testing mechanisms that operate as 'built-in headwinds' for minority groups and are unrelated to measuring job capability.[6]

A further requirement was added by the Supreme Court in another employment selection case:[7]

> If an employer does then meet the burden of proving that its tests are 'job related', it remains open to the complaining party to show that other tests or selection devices, without a similarly undesirable racial effect, would also serve the employer's legitimate interest in efficient and trustworthy workmanship.

This approach makes the employer take into account the effects of social and economic discrimination for which they are not directly responsible.[8]

In Britain the idea was slow to develop. The White Paper *Equality For Women* (1974) did not include the concept, limiting discrimination actions to an intention-based approach. It was only after a visit to the United States by the then Home Secretary, Roy Jenkins, that an indirect discrimination clause was added to the Sex Discrimination Bill. No attempt was made to add the concept to the Equal Pay Act 1970 and, as we shall see later (chapter 5), it is only recently and under much confusion that the concept has been applied to equal pay claims, despite its potential in reducing the effects of occupational segregation on pay differentials.

The Legal Basis

In British law the concept is defined in a complicated and procedural fashion. Instead of applying a straightforward 'effects' doctrine the

British courts and tribunals have frequently scuttled the indirect discrimination claim in a sea of semantic inquiries as to the meaning of particular words.[9]

The legal structure of an indirect discrimination claim comprises three elements: the requirement or condition, evidence of inability to comply and detriment suffered by the applicant. If these are proven the burden of proof then shifts to the respondent to show that the requirement or condition is justifiable.[10]

The Requirement or Condition

The requirement or condition may be written or unwritten, formal or informal; the particular form is irrelevant. In fact the industrial tribunals and the Employment Appeal Tribunal have not taken a narrow legalistic approach to identifying the discriminatory requirement or condition. Instead, by looking at the general policy objectives underlying the Sex Discrimination Act 1975, the Employment Appeal Tribunal has displayed great flexibility in construing particular employment practices as requirements or conditions even where these practices have not been distilled into formal rules. Yet the process of definition is difficult, and it is not altogether clear how much help the tribunal will give the complainant in the formulation of her complaint.

In *Francis* v. *British Airways Engineering Overhaul Ltd*[11] the Employment Appeal Tribunal suggested a different formulation of the complaint so as to bring the case within the Sex Discrimination Act 1975. In so doing, the Employment Appeal Tribunal indicated that a case of indirect discrimination could have been made out at first instance.

The facts of the case concerned the structure of British Airways engineering and maintenance department. There were six categories of employees classified into six Schedules. The complainant represented thirteen other women co-workers who were in Schedule VI, which was composed predominantly of women workers. No women were employed in Schedules I–V, which were the higher grades. Within Schedules I–V there were two or more divisions and opportunities of promotion to a higher division within each Schedule. There was no possibility of promotion within Schedule VI. The original complaint specified a claim of indirect discrimination and the employers asked for particulars of the precise requirement or condition alleged to have been applied. The reply was phrased as follows: '(a) The implicit requirement that the applicant move to other grades of employment in order to seek promotion. (b) By not setting up a careers structure in the applicants' grade to enable the applicants to progress'. The employers contended that no requirement or condition had been applied to Schedule VI employees so the claim of indirect discrimination was not made out. Ruling on the preliminary point the industrial tribunal upheld the employer's contention. The

Employment Appeal Tribunal reformulated the condition or requirement along the following lines: '[L]ooking at the employees in Schedules
I–VI as one class, in order to be eligible for promotion on the basis of
time served and experience an employee must be employed under
Schedules I–V'. It seems very likely that, given that no women were
employed in Schedules I–V, and given that Schedule VI was predominantly composed of women employees, had the Employment Appeal
Tribunal's formulation been used at first instance the complainants
would have succeeded. On appeal, however, it was too late to consider a
reformulation of the point because it was considered inappropriate to
consider the appeal on a different basis from that litigated before the
industrial tribunal. The reasoning behind this refusal to apply the new
formulation to the complainant's advantage was that she had received
legal advice which had defined the precise condition or requirement with
great particularity for the industrial tribunal. It had been agreed by the
solicitors for both parties that the industrial tribunal should decide as a
preliminary point whether the applicant's case disclosed any discrimination within the Sex Discrimination Act 1975. For the Employment
Appeal Tribunal to apply its new and better formulation might have
raised different factual questions which were not dealt with at first
instance, and this, it was argued, would have been unfair to employers.

While the Employment Appeal Tribunal's concern for justice to both
parties is desirable the case reveals the semantic difficulties for the
unwary and the need for careful formulation of the issues. It is tempting
to suggest that expert professional help is necessary for an indirect
discrimination claim, but an alternative possible interpretation is that the
litigant in person may do better than the claimant whose lawyers are
unaware of epistemological issues. The litigant in person may receive
help from the industrial tribunal in choosing a form of words which
brings the complainant within the Sex Discrimination Act 1975.[12]

This point can be further demonstrated from the cases on dismissal for
pregnancy discussed in chapter 3, where the issue of seeing a claim of
discrimination is viewed in the context of section 1 of the Sex Discrimination Act 1975 as a whole. It is not clear whether – if the applicant
refers in general terms to discrimination, or in particular only to direct
discrimination – the tribunal will, of its own accord, consider the claim
under both the direct and indirect discrimination provisions. It has been
suggested by Michael Rubenstein[13] that, where a woman complains of
unlawful discrimination under the Sex Discrimination Act 1975, there is
no requirement for her to bring the claim under section 1(1)(a) or section
1(1)(b) in the sense of nominating the relevant subsection. His view is
that the tribunal must look at the evidence as a whole and not artificially
treat the two subsections as if they were two entirely different claims. If
tribunal proceedings are to be informal and non-technical, and if the
spirit of the Act is to be implemented, then this view must be correct.

In fact industrial tribunals and the Employment Appeal Tribunal have been sensitive to issues of sex discrimination by taking a wide view of accepted and official employment practices even though they could not be formally classified as 'conditions or requirements'.

Since Britain has the highest percentage of part-time workers in Europe it is not surprising that the issue of employment practices in relation to part-time work has played an important part in the cases litigated under the indirect discrimination provisions.

One of the earliest claims, *Meeks* v. *National Union of Agricultural and Allied Workers*,[14] concerned the different rates of pay for full-time and part-time work. Although the claim failed because it concerned contractual terms of employment, and was thus excluded from the 1975 Act, it is illuminating in that it reveals a flexible approach to interpretation. Surprisingly the industrial tribunal rejected the employer's contention that a differential in pay could never come within the ambit of a 'requirement or condition'.[15] Instead it agreed with the employee's submission that the statutory words could be satisfied by formulating a requirement of 'you must work thirty-five hours per week or else you will get a lower hourly rate of pay'.

Turning to more successful cases, age bars have been found to be discriminatory. In *Price* v. *Civil Service Commission* (No. 2)[16] the complaint concerned the Civil Service practice of advertising jobs at the grade of Executive Officer as being open only to candidates aged between seventeen and a half years and twenty-eight years. This requirement was found to operate indirectly against women applicants, who would have greater difficulty than men in complying because of absences from the labour market as a result of child-bearing and child-rearing duties.

Age bars may be discriminatory in other areas and there are indications that the *Price* decision has made employers rethink their hiring practices since age requirements are now generally omitted from advertisements. But there still remain a number of hiring practices which remain unchecked. A case in point is the practice of hiring academic staff in universities, either on the lowest points of the salary scale or in the case of the 'new blood' posts where applicants were required to be aged under thirty-five. The latter was in fact scrutinized and held to be indirectly discriminatory in the case of *Huppert* v. (1) *University Grants Committee*, (2) *University of Cambridge*.[17]

An example of how indirect discrimination can attack discriminatory practices based on historical or customary practice is seen in the decision of *Steel* v. *Union of Post Office Workers*.[18] Here a practice of according priority in the allocation of postal rounds on the basis of seniority was shown to be a discriminatory 'condition or requirement'. Until 1 September 1975 women were employed by the Post Office only on a temporary basis. Although the policy was reversed, and women were employed on the same terms as men, seniority only dated from the date on which women became permanent employees.

Mrs Steel had been employed by the Post Office since 1971, but when she applied for a different postal round she was passed over in favour of a younger man who had been employed on a permanent basis since 1973. Here the 'condition or requirement' was a practice (agreed with the trade union) that 'the successful applicant for a walk must be the most senior in the roll of permanent full-time postmen'.

It is important that informal or customary practices may be subject to scrutiny in this way, especially where such practices have been legitimized through custom and long usage, and particularly in occupations which have been dominated by male employees and where management colludes with trade unions at the expense of women workers. This view shows a far-sighted awareness on the part of the legislature and the courts when drafting and interpreting the legal provision. Laurence Lustgarten explains why this flexible approach was taken:

> so long as . . . [the condition or requirement is] used to restrict employ-
> ment, [the] particular *form* – written or unwritten, a purely managerial
> decision or a shop-floor understanding reached between workers and
> managers – is irrelevant to their legality. This is a key point, for the charac-
> teristic preference in British industrial relations for shared understandings,
> custom and informal methods of settling disputes rather than formal
> agreements and precise interpretations, would make anti-discrimination
> laws a nullity if they could be applied only to formally proclaimed rules.[19]

A good example of the usefulness of this approach is the attitude taken towards selection for redundancy. While a seniority model 'last-in, first-out' is an established industrial relations practice,[20] the recent recession has seen other forms of dealing with work shortages, such as early retirement schemes, and some of these have been challenged under European Community Law.[21] There has also been a tendency for unions to negotiate other kinds of agreements such as a 'part-timers first' policy as a covert way of protecting male jobs.[22] Such a policy has a disproportionate impact upon women workers since more part-time workers are women. However, it is advantageous to employers, since employees working under a contract of less than sixteen hours per week are not eligible for a redundancy payment or an unfair dismissal claim.[23] It is not surprising, therefore, that Alice Leonard reports that one-third of the claims in her study of sex discrimination claims before industrial tribunals involved an aspect of dismissal.[24]

In *Clarke and Powell* v. *Eley (IMI Kynoch) Ltd*[25] the employers and the union opted for a 'part-time workers first' scheme before the application of the customary 'last-in, first-out'. The employers contended that the words 'requirement or condition' should be construed to mean 'a qualification for holding a position but not a qualification for immunity from disadvantage'. Both the industrial tribunal and the Employment

Appeal Tribunal rejected this in favour of the broad formula 'to rank in selection for redundancy by virtue of service in unit and the principle of last in first out, the applicant had to be employed full-time'. This approach was subsequently adopted with less favourable results in a later 'part-timers first case', *Kidd* v. *DRG (UK) Ltd*,[26] based on sexual and marital indirect discrimination.

In other cases the Employment Appeal Tribunal has refused to be swayed into adopting a restrictive stance. In *Home Office* v. *Holmes*[27] the complainant was a single mother who worked as an executive officer for the Home Office. It was departmental policy not to employ part-time workers. After the birth of her second child Ms Holmes asked to return to work on a part-time basis. Under the maternity protection provisions of the Employment Protection (Consolidation) Act 1978 (as amended by the Employment Acts 1980 and 1982) a woman is entitled to return to the job originally specified in the contract of employment, and on terms and conditions which are not less favourable than would have been applicable to her had she not been absent on maternity leave.[28] The application for part-time work was refused. On her return to work Ms Holmes complained to an industrial tribunal that she had been discriminated against contrary to sections 1 and 6 of the Sex Discrimination Act 1975. The Home Office unsuccessfully argued that the terms of full-time service were so fundamental that they could never amount to a requirement or condition: they related to the whole job. In rejecting this submission the Employment Appeal Tribunal state that the words 'requirement or condition' were clear words of wide import fully capable of including any obligation of service whether for full or for part-time.

While not establishing a general principle this case has opened up the possibility of challenging the way employers organize work, particularly in a refusal to consider patterns of work favourable to women with domestic responsibilities such as job-sharing, job-splitting and flexi-time.[29]

There is a wide range of possibilities for the extension of this approach, especially in the area of 'informal' employment practices which may operate to the detriment of women: for example, allocation of overtime working, informal 'word-of-mouth' recruitment practices, lack of child-care facilities on retraining or refresher courses, and informal promotion procedures. The Employment Appeal Tribunal seems to be sensitive to some of these issues. For example, an informal promotion procedure was subject to scrutiny in *Watches of Switzerland* v. *Savell*,[30] albeit in somewhat convoluted wording:

> [T]hat to be promoted to the post of manager in a London branch of the retail business owned by the appellant one must satisfy the criteria of a vague, subjective unadvertised promotion procedure which does not provide any or any adequate mechanisms to prevent subconscious bias unrelated to the merits of candidates or prospective candidates for the post of manager.

Evidence of Ability to Comply

Once a condition or requirement has been established the woman must show that the effects are such that the proportion of women who can comply with it is considerably smaller than the proportion of men who can comply with it.[31] The indirect marital discrimination provisions follow a similar test, using married and single persons of the same sex as the comparators.[32] This statutory definition lacks precision, and yet is central to the concept of indirect discrimination.

The words 'can comply' have been subject to restrictive definition. For example the industrial tribunal, in *Price* v. *Civil Service Commission*, interpreted them to mean merely a physical possibility. If this interpretation had been upheld it would have precluded all applications which raised the issue of women's domestic responsibilities. Fortunately the Employment Appeal Tribunal rejected such an approach, substituting instead: 'It should not be said that a person "can" do something merely because it is theoretically possible for him to do so; it is necessary to see whether he can do so in practice.'[33] This interpretation has, however, received a setback by the majority decision of the Court of Appeal in *Turner* v. *Labour Party and the Labour Party Superannuation Society*.[34] Here a pension scheme which provided automatic pensions for surviving spouses upon the death of a member, but applied conditions for a pension to be granted to a survivor of an unmarried member, was held not to the detriment of a divorcee because the conditions for benefit from the pension fund were to be satisfied at a future date: 'It cannot be said of a single woman that she "cannot" marry. She may not want to marry and cannot be compelled to marry, but she can marry.'

Use of Statistical Evidence. Adducing evidence of the smaller proportions of women who can comply has not received a definitive interpretation. Few attempts have been made to elucidate what kind of statistical evidence may be presented, how it should be analysed and the limitations of a statistical approach. This is in contrast to the United States where, since the decision in *Griggs*, statistics have played an important role in sex discrimination claims. In American case law statistical evidence can be categorized as falling into two broad areas of comparison: 'pass/fail' statistics and 'population/workforce' statistics. The 'pass/fail' comparison involves comparison between the percentage of the protected group who can satisfy a condition laid down by the employer with the success rate of the majority group. 'Population/ workforce' comparisons compare the availability of the protected group in the general population or labour force in a relevant geographic area with the percentage of that protected group in the employer's workforce.

One problem in Britain with the use of this type of comparison is that employers are not required to keep statistics on the composition of their workforce.[35] While general statistical information is available, it has been argued that the lack of precise and accurate statistics provides an insurmountable hurdle for victims of indirect discrimination.[36]

Pools and Proportions. The woman must show that the effects of the apparently neutral requirement or condition are such that the proportion of women who can comply with it is considerably smaller than the proportion of men who can comply. This implies that there must be a pool from which the proportions can be drawn so that a comparison can be made. Little guidance has been given as to how this exercise should be carried out. The original Home Office guide[37] offered the following advice:

> Questions may also arise as to the groups from which the proportions of men and women who can comply with a condition or requirement are to be drawn for the purposes of comparison. The answers will depend on the particular circumstances of each individual case. For example, the relevant groups of men and women in one case may be the men and women employees at a factory; in another the men and women inhabitants of a particular area; and in yet another the male and female populations in the country as a whole.

The Home Office does not go as far as illustrating instances in which each of the examples applies. While the issue is a question of fact to be determined by industrial tribunals, inconsistencies of approach have arisen, and there is a growing tendency for tribunals to rely on 'common-sense' knowledge rather than hard empirical evidence.

Early cases reveal an attempt to deal with statistical evidence presented to industrial tribunals. For example in *Meeks* v. *NUUAW*[38] statistics were presented from the *New Earnings Survey 1974* to show that 32 per cent of all women worked on a part-time basis, whereas only 3 per cent of men did so. Despite the fact that the evidence was not disaggregated showing the differences between married and single women (the point of the claim was that married women were more likely to work part-time because of family commitments) the industrial tribunal accepted that appropriate comparisons could be made from this evidence.

Statistical evidence was given appellate acceptance in the *Price* case, where it was held that the appropriate pool was all suitably qualified men and women who could apply for the post in question.[39] The evidence had to be available from a statistician who could be cross-examined as to the proper analysis and inferences to be drawn from the evidence. However, in a later case decided under the Race Relations Act 1976, the Employment Appeal Tribunal voiced an opinion that industrial tribunals should not be over-concerned with elaborate statistical evidence.[40] While the industrial tribunals have in fact used a mixture of evidence ranging from a psychologist[41] to witnesses familiar with the industry in question,[42] there has been a drift in more recent decisions to rely upon 'general knowledge and experience'.[43] On the one hand it could be argued that such a 'common-sense' approach has value in that a case will not automatically fail due to the unavailability of the necessary statistical evidence. On the other hand reliance upon a limited amount of 'common-sense' knowledge may mask discriminatory perceptions of the role of women in society. In relation to *Holmes*, for example, there is a wealth of evidence available on the participation of women with dependants in the labour market,[44] and if this had been used in a rigorous way the decision could have had a wider impact.

The limitations are seen in the *Kidd* v. *DRG (UK) Ltd.*,[45] where the delineation of the pool was a contentious issue. Counsel for the complainant argued that the whole population should be looked at, whereas counsel for the respondent limited it to the workforce under scrutiny. The industrial tribunal initially chose to look only at households with young children who required so much care that looking after them could not be combined with full-time employment. This was confirmed by the Employment Appeal Tribunal, since this approach would fulfil the statutory requirement imposed by section 5(3) of the Sex Discrimination Act 1975 which states that: 'A comparison of the cases of persons of different sex or marital status under section 1(1) or 3(1) must be such that the relevant circumstances in the one case are the same, or not materially different, in the other.' This comparison ignores the fact that most young children live in households with a married couple, and thus the comparisons between men and women who could comply with the requirement to work full time became unduly restrictive.

Prior to the decision in *Kidd*, motherhood, especially the role of caring for young children, had been treated by the tribunals and official discourse generally as a major factor limiting women's participation in the labour market. This 'social fact' was challenged by the industrial tribunal and the Employment Appeal Tribunal in *Kidd* when it was alleged that:

> [M]others of young children in the modern community are no longer conforming universally to the traditional notion that their place is in the home; and that there are plenty of couples (married and unmarried) today with young children, where the male partner stays at home for the whole or part of the time to release his female partner to undertake full-time work.[46]

No evidence was given for this new 'social fact'.

One of the problems with looking at households with children is that it assumes that all adult members of the household are equally incapacitated by the presence of children (or indeed others who need care), and this overlooks the sexual division of labour.

The Equal Opportunities Commission[47] points out that it is difficult to separate the delineation of the pool from the condition or requirement that creates it, and from the justifiability of the continued application of the requirement. We have argued elsewhere[48] that the correct pool should be those at risk under the first element of the statutory definition of indirect discrimination: that is, those at risk under the ostensibly gender-neutral requirement or condition. Having identified those at risk the appropriate comparison is between those who can comply with the requirement and those at risk under it. In the particular circumstances of *Kidd* those at risk are part-time workers, and those who can comply are full-time workers. Thus the compliance of married women was the issue, not the presence of children in the household. In fact the issue of child care is only one reason why married women work part-time; in addition to other domestic responsibilities state policies such as the tax and social security thresholds provide incentives for married women to work part-time rather than full-time.[49]

A final problem with the approach in *Kidd* was the apparent lack of appropriate statistical evidence. It seems that once the pools were identified both tribunals wanted to hear statistical evidence about households with children. Extracts were produced from the National Census figures which were held to be 'too broadly based', and which merely confirmed that more full-time jobs are held by men than are held by women. The Employment Appeal Tribunal wanted figures as to the effect as between the sexes, or as between unmarried and married persons, of responsibility for children as a factor potentially precluding the acceptance of a full-time job. While such evidence is now widely available it is submitted that the statistical evidence of women's or married person's lesser ability to comply is enough to show a *prima facie* case of indirect discrimination. The reasons for that inability rank as supplementary.

A more responsive approach to the question of comparability is seen in a case taken under the European Community Equal Treatment Directive.[50] In *R. v. Secretary of State for Education, ex parte Schaffter*[51] the statutory scheme for the provision of education grants provided that hardship grants for lone parents were only available for parents who had once been married. The Secretary of State argued that the appropriate pool was single lone parents, and within this pool there was no significant difference between the percentage of female lone parents and male lone parents. There was, however, a decisive difference between the percentage of lone parents who were female and the percentage of lone parents who were male. Mr Justice Schiemann discerned the danger of falling into the trap of incorporating discrimination into the way the groups for comparison are defined, by concentrating too much attention on the requirement that like be compared with like. Instead, the overriding principle was that indirect discrimination claims were about 'a practice working in reality in such a way that many more women than men are adversely affected by it'. The appropriate pool for comparing the proportions of men and women who could comply with the eligibility requirement was a pool of all students with dependent children claiming grants. Since there were four times as many female lone parents ineligible for hardship grants as male lone parents ineligible there was a *prima facie* case of indirect discrimination.

Surprisingly the phrase 'considerably smaller' has not yet received a definitive interpretation.[52] The Equal Opportunities Commission[53] has asked for statutory guidance on the matter. The Commission for Racial Equality supports the convention adopted in the United States known as the 'four-fifths' rule, whereby adverse impact is shown if there is a 20 per cent difference in impact between the racial groups involved. This has been rejected by the Equal Opportunities Commission for sex discrimination cases, since the effects on women of many requirements and conditions will vary according to the point in the woman's life cycle at which they are applied. The application of this principle links in to the necessity of the statistical data becoming available.

Detriment

Although indirect discrimination is a group issue the applicant must establish a personal *locus standi* by showing that she has suffered a 'detriment' because she cannot comply with the requirement or condition. When the Sex Discrimination Bill was first proposed it contained no requirement of detriment but spoke of an 'unfavourable' requirement or condition. This was removed during the Standing Committee Debates.[54] At the Report Stage in the House of Commons the government successfully introduced an amendment adding the requirement of detriment. This reason for this was explained by Mr John Fraser, Under-Secretary of State for Employment: 'there must be a particular victim of indirect discrimination, and she must, for obvious reasons, be one of the women who are unable to qualify for the benefits.'[55]

In looking through the case law, however, there has been some confusion as to what exactly the applicant must prove. In *Clarke and Powell* v. *Eley (IMI Kynoch) Ltd*[56] it was emphasized that only one point in time is being looked at: 'the only material question is whether *at the date of the detriment* she can or cannot comply with the requirement. If she can, paragraph (iii) is not satisified, if she cannot, it is satisfied.' It was irrelevant that at some earlier date the complainant could have avoided the detriment by complying with the requirement; equally it was irrelevant that at some future date the requirement could be complied with.[57]

In *Price* v. *Civil Service Commission*[58] the Employment Appeals Tribunal held that 'it should not be said that a person "can" do something merely because it is theoretically possible for him to do so: it is necessary to see whether he can do so in practice'.[59]

However in the more recent case of *Turner* v. *Labour Party*[60] the Court of Appeal seems to have ignored past interpretations. Here a pension scheme which provided automatic pensions for a surviving spouse upon the death of a member, but applied conditions for a pension to be granted to a survivor of an unmarried member, was not to the detriment of a divorced woman because she 'cannot comply with it', on the grounds that the conditions for benefit from a pension fund were regarded as having to be satisfied at a future date.

In *Watches of Switzerland* v. *Savell*[61] Mrs Savell was asked to prove that, as a woman, she could not achieve promotion, and indeed, because she had been promoted in the past and might therefore achieve promotion in the future, the element of personal detriment could not as a matter of law be said to have been shown. The reasoning here seems confused in many respects, since it was accepted that the promotion procedures were biased against women and the applicant was able to show a failure to promote her in a particular instance, thus satisfying the test of necessary detriment. The decision focuses upon past behaviour (and therefore past ability to comply) and hypothetical future behaviour rather than the present factual situation on which the complaint is based. It would also seem to conflate the two separate tests showing the ability of a smaller proportion of women than men to comply with the discriminatory effect on the group and the test of personal detriment giving the necessary *locus standi*. The heavy burden imposed upon Mrs Savell, of proving it was impossible for a woman to be promoted under the alleged discriminatory procedures, is therefore a misapprehension of the statutory test.

For the most part proving the group inability to comply with a condition or requirement will reveal the element of personal detriment to the applicant. The issue has not been fully discussed in British law – often because respondents are willing to admit that if it is shown that the condition or requirement is discriminatory the applicant would suffer a detriment. From the successful cases on indirect discrimination various accepted employment practices have now become suspect: failure to be considered for employment because of an age bar (*Price*), lack of choice in carrying out employment duties (*Steel*), selection of part-time workers first for redundancy (*Clarke and Powell*), refusal of part-time employment to a mother (*Holmes*). The last case is particularly interesting in that the industrial tribunal took the view that the full-time-only requirement was to Ms Holmes's detriment in that she was unable to comply with it because parental responsibilities prevented her from carrying out a 'normal' full-time week's work. In trying to fulfil all these obligations she had to suffer excessive demands on her time and energy. Very rarely is this 'double burden' recognized in legal discourse which seeks to achieve parity of treatment between perceived equals in the labour market.

This evidentiary requirement of detriment poses a question, to date unresolved, of whether the woman merely has to show that she has suffered a detriment or whether she has to go further and prove that, but for the alleged discriminatory condition or requirement, she would have received a benefit or not suffered a detriment. For example, the applicant would have got the job or would not have been selected for redundancy.[62]

A final point is why should discriminatory practices be illegal only when the woman can show a personal detriment? This has been a problem in bringing sexual harassment claims under the indirect discrimination provisions, in that the woman must take steps such as to be moved to another department or establishment, or leave her job altogether.[63] A more recent decision under the Race Relations Act 1976 has been more helpful, in that the creation of an unpleasant working environment may be a sufficient detriment to bring a claim of racial discrimination and this may be the way forward for expanding the concept of sex discrimination in working conditions.[64]

Surprisingly the Equal Opportunities Commission 'found no grounds for considering that the interpretation by the courts of what constitutes a detriment gives cause for concern, but this is nonetheless an issue which is being monitored by Commission staff'.[65] Given the complexity of the issue, and the scope for semantic diversions, it is strange that the Equal Opportunities Commission wishes to adopt only minor amendments to the concept whereas elsewhere it suggests that the wording of the Act be expanded and clarified to make it clear that any practice or policy having an adverse impact upon women could be challenged.[66]

Justifiability

Once a *prima facie* case of indirect discrimination has been established the burden of proof shifts to the employer, and effectively the issue becomes one of how justifiable are the discriminatory practices. The defence to the indirect discrimination action was subject to scrutiny by Parliament as attempts were made to substitute the word 'necessary' for 'justifiable'. From the explanations given at the House of Commons Committee Stage of the Sex Discrimination Bill it is clear the drafters intended a job-related, *Griggs*-style interpretation of the defence.[67] As Breen Creighton[68] points out, since 'justifiable' is a broader concept than 'necessary' it is possible for it to be interpreted in such a way as to render the whole concept of indirect discrimination meaningless.

While the application of the defence is a question of fact in each case the appellate courts and tribunals have supplemented the statutory language with their own tests as to how justifiability is shown. Originally the Employment Appeal Tribunal demanded a strict interpretation of 'justifiable', equating it with necessity rather than purely administrative convenience. Drawing upon the 'business necessity' test expounded in the *Griggs* case, Phillips J. in *Steel* v. *Union of Post Office Workers* argued that:

A similar approach seems to us to be proper when applying s.1(1)(b)(ii) of the Sex Discrimination Act 1975. . . . [A] practice which would otherwise be discriminatory, which is the case here, is not to be licensed unless it can be shown to be justifiable unless its discriminatory effect is justified by the need – not the convenience – of the business or enterprise.[69]

This rigorous interpretation has gradually been watered down by a series of decisions under the Race Relations Act 1976. Firstly, the Scottish Employment Appeals Tribunal in *Singh* v. *Rowntree MacIntosh*[70] interpreted 'justifiable' as meaning a 'reasonable commercial necessity'. A later Court of Appeal ruling replaced this interpretation by a looser form of wording summarized by Eveleigh LJ: 'if a person produces reasons for doing something which would be acceptable to right thinking people as sound and tolerable reasons for so doing then he has justified his conduct'.[71]

Two cases show the inconsistencies which may arise as a result of this subjective approach. In *Home Office* v. *Holmes*[72] the industrial tribunal and the Employment Appeal Tribunal held that the 'full-time work only' requirement was not necessary. Efficiency could be maintained (and even increased) without it, and the discriminatory effect it produced outweighed the need for it. Evidence was produced in the form of two departmental reports recommending greater flexibility for part-time work. Both reports suggested the use of part-time work could lead to greater efficiency, although it was recognized that this might not apply to all jobs, particularly those requiring continuity and supervision. Ms Holmes successfully argued that these problems would not arise in her own job, since she was employed upon casework organized from a common queue and the work did not necessitate reporting to a particular executive officer if problems arose. It was argued that the advantages of part-time work, in particular the retention of trained and experienced staff, outweighed the disadvantages. The industrial tribunal accepted this argument, pointing out that the Home Office had not entertained the feasibility of part-time working, and had not assessed the discriminatory effects of the ban in relation to their own organizational requirements.

On appeal the Employment Appeal Tribunal refused to accept the Home Office's contention that since most of industry and the public sector was run on a full-time basis it was self-evident that a full-time work requirement was justified. In particular the Employment Appeal Tribunal was anxious to assert that the defence was not a mere formality. The industrial tribunal had entered a caveat that if the demand for part-time work became excessive, or created difficulties which could not be overcome, the Home Office might be able to justify the requirement. This caveat was repeated by the Employment Appeal Tribunal, which stressed that the case stood on its own particular facts. The rider was added quite clearly in response to the publicity surrounding the case since

Counsel for the Home Office had invited the Employment Appeal Tribunal: 'to envisage the shock to British industry and to . . . national and local government administration which . . . would be bound to be suffered if, in addition to all their other problems they now had to face a shoal of claims by women workers alleging it would be discriminatory to refuse them part time status'.[73]

In *Kidd* v. *DRG (UK) Ltd*[74] the employer was able to show that the requirement of full-time work was justifiable. The Employment Appeal Tribunal recognized that while the advantages of full-time work to the employer were only marginal, and on their own of little account, they might have cumulative disadvantages. These amounted to the fact that employing two shifts of part-timers necessitated more employees than one shift of full-timers; increased length of staff records and the additional time to compile them increased administrative and personnel functions; and incurred more laundering of uniforms and a 'mild degree' of disruption when shifts changed over. The Employment Appeal Tribunal stated that the industrial tribunal's decision reflected 'a realistic recognition of the fact that under the competitive conditions of modern industry small advantages of that kind, though singly they be of little account, can cumulatively make a crucial difference between success or failure in attracting or maintaining orders'. This trend of interpretation reveals important limitations on the concept of indirect discrimination. As Lord Wedderburn[75] comments:

> This judgment confirms the influence of the recession and of changes in prevailing philosophy upon the courts. The barrier of 'business necessity' stood firm in the 1970s against indirect discrimination. In the 1980s the market-oriented demand for competitiveness sways the judges to accept in its place the judgment of 'right-thinking' people and marginal influences on the bottom line.

The decision exposes a tendency towards managerial bias. While a balance must be held between the needs of industry and the prevention of sex discrimination, emphasis seems to be placed by the interpreters upon the problems encountered by employers in organizing their workplace. This overlooks the problems of women in complying with the full-time work requirement. Surely this is against the spirit of the legislation? While there is plenty of evidence available to show the importance of part-time work for women to reconcile the demands of domestic and economic pressures, this kind of evidence was ignored in the *Kidd* decision. In particular the Employment Appeal Tribunal seems to have lost sight of the fact that 'justifiable' should relate to the demands of the employment in question; in other words, the condition or requirement should be job-related.[76]

The major factor in this reasoning stems from the dictum of Eveleigh LJ in *Ojutiku* v. *Manpower Services Commission*,[77] that justifiability is

tantamount to reasonableness. Leonard[78] points to the tendency of
industrial tribunals to misapprehend the nature of the justifiability test,
and instead apply a test of reasonableness as understood under the unfair
dismissal legislation when the reasonableness of an employer's actions is
assessed in relation to the circumstances surrounding a dismissal.[79]
Parallels may also be drawn between the decision in *Kidd* and the judicial
reluctance to interfere in an employer's economic decisions unless it can
be shown that the employer has acted unreasonably.[80] Whereas unfair
dismissal claims turn on their own particular facts, and merit an
individualistic approach, indirect discrimination is concerned with group
characteristics and the justifiability of a particular employment policy on
particular groups. Thus the way in which the issue was examined in both
the *Holmes* and *Kidd* decisions led to a particular underplaying of the
socioeconomic implications of the decisions, precluding any wider discussion of the role of women in the labour market, and how they might
be discriminated against by particular employment practices.[81]

The consequences of treating the issue of 'justifiability' as a question
of fact were predicted in *Clarke and Powell* v. *Eley (IMI Kynoch) Ltd*:

> To decide whether some action is 'justifiable' requires a value judgement to
> be made. On emotive matters such as racial or sex discrimination there is no
> generally accepted view as to the comparative importance of eliminating
> discriminatory practices on the one hand as against, for example, the
> profitability of a business on the other. In these circumstances, to leave the
> matter effectively within the unfettered decision of the many Industrial
> Tribunals throughout the country, each reflecting their own approach to
> the relative importance of these matters, seems to us likely to lead to widely
> differing decisions being reached.[82]

The Employment Appeal Tribunal has frequently accepted that in some
decisions a different tribunal might come to a different conclusion.[83] The
difficulty with this approach is that employment practices affecting large
groups of women are being tackled, and it seems both inequitable and
inefficient that each individual affected should be subject to a judicial
lottery as to whether the practice is lawful or not. If indirect discrimination is to hold future potential for class actions greater emphasis must
be placed on preparing the evidence for an investigation of the discriminatory effects of employment practices, rather than focusing attention on
how far individual discriminatory actions will be tolerated.

The defence may be tightened up in the future by the application of the
European Court of Justice ruling in *Bilka-Kaufhaus GmbH* v. *Weber
von Hartz*.[84] This provided that in a defence to a charge of indirect
discrimination in an equal pay case it is for the national court to apply a
threefold test: the policy must be based on objectively justified factors
unrelated to any discrimination on grounds of sex, the means chosen for
achieving the objective must correspond to a real need on the part of the
undertaking, and be appropriate with a view to achieving the objective in

question, and be necessary to that end. The final gloss added to the American defence, that the employee may show alternative less discriminatory measures are appropriate, has not been added.[85]

The *Bilka* ruling was first applied to challenge an action of the state in *R v. Secretary of State for Education, ex parte Schaffter*.[86] It was held that it was for the Secretary of State to show that the advantages of the distinction drawn between single and married lone parents were such that, giving due weight to the principle of proportionality, the unequal treatment of women was justified. All the Secretary of State had done was to state that the purpose of the regulations was to benefit lone parents. That did not amount to a justification.

The Future Potential for Indirect Discrimination

Despite the reservations drawn in this chapter it is perhaps illuminating to consider that of the twelve member states of the European Community only two, the United Kingdom and the Republic of Ireland, have a doctrine of indirect discrimination enshrined in legislation. In Ireland indirect discrimination is defined as:

> Where because of his sex or marital status a person is obliged to comply with a requirement, relating to employment or membership of a body, which is not an essential requirement for such employment or membership and in respect of which the proportion of persons of the other sex or (as the case may be) of a different marital status but of the same sex able to comply is higher.[87]

This legal definition is not dissimilar from the definition given in British law, and the Irish Labour Court has defined requirements of mobility, minimum height, upper age limits, recruitment through a training school and refusal of employment on grounds of pregnancy as amounting to indirect discrimination. However, Angela Byre[88] reports that rulings of the Labour Court have had little general impact upon employment practices since they have been implemented only in relation to individual cases, and there is no provision to render discriminatory practices unlawful.

The concept of indirect discrimination has been included in some of the secondary legislation implementing the equal treatment principle in European Community law. The phrase has been added without further clarification of its legal meaning and how it is to be proven and defended. In proposing a European Community solution (which would take precedence over national law) Byre suggests that regular monitoring of employment practices and national legislation is a good starting point to expose discriminatory practices, particularly those that have been embedded in industrial relations practice, and to raise consciousness, not only amongst women, but also amongst employers and trade unionists. Once identified, she argues, these practices need to be countered by finding alternative, non-discriminatory ways of implementing employment policies, as well as the initiation of positive action programmes to enable women to make up for lost ground.

Conclusions

This chapter has argued that, while in theory the doctrine of indirect discrimination provides a legal mechanism whereby the goal of equality of opportunity is pursued rather than a goal of equality of treatment, the reality is that the way the concept has been translated – through a complicated procedural mechanism, the lack of available data and statistics, and preconceived judicial ideas of the way society is organized – preclude any radical thought to using the idea as a means of pursuing a focus upon differences rather than assimilation between the social roles of men and women. Peter Fitzpatrick,[89] in looking at the form of law and the mode of adjudication in employment cases concerned with racial discrimination, argues:

> A detailed study of such instances showed that there were certain persistent limits, certain bounds beyond which law did not proceed in countering racism. What, in an immediate sense, stood on the other side of those bounds and checked law's advance was the power and autonomy of employers. Law thus marked out areas in which the racism of employers could operate.

As this chapter reveals, the word 'sexism' could readily be substituted for the word 'racism' in the above quotation. The legal discourse surrounding the operation of the indirect discrimination provisions recognizes the goal of accommodating difference into a concept of equality of opportunity, but that discourse is limited through technical, procedural qualifications and a judicial reluctance to widen the ambit of the debate over equality. Without such changes indirect discrimination will remain limited in its application, and will not realize the ambition envisaged by the Equal Opportunities Commission of this 'powerful innovation'.[90]

Notes

1 Indirect discrimination is legally defined in the Sex Discrimination Act 1975, section 1(1)(b). A person indirectly discriminates against a woman (in the contexts of employment, education and the provision of goods, facilities, services and premises) if he applies to her a requirement or condition which he applies or would apply equally to a man but (i) which is such that the proportion of women who can comply with it is considerably smaller than

the proportion of men who can comply with it, and (ii) which he cannot
show to be justifiable irrespective of the sex of the person to whom it is
applied, and (iii) which is to her detriment because she cannot comply with it.
The concept has also been used in European Community legislation, and
now extends to look at discrimination in state and occupational social
security measures (see chapter 7).

2   See recognition of this by Lord Lowry in *Wallace* v. *South Eastern
Education and Library Board*, [1980] IRLR 193.

3   'Institutional discrimination', 2 *Oxford Journal of Legal Studies* 303 (1982).

4   401 US 424 (1971).

5   For background see McCrudden, C., op. cit. note 3; Rustin, B., *Strategies
for Freedom: The Changing Patterns of Black Protest* (New York, Columbia
University Press, 1976); Rainwater, L. and Yancey, W. L., *The Moynihan
Report and the Politics of Controversy* (Cambridge, Mass., Harvard
University Press, 1967); Burstein, P., *Discrimination, Jobs and Politics*
(Chicago, University of Chicago Press, 1985).

6   supra note 4; at p. 431.

7   *Albermarle Paper Co.* v. *Moody*, 422 US 404 (1975).

8   The concept was extended to sex discrimination in *Dothart* v. *Rawlinson*,
433 US 321 (1977), where minimum height and weight requirements for
prison employees were held to be indirectly discriminatory against women,
and therefore contrary to Title VII.

9   Vestiges of an intention-based approach to discrimination also remain since
section 66(3) of the Sex Discrimination Act 1975 precludes an award of
compensation if the respondent successfully argues that he did not intend to
treat the applicant unfavourably.

10   For further discussion and comparison with the United States see Pannick,
D., 'The burden of proof in discrimination cases', 131 *New Law Journal* 895
(1981).

11   [1982] IRLR 10.

12   Compare with Alice Leonard's findings on the effect of legal advice and its
relationship with the success of claims. From Department of Employment
statistics on industrial tribunal hearings of equal pay and sex discrimination
claims, applicants with legal representation were successful twice as often as
those who had trade union representation or were self-represented (*Pyrrhic
Victories*, London, HMSO, 1987).

13   [1983] IRLR 137. The Equal Opportunities Commission seems to suggest
that the applicant should make a choice, see *Legislating For Change*
(Manchester, 1986), pp. 10–13, although in discussion with their legal
officers they confirm that applicants in doubtful cases are advised to plead in
the alternative.

14   [1976] IRLR 198.

15   See, however, section 6(6) of the Sex Discrimination Act 1975.

16   [1978] IRLR 3.

17   8 *Equal Opportunities Review*, 38 (1986).

18   [1977] IRLR 288.

19   *Legal Control of Racial Discrimination* (London and Basingstoke,
Macmillan, 1980) at p. 43.

20 One which was not necessarily seen as discriminatory in either the Standing
    Committee debates on the Sex Discrimination Bill since John Fraser, Under-
    Secretary of State for Employment used 'last-in, first-out' as an example of a
    policy which was 'justifiable' (Standing Committee B, 24 April 1975, col. 71)
    or by the Employment Appeal Tribunal in *Clarke and Powell* v. *Eley (IMI
    Kynoch) Ltd*, [1982] IRLR 482. Title VII (section 703(h)) of the US Civil
    Rights Act 1964 allows an employer to apply a bona-fide seniority system as
    long as it does not intend to discriminate on invidious grounds. Cf. *Robinson*
    v. *Lorillard Corp.*, 444 F. 2d. 791, 799 (1971) where the United States Court
    of Appeals held that pressure from trade unions or an agreement with a trade
    union cannot, of itself, justify a practice which has a disproportionate
    adverse impact on women or minority groups under Title VII. See also US
    Commission on Civil Rights, *Last Hired, First Fired* (Washington, 1977).
21 Case 19/81, *Burton* v. *British Railways Board*, [1982] 2 CMLR 136; Case
    151/84, *Roberts* v. *Tate and Lyle Industries Ltd*, [1986] IRLR 150; Case
    262/84, *Beets-Proper* v. *F. Van Lanschot Bankiers NV*, [1986] ICR 706.
22 For further discussion see Earnshaw, J., *Sex Discrimination and Dismissal:
    A Review of Recent Case Law*, University of Manchester, Department of
    Management Sciences, Occasional Paper no. 8505 (1985).
23 This is discussed further in chapter 6.
24 *The First Eight Years* (Manchester, Equal Opportunities Commission, 1986)
    p. 22.
25 [1982] IRLR 482. For background to this case see Sedley, S., 'Pin money: a
    test case on discrimination against part-time workers', in P. Wallington
    (ed.), *Civil Liberties 1984* (Oxford, Martin Robertson, 1984).
26 [1985] IRLR 190.
27 [1984] IRLR 299.
28 Section 45. The right is circumscribed in that section 45 of the Employment
    Protection (Consolidation) Act 1978 does not apply to employers who
    employ five or fewer employees, and who can show it is not reasonably
    practicable to permit the woman to return to her original job or offer not less
    favourable, alternative employment. Irrespective of the size of the firm an
    employer may have a good defence to an unfair dismissal claim if he can
    show it is not reasonably practicable to reinstate the woman in the original
    job and alternative employment is offered which is accepted or unreasonably
    refused (section 56A(2)–(4)). Suitable alternative employment may also be
    offered if the job has become redundant (section 45).
29 *Wright* v. *Rugby Borough Council*, (1984) COIT No. 235 28/84. Here an
    industrial tribunal held that an employer indirectly discriminated by
    refusing to allow a woman to work flexible hours so that she could combine
    her job with family commitments. Cf. *Fulton* v. *Strathclyde Regional
    Council* (EAT, Scotland, 15 January 1985). The Scottish Employment
    Appeal Tribunal was reluctant to act on 'alleged' social trends as to the
    prevalence of part-time work among women and refused to apply *Holmes* to
    part-time workers who wanted their employer to introduce a job-sharing
    scheme. Subsequent cases of *Hicks* v. *North Yorkshire County Council*
    (COIT 1643/117) and *Guthrie* v. *Royal Bank of Scotland plc* (COIT
    31796/86) have upheld the claim of indirect discrimination for failure to
    accept a return to work on a part-time basis after maternity leave, although

the Employment Appeal Tribunal is still prepared to uphold the defence if particular justifications are advanced; see *Greater Glasgow Health Board* v. *Carey* [1987] IRLR 485.

30   [1983] IRLR 141.

31   Section 1(1)(b) Sex Discrimination Act 1975.

32   Section 3(1)(b) Sex Discrimination Act 1975.

33   Contrast the Court of Appeal decision in a Race Relations Act 1976 case, *Perera* v. *Civil Service Commission*, [1983] IRLR 166, where criteria taken into account by an interviewing board were held not to be a 'requirement or condition' because none of the factors in question 'could possibly be regarded as a requirement or condition in the sense that lack of it . . . would be an absolute bar'.

34   [1987] IRLR 101.

35   Compare the proposal of the Commission for Racial Equality recommending mandatory record-keeping of racial statistics (*The Race Relations Act 1976 – Time For Change?* (London, 1983) at pp. 7 and 14.

36   See Redmond, M., 'Women and minorities', in R. Lewis (ed.), *Labour Law in Britain* (Oxford, Basil Blackwell, 1986).

37   A *Guide to the Sex Discrimination Act 1975* (London, EOC, 1975) p. 4.

38   Supra note 14.

39   Compare *Wright* v. *Civil Service Commission* (London Central IT Case No. 9324/79/3), where the pool was restricted to those who fulfilled the necessary conditions for promotion by those already employed by the Civil Service.

40   *Perera* v. *Civil Service Commission* (No. 2), [1983] ICR 428.

41   *Watches of Switzerland* v. *Savell*, [1983] IRLR 141.

42   *Meeks* v. *NUUAW*, [1976] IRLR 198.

43   *Home Office* v. *Holmes*, [1984] IRLR 299.

44   See, for example, Elias, P. and Main, B., *Women's Working Lives: Evidence from the National Training Survey*. Research Report, Institute For Employment Research, University Of Warwick, 1982.

45   [1985] IRLR 190.

46   Ibid., at p. 195.

47   *Legislating For Change*, op. cit. note 13, p. 12.

48   14 *Industrial Law Journal* 252 (1985).

49   See Disney, R. and Szyszczak, E., 'Protective legislation and part-time employment in Britain', *British Journal of Industrial Relations*, 22, 78 (1984); Szyszczak, E., 'Employment protection and social security' in R. Lewis, (ed.), *Labour Law in Britain* (Oxford, Basil Blackwell, 1986).

50   Council Directive 76/207/EEC OJ L 39/40.

51   [1987] IRLR 53.

52   Note the case of *Wong* v. *GLC*, (unreported) 15 October 1980, where the EAT decided that if a requirement or condition excluded *all* of one racial group then as none could apply the proportions test could not be applied, since nil was not a proportion. Compare with *Greencroft Social Club and Institute* v. *Mullen*, [1985] ICR 796, which disapproved of *Wong* as running counter to the spirit of the legislation.

53   *Legislating for Change*, op. cit. note 13, p. 13.

54   Standing Committee B (24 April 1975), cols 79–80.

55 893 HC 1491–2 (18 June 1975).
56 See note 20.
57 *Steel* v. *Union of Post Office Workers*, [1977] IRLR 288.
58 [1978] IRLR 3.
59 This approach was approved of by the House of Lords in *Mandla* v. *Dowell Lee*, [1983] 2 AC 548: 'the word "can" must have been intended by Parliament to be read not as meaning "can physically", so as to include a theoretical possibility, but as meaning "can in practice" '.
60 [1987] IRLR 101.
61 [1983] IRLR 141.
62 Compare Pannick, D., *Sex Discrimination Law* (Oxford, Clarendon Press, 1986) at p. 55: 'Section 1(1)(b)(iii) does not require the complainant to show that but for the impugned requirement or condition she would have been appointed to the job or received the other benefit (or avoided the detriment) at issue. Section 1(1)(b) is concerned to ensure fair consideration of individuals for the relevant opportunities or disadvantages.'
63 *Porcelli* v. *Strathclyde Regional Council*, [1986] ICR 564.
64 *De Souza* v. *Automobile Association*, [1986] IRLR 103.
65 *Legislating for Change*, see note 13.
66 Ibid., p. 14.
67 See HC Standing Committee, cols 35–6 and 57–80, 22 and 24 April 1975, and HL Debs, vol. 362, cols 1014–22, 14 July 1975.
68 Creighton, W. B., *Working Women and the Law* (London, Mansell, 1979) at p. 162.
69 [1977] IRLR 288 at p. 291.
70 [1979] ICR 554.
71 *Ojutiku* v. *Manpower Services Commission*, [1982] ICR 661, at pp. 667–8.
72 [1984] IRLR 299.
73 Ibid. at p. 301.
74 [1985] IRLR 190.
75 *The Worker and the Law* (3rd edn, Harmondsworth, Penguin, 1986), at p. 470.
76 This retreat from the *Griggs* approach is paralleled under the Race Relations Act 1976 in *Raval* v. *Department of Health and Social Security*, [1985] IRLR 370.
77 See note 71.
78 *Judging Inequality* (London, Cobden Trust, 1987) ch. 2.
79 Section 57(3), Employment Protection (Consolidation) Act 1978.
80 For discussion of the implications of this approach in relation to the unfair dismissal provisions see Collins, H., 'Capitalist discipline and corporatist law', 11 *Industrial Law Journal* 78, 170 (1982). Cf. Elias, P., 'Fairness in unfair dismissal: trends and tensions', 10 *Industrial Law Journal*, 201 (1981).
81 See M. Rubenstein, [1984] IRLR 198, who argues that it is debatable whether the decision in *Holmes* is binding upon the Home Office except in the specific circumstances of Ms Holmes.
82 Supra note 20, at p. 254.
83 For example see *Home Office* v. *Holmes,* [1984] IRLR 299, and for a Race Relations Act 1976 case see *Raval* v. *Department of Health and Social Security*, [1985] IRLR 370.

84   Case 170/84, [1986] 2 CMLR 707, discussed in detail in chapter 5.
85   *Albermarle Paper Co.* v. *Moody,* supra note 7.
86   [1987] IRLR 53.
87   Section 2, Employment Equality Act 1977.
88   *First Report of the Network of Experts Set Up to Monitor the Application of Equal Treatment Legislation*, V/1035/84-EN, Brussels (1984).
89   'Racism and the innocence of law', 14 *Journal of Law and Society*, 199 (1987) at p. 130.
90   *First Annual Report* (London, HMSO, 1976) at p. 4.

Chapter 5

Equal Pay and Wage Discrimination

The Economic Background

As with the sex discrimination legislation, doubts have been expressed over the operation of the Equal Pay Act 1970. These range from conservative suspicion of any intervention in the market for rates of pay, to feminist disillusionment with the inability hitherto of the Equal Pay Act to achieve parity between male and female wages or even to remove aspects of sex discrimination in the wage determination process.[1] Unlike sex or race discrimination, equality of pay is a more tangible concept and the effects of the legislation can be seen in concrete statistical evidence. Perhaps the most obvious evidence of disillusionment is the rapid decline in the number of equal pay applications: from a total of 1,742 in 1976 to thirty-nine in 1982.[2] The first two years of the new equal value claim after 1983 saw some 600 applications being lodged, of which only four had completed the procedure by the end of 1985.[3]

These figures lead many commentators to argue that the Equal Pay Act has outlived its usefulness. If we look at the effects of the legislation on male and female earnings we see that in 1970 women's hourly earnings were 58 per cent of men's. By 1977 they had increased to 68 per cent of men's, and since then this differential has remained fairly constant. Some commentators have argued that even this limited impact owes more to other strategies such as incomes policies in operation at this time.[4] Research by Tony Zabalza and Zafiris Tzannatos, however, confirms that most of the reduction in the male–female differential in the mid-1970s is due to equal pay legislation.[5] Thus a case can be made out showing that the legislation has had a significant impact, despite apparent contrary evidence.

The methodology of using this kind of evidence to assess the impact of the legislation has several drawbacks. By taking average wages in this way it makes the implicit assumption that in an 'ideal world' men and women would compete on relatively equal terms in the labour market, thereby carrying out similar work, working in similar places and at similar times. Taking average pay for men and women ignores the fact that women are a heterogeneous group, and that differences in, for example, race and age are not significant factors in the determination of pay.[6] Thus much of the issue of inequality of pay is hidden, since such general statistics fail to capture the variety of experiences and differences between male and female work and the rates of pay attributed to that work.

Some of these differences lie in the fact that women's employment is concentrated into jobs where, for example, unionization is weak, and where there is little likelihood of improvement in overall wage rates. Examples are the 'female' occupations such as hairdressing or the clothing industry. For some of these industries the Wages Councils help to maintain a basic minimum wage,[7] but whether they will continue to do so is a matter of speculation since the Wages Councils have been singled out by the Conservative government at least for 'streamlining', if not abolition, in the new wave of deregulating the labour market.[8] Equally any attempts to introduce a minimum wage would also seem inappropriate in the new era of deregulated labour markets.[9]

Women have also traditionally carried out home-working and part-time work, although during the recession we have seen a qualitative change in this type of work.[10] Figures from the *New Earnings Survey* reveal that this type of work continues to attract lower rates of pay than 'normal' full-time work carried out in factories or firms.[11] Other new forms of organizing work are also emerging, such as 'networking'.[12] While these new forms of work are used to evade employment protection legislation they are also useful ways of segregating workforces in the same way that homeworking has been used to prevent comparability in equal pay claims.

Another important factor is that the composition of many women's pay packets is different from many men's. In the 1985 *New Earnings Survey* it was found that 39 per cent of male workers received overtime payments, compared with only 17 per cent of women, and that 16 per cent of men and only 12 per cent of women received shift premiums. Thirty-nine per cent of men received additional payment by results, so-called 'productivity payments'. In a survey carried out for the Department of Employment it was found that although men and women were being paid the same basic rates, and working the same hours, there was still a difference in take-home pay attributable to the fact that: 'Men work more overtime, do more shiftwork, have been employed for longer to qualify for length of service awards and hold a disproportionate number of merit or responsibility positions.'[13] Such forms of incentive payments are not found in all occupations, and are notably missing from occupations where women are crowded – for example, teaching, nursing, secretarial and services sector work. The inclusion of productivity deals into male wages further reveals the significance and relationship of men to paid work and unpaid domestic work. For many women the opting for productivity deals through overtime or special shift-working is simply not possible, either because of the constraints of domestic commitments or because of lack of adequate child-care facilities.

Definition of Pay

The concept of what constitutes 'pay' is important under the Equal Pay Act, but the notion of what constitutes 'pay' is an increasingly complex concept to unravel. On the one hand it is the central focus of any employment relationship, since it is concerned not only with the amount of 'take-home' pay but encompasses many other rewards in the form of fringe benefits, paid holiday entitlements and occupational insurance schemes. However the concept of 'pay' also has repercussions for the calculation of awards in the context of employment protection rights (compensation for redundancy, unfair dismissal) and the earnings-related supplement to the state pension and (when it existed) the earnings-related supplement to unemployment benefit. Thus the issue of equal pay has a wider dimension than simply the structure of wage or salary rates.

In fact 'pay' is given an ambiguous definition in the Equal Pay Act. This is because the Equal Pay and Sex Discrimination Acts were intended to be mutually exclusive. The Equal Pay Act covers the terms and conditions of the contract; if less favourable treatment relates to the payment of money regulated by a contract of employment the Equal Pay Act applies.[14] If less favourable treatment relates to a matter not included in the contract (either expressly or by virtue of the operation of the equality clause) only the Sex Discrimination Act applies.[15]

Section 6 of the Equal Pay Act excluded from the operation of an equality clause terms relating to the operation of protective legislation, special treatment of women in connection with pregnancy or childbirth, and terms relating to death or retirement or to any provision made in connection with death or retirement except terms relating to membership of an occupational pension scheme. Although European Community law has played a significant role in opening up the blanket exemption to terms relating to death or retirement in section 6 of the Equal Pay Act,[16] this has worked to the applicant's disadvantage in the first equal value claim to proceed through the British courts. In *Hayward* v. *Cammell Laird Shipbuilders Ltd*,[17] the Court of Appeal has held that equal pay for work of equal value is achieved if, overall, the terms and conditions of the woman's contract are not less favourable than those of male comparators. Although Julie Hayward's basic pay and overtime rates were lower than those of her male comparators she also received a paid meal break, additional holidays and better sickness benefits. The employers contended that when these were taken into account Ms

Hayward was better off than the comparators. Although the industrial tribunal and the Employment Appeal Tribunal did not accept the employer's valuation, both tribunals and the Court of Appeal accepted the argument that section 1(2)(c) of the Equal Pay Act should be interpreted to include not just basic pay but other benefits included in the pay package.[18]

This decision may have positive results in other cases because it leaves unanswered the question of whether the effect of a finding that two jobs are of equal value leads to the result that *all* the benefits of the man's contract must be applied to the woman's contract in order to achieve equal pay. This may have far-reaching consequences, particularly in the light of the ruling in *Bilka Kaufhaus GmbH* v. *Weber von Hartz*,[19] that discriminatory access to occupational pension schemes may fall within Article 119 EEC. Part-time workers are often not covered by occupational schemes, and one of the purposes of segregation of workforces is to exclude certain classes of workers from fringe benefits. These may have a significance beyond purely monetary consequences: access to a company car, to expense accounts, relocation expenses or occupational social security schemes are often used to reinforce a status hierarchy within a firm.

Several other reasons can be put forward to explain why, despite the Equal Pay Act, there remains a significant differential between male and female pay. Commentators have pointed to the maintenance by unions of a 'family wage', the effects of both horizontal and vertical segregation within the workforce, the definition of skill, changes in the labour market over the past century, and particularly the current widening of the dispersion of pay caused by mass unemployment and the introduction of new technology.[20] While various factors would seem to contribute to an explanation of the causes of pay inequality the law has perceived the issue and focused attention on a somewhat narrow formulation of pay inequality.

The historical background to the Equal Pay Act has been charted in chapter 2. There it was seen that, mainly due to historical processes, Britain has followed the United States in adopting separate strategies for dealing with equal pay and sex discrimination. This is a significant factor in analysing the effect of the equal pay legislation. In Britain equal pay has a longer history than both sex and race anti-discrimination laws and, as in the United States, the equal pay legislation is conceptually more at home within the legislation relating to 'fair labour standards', interwoven with industrial relations and economic factors rather than a concept of civil liberties. Indeed, in the late 1960s any attempts to introduce wider legislation to deal with equality of opportunity issues were considered inappropriate at the time.[21] This separation of equal pay from equal opportunity is a major weakness in the structure of anti-discrimination legislation since it circumscribes the discourse on inequality of pay. This is because an inquiry as to how far differences between male and female wages are due to sex discrimination through lack of equality of opportunity, and the wider social and institutional issues which interact with the workings of the labour market, is precluded. At present the legislation permits only a narrow inquiry focusing upon individual employers' actions and policy choices.

Equal pay claims involve more than the mere equalization of wage rates. In addition they have much to do with how women's work is organized and perceived, and the status accorded to women's work. Surprisingly these issues have received minimal attention in the legal discourse on pay equality. The point is illustrated in a newspaper report of a job evaluation exercise carried out between local authority workers. Under a heading 'Home helps get boost in status' it is reported that: 'A new pecking order among one million council workers in which home helps are elevated above the industrially-powerful dustmen has been agreed between employers and unions.' Later in the report it is acknowledged that:

> The fact that the unions have agreed the new structure means they have taken on board the widespread criticism that workers with the most industrial muscle do not necessarily deserve the highest rates of pay. The deal involves a major shift for the labour movement, which always paid lip-service to the importance of the 'caring services', but could never agree a method of reflecting the concept of social usefulness in the determination of pay levels. [22]

In fact the whole issue of sex-based wage discrimination is still being debated at a controversial level in the 1980s. [23] This debate has intensified after calls for a 'comparable worth' or 'equal pay for work of equal value' concept in law. [24] Prior to this, in Britain and the United States, equal pay legislation adopted a stance of assimilation: so long as women are similarly situated with men then justice demands equal remuneration. The flaw in this argument is that while women's participation in the labour market has increased significantly since the Second World War, the reality of their situation is that few women behave like men in the labour market. Instead their participation is limited because of differences in education and training, child-bearing and child-rearing roles or other domestic obligations. When in the labour market, women undertake frequently what is perceived of as traditionally 'female' work, or they work at different hours in part-time, temporary, shift-work jobs or in different places, crowded into unskilled grades or home-working jobs.

In contrast the thesis of the equal pay legislation sees women and men as isolated and equal individuals competing with each other in the labour market. Not only does the thesis overlook the lack of equality of opportunity in allowing women to compete on the same terms as men, or the inequalities in the sharing of domestic responsibilities, but it also ignores the influence on pay differentials of historical factors such as the maintenance of a family wage and the political processes of defining and constructing skills within the labour market.

Therefore the issue of equal pay is a controversial idea at both the economic and legal level. While it is appreciated that inequalities exist in various forms in the labour market there is disagreement as to how far these inequalities can be viewed as 'discrimination' and how far law, and in particular the judicial forum, can and should intervene to redress these inequalities. In the United States doubts have been expressed as to whether judges are themselves better at making a 'second guess' at improving the imperfections of a flawed labour market. It is acknowledged that the judicial forum is not the most practical for eradicating discrimination.[25] Since the introduction of equal pay legislation perhaps more gains have been made through the use of the legal concept in collective bargaining[26] and even industrial action.[27] Similarly it is acknowledged that the Equal Pay Act (even as amended) cannot work alone, and other measures such as positive action, contract compliance[28] and the use of the Sex Discrimination Act to break down institutional barriers to job segregation all have a role to play in eradicating wage discrimination.

The rest of this chapter will analyse the framework of the equal pay legislation and the definitions of discrimination used to determine a legal remedy for pay inequality. In so doing we will discuss the various conceptual and procedural mechanisms which might be implemented to link further the concept of pay inequality with sex discrimination.

Procedural Mechanisms

Although the Equal Pay Act 1970 offered various procedural means of initiating equal pay claims, the right of an individual to take a complaint to an industrial tribunal was given paramount importance in the legislative strategy. Such an approach is limited conceptually, because although it is possible for several concurrent claims to be heard at the same time it isolates the individual claim and thus distracts from wider issues such as the division of domestic responsibilities, lack of equality of opportunity and the role of female labour in the labour market. Attention is focused only on the individual position.[29] Using the new equal value provisions claims have been brought involving large numbers of applicants within a single suit,[30] but the issue still remains one of limited comparability, that of comparing similarly situated employees working for the same employer.

Despite the resultant emphasis upon individual enforcement the state does not facilitate access to the industrial tribunals by extending legal aid. Assistance through the Equal Opportunities Commission is limited by financial constraints upon that body,[31] and in the absence of strong trade union support, civil liberties organizations or other pressure groups, women are left to finance their own claims. From Alice Leonard's study the importance of some kind of representation at the tribunal hearing emerges. Where both employer and employee had representation the applicant success rate was 46 per cent, but where the employer was legally represented and the employee self-represented the applicant success rate was only 23 per cent.[32]

In times of recession and job loss, equality of opportunity might be seen as a lower priority for the trade unions than retaining and maintaining wage differentials. Statistics for the period 1976–83, however, reveal that, in equal pay cases, 49 per cent of male applicants and 47 per cent of female applicants had a trade union representative.[33] Further evidence shows that many of the larger unions have used the principle of equal pay for work of equal value coupled with the threat of a tribunal case as a new weapon in attempts to disrupt pay structures.[34] The relationship may be two-way, therefore. The more likely the claim is to be successful the more the union may be prepared to fight it and represent the claimant, and also the probability of union support will be greater the more the union wants to disrupt the pay structure.

In addition to representation of the parties the Advisory, Conciliation and Arbitration Service is available to effect a conciliation, but evidence varies as to how helpful and impartial this is to applicants.[35]

Discrimination cases were allotted to the industrial tribunals since it was envisaged that they would form the 'nucleus of a system of labour courts'.[36] There have been doubts expressed whether these are the right forum to deal with discrimination issues, and whether the personnel who staff them are sufficiently trained in discrimination law[37] or display an 'understanding of discrimination or empathy with its victims'.[38] It is still the case that women are underrepresented as members of industrial tribunals. Women compose only 7 per cent of industrial tribunal chairs and 21 per cent of panel members. Leonard found that, in her study of cases heard between 1980 and 1982, 23 per cent of equal pay cases were heard without a woman present. When Leonard investigated whether the presence of a woman member on the industrial tribunal panel made any difference to the outcome of the discrimination cases she discovered that panels with a woman member did decide more often in the applicant's favour than did all-male panels. While there are grounds for arguing that the presence of a female member in the tribunal might be advantageous, not only to put female applicants at their ease but also to bring some female experience of discrimination into the decision-making process, the structure of the institutional arrangements do not necessarily facilitate this dimension, particularly for the lay members of tribunals. As Michael Rubenstein has observed of the lay members of the Employment Appeal Tribunal: 'the lay member is much more likely to put forward collectivist values designed to ensure that agreed procedures or pay structures are not disrupted than to champion attempts by members of disadvantaged groups to assert individual rights at the expense of the status quo'.[39] The research by Linda Dickens on unfair dismissal indicates that lay members of tribunals exert less influence, particularly where the issue is presented as a legal one.[40]

The crisis in confidence in the industrial tribunals is also borne out by statistical evidence. At the beginning of this chapter we referred to the enormous decrease in applications under the Equal Pay Act 1970 before it was amended in 1983. Furthermore there is evidence that from 1976 to March 1985 only 9.7 per cent of equal pay cases heard by tribunals were successful.[41]

Conceptual Issues

The Concept of Discrimination

The Equal Pay Act does not give a precise definition of pay discrimination. The words 'less favourable' are used in section 1 of the Act, and reliance is placed upon the definitions contained in the Sex Discrimination Act. Article 119 EEC gives only a limited explanation of what constitutes discrimination.[42] This would seem to be illustrative rather than exhaustive, since the European Court of Justice has built upon Article 119 EEC to include both direct and indirect discrimination. Surprisingly, the concept of positive discrimination seen in governmental or corporate policy in terms of giving preferential treatment to a minority or disadvantaged group (usually in hiring or promotion practices) does not seem to have a place in tackling directly the issue of wage discrimination. Such a policy would be a useful way of counteracting low pay in a segregated workforce, by bringing a group of female workers up to a comparable wage level in occupations dominated by male workers. To date such policies have not received any widespread use.

We have already seen that in differentiating between direct and indirect discrimination under the Sex Discrimination Act the applicant must take care in presenting the claim because of differences in proof and the application of the defence. Such distinctions have not been so fully articulated under the Equal Pay Act. Direct discrimination, as we have seen, occurs when a woman is treated less favourably than a man is or would be treated on the grounds of sex. This definition is not applied fully to the Equal Pay Act because hypothetical comparisons are not allowed.[43] Indirect discrimination, in contrast, moves away from making direct comparisons, to scrutinizing pay policies to see if they have an adverse or disparate effect upon women. As we have seen, indirect discrimination is defined in a complicated and procedural form under the

Sex Discrimination Act. It was not until the Employment Appeal Tribunal decision in *Jenkins* v. *Kingsgate (Clothing Productions) Ltd* (No. 2),[44] that it was accepted that indirect discrimination could apply to equal pay claims. Even then it was unclear whether the procedural form of the Sex Discrimination Act should apply, and how far intention to discriminate was relevant.

This uncertainty was due to the fact that the concept of indirect discrimination in equal pay matters was introduced into British law through the use of a preliminary reference to the European Court of Justice. For some time the scope of European Community law was uncertain because of the ruling of the European Court of Justice in the second *Defrenne* case, which attempted to limit the direct applicability of Article 119 EEC.[45] A distinction was drawn between 'direct and overt' discrimination and 'indirect and disguised discrimination', which could only be identified with the aid of more detailed implementing provisions at either the Community or national level. Only as regards the former situation would Article 119 EEC be directly applicable – that is, give rise to rights directly enforceable before national courts. The distinction was followed by the European Court of Justice in *Macarthys* v. *Smith*, but in the Opinions of Advocate-General Warner in *Worringham and Humphreys* v. *Lloyds Bank* and *Jenkins* v. *Kingsgate* disquiet was expressed over the distinctions, and the European Court of Justice responded to the requests for clarification when it abandoned the phrases and instead spoke of Article 119 EEC applying directly 'to all forms of discrimination which may be identified solely with the aid of the criteria of equal work and equal pay referred to by the article in question, without national or Community measures being required to define them with greater precision in order to permit their application'.[46] In bringing indirect discrimination into the direct effects of Article 119 EEC in the *Jenkins* case the European Court of Justice created uncertainty as to the scope of the concept. This stemmed from the wording of the judgment. The Court did not seem to apply an 'effects' doctrine as understood in American law, but rather seemed to imply that an *intention* to discriminate was necessary. This is how the national courts in *Jenkins and Bilka-Kaufhaus GmbH* v. *Weber von Hartz* construed the judgment until the point was clarified by Advocate-General Darmon in *Bilka*. He explained that Article 119 EEC did not apply only to deliberate discrimination. Rather it was the Court's intention to indicate that the absence of discriminatory intent on the employer's part was not enough to justify a finding that a provision which in fact placed women at a disadvantage was not contrary to the prohibition on discrimination; the intention to discriminate being only a specific instance of the application of Article 119 EEC.

This retrospective interpretation of the *Jenkins* case by the Advocate-General seems difficult to reconcile with the judgment of the European

Court of Justice. It could be argued that, despite the statistical evidence presented in the case, the Court was ambiguous in confronting the gender aspects of the use of part-time work and the disparate impact upon women of pay practices towards part-time workers. In *Jenkins* the European Court of Justice held that a difference in pay between full-time and part-time workers was not incompatible with Article 119 EEC unless it was an indirect way of reducing the pay of part-time workers on the ground that that group was composed exclusively or predominantly of women. Even then the employer was able to justify the pay policy on the ground that it was objectively justified to achieve a particular economic end.

In *Bilka* an equally narrow view of discrimination was taken, in that while an occupational pension scheme excluding part-time workers was open to scrutiny it was held that Article 119 EEC imposed no obligation upon employers to take account of family responsibilities in organizing pension schemes. The mere fact that the measures affected a greater number of women than men would not infringe Article 119 EEC if the employer could show that the measures met a genuine need of the enterprise and were necessary for that purpose. The focus of this discrimination model, therefore, has been upon the defence to the claim rather than a close scrutiny of the *effects* of a particular policy.

Like Work

In facilitating individual access to the industrial tribunals the Equal Pay Act 1970 (as amended) employs three concepts. The first implies an equality clause in a contract of employment which modifies other terms and conditions of employment so as to eliminate inequalities between men and women in the same employment on like work.[47] In interpreting this clause the tribunals have followed an approach evidenced elsewhere in labour law of looking at the total job package together with the employee's task specification. According to the authors of one of the leading labour law texts, Paul Davies and Mark Freedland, such an approach reflects 'the very stuff of which much plant-and-company wide collective bargaining about pay consists'.[48] This approach, however, ignores how the decisions were made, the assumptions about the value of the work involved and the relative bargaining strengths of the parties. In other words, it takes as definitive the job package given. In particular, the legal discourse has been silent in definitions and control over skill. But as feminist historians and economists have shown, the historical relationship between sex, skill and control over work had less to do with the content of the job and had more to do with the bargaining power and gender of whoever was doing the work.[49] This 'hidden agenda' remains unseen in the legal attempt to redress the inequality of pay.

Aspects of the 'feminization' of particular kinds of work are also lost in the present inquiry required by law as to whether jobs are sufficiently similar to warrant comparison. This is seen clearly in office jobs. As male clerks disappeared they were replaced by women with new skills in typewriting and shorthand. These women also took over extra duties not expected from men: 'The female secretary looked after her boss as only a woman could. She brought him cups of tea, dusted his desk, dialled his telephone calls, took his suits to the cleaners, bought presents for his relatives . . . became, in short, the office wife.'[50]

The concept of defining aspects of skill is also complex in the cluster of 'female' jobs that have built into them the notion of 'service with a smile'. This may be where being presentable, helpful and friendly are inbuilt ingredients of a job – for example, personal secretaries or receptionists. Or where individuals are rewarded for good service by the notion of personal tips. The tips not only reward skills, but also measure success. The hidden agenda behind the definition of these skills is complex. In reality such payment systems hide the fact that such jobs are not paid an economic rate. They may do more. They may reinforce segregation and may be used to create hierarchies, 'discipline' female labour into subservience and also reinforce social relationships. The point is illustrated by Catharine MacKinnon's work on sexual harassment in quoting a waitress's experience of her work: '[Men think] they have a right to touch me, or to proposition me because I'm a waitress. Why do women have to put up with this sort of thing anyway? You aren't in any position to say "get your crummy hands off me" because you need the tips. That's what a waitress job is all about.'[51]

These kinds of jobs are not exclusively filled by women – some hairdressers are men, and male taxi-drivers, waiters and porters also rely upon tips to boost low incomes. But where job definitions have strong links with domestic work we find that women are expected to bring special attributes to the labour market, though the skills involved are often overlooked or undervalued. In so far as gender is a silent part of the job description this can be seen as unlawful discrimination.[52]

Despite the weaknesses inherent in the conceptual underpinnings of the Equal Pay Act the industrial tribunals have given a mixed reception to applications. In some cases, for instance, the tribunals have taken a fairly broad perspective and have adopted what is termed a 'broadbrush' approach in identifying 'like work' cases.[53] Trivial differences are discounted 'unless the differences are plainly of a kind which the industrial tribunal in its experience would expect to find reflected in the terms and conditions of employment'.[54] The courts and tribunals have been asked to apply a definition of equality without challenging any of the assumptions that certain types of work or behaviour are appropriate for one sex and not for the other. As Catharine MacKinnon argues: 'The functional biological differences between the sexes with respect to human reproduction is still openly adduced to support a wide-ranging set of assumptions about social roles which have nothing demonstrable to do with biology.'[55]

This is exemplified in the case of *Shields* v. *E. Coomes (Holdings) Ltd*,[56] where the work under scrutiny was described by Lord Denning in the following way: 'the man filled a protective role. He was a watch dog ready to bark and scare off intruders. . . .' Later, in describing the kind of persons undertaking the work, the judge tries to show how liberal he is in not stereotyping men and women into particular roles: '[The man] may have been a small nervous man, who would not say "boo to a goose". She may have been as fierce and formidable as a battle-axe.' In another case the same judge reveals his own perceptions of the role of the equality legislation. In dismissing a claim brought by a male applicant alleging discrimination in the employer's practice of allowing female employees to leave work a few minutes early to avoid the crush at the end of the shift Lord Denning delimited the scope of discrimination law: 'It is not discrimination for mankind to treat womankind with the courtesy and chivalry which we have been taught is the right conduct in society.'[57]

Although some tribunals have recognized the dangers of artificial differences, particularly those based on sexual stereotypes,[58] other cases reveal this is not a universal trait. Jean Coussins, for example, cites the case of *Greendale* v. *Jarman and Flint Ltd*, where an office cleaner compared her work with that of a man cleaning the warehouse. The claim for equal pay was denied partly because 'the office cleaners work in the comfortable surroundings of carpeted offices, very similar to the environment of one's own home'.[59]

The fact that a woman complainant works at a different time does not automatically preclude a finding of 'like work', but employers may justify differentials based on overtime rates or night shift premiums.[60] The tribunals seem reluctant to inquire, and would argue that due to the limitations of the legislation they are precluded from inquiring, whether or not women and men are given equality of opportunity in carrying out the work which is given preferential rewards. Such an inquiry would fall within the operation of the Sex Discrimination Act.

A major limitation of the 'like work' concept is found in the fact that the Employment Appeal Tribunal has taken an 'all-or-nothing' approach. For instance, the case of *Maidment and Hardacre Ltd* v. *Cooper & Co.*[61] involved a man and a woman engaged in exactly the same tasks for about 80 per cent of their employed time, but on different tasks for the remaining 20 per cent of the time. A claim of 'like work' was refused because of the different tasks performed, even though the differences did not occupy a significant amount of the working time. Thus one of the limitations of the 'like work' provisions is that there is no 'half-way house'; the judiciary have taken an 'all-or-nothing' approach. So where a woman is doing a job which involves greater effort, or skills, or responsibility than the job undertaken by the man there can be no claim of 'like work'.[62] This poses limitations in trying to argue a case based on wage discrimination where the woman alleges that her pay is disproportionately less (or even higher) than the work being carried out by the only available comparable males.

Work Rated as Equivalent

The second way of implementing the principle of equal pay is through the use of a job evaluation scheme. Although section 1(5) of the Equal Pay Act allows the use of job evaluation schemes to determine whether the applicant and the comparator are engaged upon work rated as equivalent, it does not make them compulsory. Job evaluation studies can only be carried out with the agreement of the relevant parties – that is, employers and workers (or their representatives).[63] Section 1(5) states that a woman is to be regarded as employed on work rated as equivalent to that of a man if the complainant's job and the comparator's job have been given an equal value in terms of the demands made on a worker under such headings as effort, skill and decision. Only quantitive studies using the factor comparison or point method are recognized under the Act, and qualitive studies using a ranking or classification method are not.[64]

At first sight job evaluation studies would seem an attractive alternative to settling issues of pay. In *O'Brien* v. *Sim-Chem Ltd* the House of Lords acknowledged the use of job evaluation schemes 'in an attempt to achieve a broadly sound pay structure',[65] but such schemes are not widespread in Britain. In the infringement action against the United Kingdom (concerning the failure to introduce the equal value concept) the government argued that compulsory use of job evaluation schemes was unacceptable given the largely voluntary nature of wage-bargaining in the United Kingdom and the expenses necessarily incurred in introducing the expertise and institutional structures required to evaluate different jobs.[66]

The traditional objective of job evaluation schemes is to provide an acceptable pay structure. Implicit within them is a status hierarchy. Often existing salaries based on market rates are used to validate the job evaluation schemes, and these may replicate and perpetuate the status quo, particularly where a professional firm of consultants has been used, since then it is more likely that labour market considerations are taken into account. Thus no attempt has been made to deconstruct the notions of skill that have developed as a means of preserving wage differentials. Now job evaluation schemes have been adopted to achieve a different objective – that of tackling sex discrimination – with little attempt to alter the structure or provide safeguards against discrimination.

Although Article 1 of Directive 75/117/EEC[67] provides that job evaluation schemes must be drawn up by the use of sex-neutral criteria, little research has been undertaken to determine what this entails.[68] It is surprising that discrimination is not more clearly defined in either the Directive or the Equal Pay Act, since job evaluation schemes can conveniently disguise and reinforce discrimination while giving the appearance of an objective and scientific approach. In the American case of *Thompson* v. *Boyle*,[69] for example, a job evaluation of a bookbinding job ascribed no points for training and experience required in sewing since 'the sewing was of the variety most women know how to perform'; meaning, therefore, that it was not a skill recognised as being of value in the paid labour market.

As with other aspects of the wage bargaining process, a job evaluation scheme relies upon a set of skills agreed between management and unions, and reflects the relative bargaining strengths not only of these parties but also of male and female workers. Thus disproportionate weight may be given to various gender-related attributes such as physical strength or manual dexterity. This is clearly acknowledged by the Advocate-General Verloren van Themaat:

> the evaluation criteria are not always neutral as between the sexes. For example, certain qualities in work could be described as typically female (for instance, dexterity, meticulousness, readiness to undertake repetitive work and so on) and are valued commensurately lower than 'male' qualities (ability to handle materials and machines, physical strength and so on).[70]

The problem of identifying discrimination becomes more important under the Equal Pay Act since a woman is precluded from bringing an equal value claim where a job evaluation scheme is in existence unless she can show that discrimination exists in the scheme. Discrimination is shown where: 'a difference or coincidence between the value set by that system on different demands under the same or different headings is not justifiable irrespective of the sex of the person on whom those demands are made'.[71] This definition of discrimination has been criticized for lack of clarity, particularly on the extent of recognition of indirect discrimination. This is particularly important in cases where women are arguing that aspects of their skill have been overlooked.[72] The British legislation has, however, been modified by the ruling of the European Court of Justice in *Bilka-Kaufhaus GmbH* v. *Weber von Hartz*,[73] which subjects the word 'justifiable' in section 2A(3) to closer scrutiny. This may have potential in challenges to job evaluation schemes on the grounds of indirect discrimination. In order to defend a claim of discrimination in a job evaluation scheme the employer must now show that there is a causal connection between any pay differentials and a genuine objective pursued by the firm, and that these differentials are necessary for that objective. In particular these conditions apply to the choice and weighting of the factors in a job evaluation scheme. In *Rummler* v. *Dato-Druck GmbH*[74] the way has been opened for the challenge to a job evaluation scheme if the choice of factors is not representative of the tasks undertaken by both sexes. In this ruling the European Court of Justice held that Council Directive 75/117/EEC does not preclude the use in job evaluation schemes of factors which favour one sex, provided the system does not discriminate overall on grounds of sex. However, if the job evaluation scheme is not to be discriminatory, criteria should be used which can measure particular aptitudes on the part of the employees of both sexes.

These rulings are important because, for the most part, job evaluation schemes have hitherto been difficult to challenge under British law.[75] Greater use could be made of the decisions to tackle the methodology and assumptions behind established schemes, particularly where disproportionate attention has been given to gender-related attributes. Even the Equal Opportunities Commission are guilty of such assumptions. In the guide, *Job Evaluation Schemes Free of Sex Bias*, a company nurse's job is compared with that of a fitter. The fitter is given six points for working conditions and the company nurse only one. Michael Rubenstein argues that no account is taken of the workplace hazards for the nurse of contracting infections, or of moving to parts of the factory to deal with serious workplace accidents.[76]

In all aspects of job evaluation certain questions relating to the gender bias of certain work and its evaluation remain unanswered. Is looking after property more important than looking after people?[77] For example, how is occasional heavy lifting to be compared with repetitive light lifting? How are the strains imposed by working in noisy offices, cramped spaces, or the operating of visual display units for long periods to be measured? How is full weight to be given to the co-ordination of women's skills? Are the various dimensions of certain jobs ignored? For instance, secretaries and receptionists contribute a variety of tasks to their work such as dictation, answering the telephone, taking messages, photocopying – all done with good grace and a smile – but many of these are overlooked when writing out a job description. The law relating to the evaluation of these tasks has yet to come up with a methodology which approaches the evaluation task in the spirit of true equality.

Work of Equal Value

The third basis of comparison is for a woman to show that her work is of equal value to that of a man in the same employment.[78] Under the Equal Pay Act (as amended) this is a residual claim, only available if a woman is not employed on 'like work' or the job is not covered by a valid, non-discriminatory job evaluation scheme. The Court of Appeal has held that a claim for equal value may be made relying directly upon Article 119 EEC.[79]

The equal value claim was introduced somewhat grudgingly after an infringement action brought by the EC Commission against the British government for failure to introduce the necessary measures to comply with Council Directive 75/117/EEC. Conservative opposition to the amendment (which did not fit in with the party's proposals to deregulate the labour market) is seen in the comments of Conservative backbencher Mr Tony Marlow, who saw the amendment as leading to a situation where '[a]ny trouble-maker . . . is going to pretend that her work is of equal value. It is an open invitation to any feminist, any harridan, or any rattle-headed female with a chip on her bra-strap to take action against her employer.'[80]

In fact the government precluded any mass surge of claims by enacting the equal value claim by means of a procedure which confounded even Lord Denning by its 'tortuosity and complexity'.[81] This did not preclude the press from sensationalizing the new claim. Such coverage has concentrated upon the costs of equal value claims both to private industry and local and central government: 'Equal pay costs set to explode', declared *The Sunday Times*.[82] The discussion of a 'comparable worth' concept in American law is equally reported in emotive language. Commenting upon the emerging case law under Title VII of the Civil Rights Act 1964, Evan Spelfogel introduces the discussion in the following way:

> There is a storm brewing on the horizon, largely unnoticed by the labor bar. In the center of this storm is the U.S. Equal Employment Opportunity Commission, led by Chair Eleanor Holmes Norton. . . . It is a storm of cyclonic proportions which, if left unchecked, may soon rip through the American economy costing untold millions of dollars to business and labor.[83]

Within European Community law little guidance is given on how equal pay for work of equal value should be assessed. In the infringement actions,[84] and also the substantive implementation of the concept in British law, the emphasis has been upon procedural aspects. These are complicated and encourage the parties to seek a conciliation of the dispute.[85] This emphasis upon conciliation is, on the one hand, a prevailing industrial relations notion, part of the attempt to keep labour law within a spirit of 'voluntarism'. On the other hand, conciliation has become an attractive proposition in other areas where women are significantly affected by the operation of the law, notably in the arena of family disputes. Portrayed as a therapeutic remedy to conflict, conciliation may mask some of the detrimental effects the procedure has on women applicants. The relegation of issues to a 'private' sphere of informal justice means that the process can be used to hide or control wider group issues of female labour which need articulation in the 'public' sphere of formal justice through the tribunals and courts. Public discussion is important to women in so far as it enables a dialectical process and the emergence of women's perspectives. It provides a consciousness-raising function. Similarly conciliation provides no checks against bias or stereotyped assumptions held by the person attempting to effect a conciliation of the dispute. As with the 'public' legal forum, women applicants are assumed to have the same bargaining power as the opposing party – the employer. A feminist critique of conciliation in family law could apply equally to the labour law arena: 'The particular invidiousness of this mode of informal justice is that it reproduces power relationships much more effectively than formal justice because of the very construction and manipulation of images of party control, privacy, neutrality and a "back to the people" grass roots appeal.'[86]

Once a *prima facie* equal value claim has been established the employer is given the opportunity of defending the claim. If this does not occur, or is unsuccessful, then the case is handed over to an independent expert who investigates the claim and sets about evaluating the jobs under scrutiny. In the amendments to the Equal Pay Act little indication of the methodology of assessing equal value claims was given, and the present guidelines neither suit industrial relations practice nor attempt to deal squarely with issues of sex discrimination. The work being compared is to be reviewed 'in terms of the demands made upon her (for instance under such headings as effort, skill and decision)'.[87] While it is presumed the list is merely illustrative, no answers are given to crucial questions such as what factors should be weighed, measured and compared (although since the factors look at the demands made on the worker, analytical methods are presumed to be used). From an industrial relations viewpoint, in looking at the *content* of jobs rather than the determination of the pay structure, the methodology is at odds with established pay bargaining.

Few restraints are placed upon the independent experts who have the duty of investigating whether the work between the applicant and the comparator is comparable. There is no indication as to what factors may or may not be taken into consideration. The only direction within British legislation is that the experts are required to take account of relevant information supplied, and representations made to them, and to 'take no account of the difference of sex'.[88] It is assumed that the experts have an insight into what constitutes sex discrimination in the wage determination process. Thus there is no attempt to delimit which aspects of the employment and pay structure are due to sex discrimination. Emphasis on job content shifts the focus of attention away from an inquiry into discriminatory factors which may determine different values given to jobs in the first place. The only time such factors are considered relevant is in the application of the defence.

Robin Beddoe[89] suggests that the experts have adopted certain attitudes such as explicit and implicit value judgments, and have drawn up inflated descriptions of job content which, together with lack of analysis of job descriptions, would be unacceptable even in a normal job evaluation exercise. In fact different methods of assessment have been used in the cases reported and it is educative to compare some of these decisions.

In *Hayward* v. *Cammell Laird Shipbuilders Ltd*[90] a version of the factor comparison method was used. The jobs under consideration were viewed as a number of key demands upon those who performed them. Unweighted factors were used having a relationship to job difficulty or value, and a decision made about those demands in terms of values rated as 'low', 'moderate' or 'high'. A female cook spent approximately 80 per cent of her time preparing meals, 15 per cent cleaning or serving and 5 per cent on miscellaneous duties. She was compared with a painter, a joiner and a thermal insulation engineer. The independent expert asked for additional comparators before concluding that the applicant was employed upon work of equal value.

In another decision, *Wells* v. *F. Smales & Sons (Fish Merchants) Ltd*,[91] we see the closest that British law can come to a class action. Fourteen female fish packers claimed their work was of equal value to a male labourer paid £6 per week more. The applicants performed a range of tasks and the expert looked at the content of the individual tasks performed by the applicants and the comparator. The component tasks were examined individually, and from these comparisons a set of 'personal values' reflecting the proportion of time spent on each was calculated. Originally the expert was reluctant to attach numerical values to the assessment, but conceded that a value had to be attached to the percentages shown in the time assessments. Scores of subfactors for each of the individual jobs performed by the applicants and the comparator were then added together to obtain total scores for each main factor. The percentages of time spent on each job were then applied and a total numerical score was calculated for each applicant and the comparator under each main factor. The values for all of the four main factors were added together to obtain a total score for each applicant and comparator.

The result was that nine of the applicants had higher scores than the comparator, and that the other five scored between 79 per cent and 95 of the comparator's score. The expert concluded that the nine applicants who scored higher than the comparator were employed on work of equal value but the five applicants who scored lower were not. The industrial tribunal concluded that the scores were so close that the difference was not relevant, and that all the applicants were entitled to equal pay.

This use of a 'broad brush' approach is adopted, as we have seen earlier, from section 1(4) Equal Pay Act, where small differences are held not to be a barrier to a finding of 'like work'. However, the lack of precision in the evaluation process may have a deleterious effect upon the applicant's claim, and this is seen in the rejection of a 'broad brush' approach by the industrial tribunal in *Brown and Royle* v. *Cearns & Brown Ltd*,[92] arguing that under the equal value provisions the evaluation was not a precise mathematical exercise.

By contrast in *Scott* v. *Beam College*[93] the flexibility of the legislation is revealed when the nature of the work indicated that a non-numerical approach be taken. Here a house mother was paid £1,500 per annum less than house fathers employed at a residential college for emotionally disturbed or deprived boys. After her request for an explanation of the differences in pay the house mother was dismissed without warning. She brought an action under the Equal Pay and Sex Discrimination Acts. In evaluating the work the independent expert chose five factors: emotional care and counselling, responsibility for maintenance and discipline, practical care of boys, practical maintenance of the college and instructional skills and responsibilities. The expert regarded the first three factors of greater importance. On the first three factors the applicant scored 'high' on the first, 'medium/high' on the second and 'high' on the third. The male comparator scored 'medium/high', 'high' and 'medium'. The work was concluded to be of equal value. This sort of approach offers potential for evaluating and giving relative values to traditional female skills found in occupations dominated by women, such as nursing, and also gives recognition to aspects of female skills and work which go unrewarded in other occupations, for example, counselling skills in teaching.

Comparability

Choice of Comparator

The fundamental basis of the approach to equal pay is one of comparability. The Employment Appeal Tribunal has held that a woman is entitled to choose the man with whom she wishes to be compared.[94] This was modified briefly by a later decision in *Pickstone and others* v. *Freemans plc*.[95] Here the Employment Appeal Tribunal ruled that since equal value is a residual right a claim could not be brought on these grounds if the woman is employed on 'like work' or 'work rated as equivalent' to that of a man other than her comparator. The consequences of this ruling would result in the tribunal substituting its own comparator for the woman's choice. This would allow employers to minimize equal pay claims by ensuring that there was always a 'token man' engaged upon 'like work' to preclude equal value claims. The Court of Appeal has since held that while section 1(2)(c) Equal Pay Act precludes a claim for work of equal value where there was a man employed on 'like work', Article 119 EEC may be relied upon directly in the national courts. [96]

It is not necessary for the woman to choose a man employed contemporaneously: reference has been made to a predecessor[97] and a successor,[98] although employment at a different time may be a factor giving rise to a successful defence of the equal pay claim. [99] The use of these temporal comparisons allows women some buttress against economic factors when women may be moved in and out of certain jobs in responses to market considerations.

Unlike the Sex Discrimination Act 'hypothetical' male comparisons are not permitted under the Equal Pay Act, and it seems that such comparisons are not within the direct effects of Article 119 EEC. However, if the applicant can show a *prima facie* case of disparity without knowing the actual names of comparators she may initiate proceedings and then try to obtain the relevant names by discovery. [100] In an equal value claim the independent expert may ask for additional comparators to be included in the evaluation exercise. [101]

The major limitation of the British law is that the comparison must be made with a comparator of the opposite sex in the 'same employment'. A man is to be treated in the 'same employment' as a woman if he is employed by the same employer in the same establishment. Comparison can only be made with employees at another establishment if there are common terms and conditions of employment generally for employees of the relevant classes and the employers are 'associated'. [102] An employer can minimize equal pay claims, therefore, through the use of home-working or employment of subcontractors. The interpretation of the Court of Appeal in *Leverton* v. *Clwyd County Council*[103] has limited the scope of comparison even further. Here a local authority nursery nurse tried to compare her work with that of higher-paid male clerical staff employed at different establishments but covered by the same collective agreement. Despite several common terms in both contracts the Court of Appeal held that differences in the hours of work and holidays meant that common terms and conditions were not observed between the two employments. [104]

This constraint on the choice of comparator explains one of the limitations on the scope of the equal pay principle, particularly as it operated under the 'like work' and 'work related as equivalent' provisions of the Equal Pay Act. One of the major impediments to reducing the male/female differential is that the consequences of segregation of men and women into different occupations makes it difficult for a woman to find a comparable man doing similar work in a given occupation within the same employment. Indeed, some commentators have suggested that the implementation of the Act has led to even greater segregation by employers in an attempt to minimize equal pay claims. [105] The new equal value provisions only open up comparisons between different occupations in the same employment. Such comparisons do not overcome the problem of low pay in female-dominated occupations.

While there has been some improvement in terms of greater representation of women in the previously male-dominated areas of life, detailed research into occupational segregation shows that the segregation of women at the lowest levels of responsibility and remuneration is continuing.[106] The study commissioned by the Department of Employment in 1980[107] revealed that in this century the likelihood of men doing work in an occupation composed of nearly all male workers increased. Forty-five per cent of women and about 75 per cent of men worked in totally segregated jobs. This trend has been reinforced by the restructuring of the labour market, particularly the decline of jobs in the manufacturing sector and the growth of jobs in the service sector. Although this is an area where the Sex Discrimination Act could be used in conjunction with the Equal Pay Act to produce a coherent code of equality, John Hutton[108] argues that the Act has not been effective in allowing women to break into areas of male dominance but rather male applicants (perhaps as a result of the recession and the erosion of jobs in areas like the manufacturing sector) have used the Act to enter areas of traditional female employment such as the retail trade, catering and clerical work. Other factors may also be influential, particularly the trend towards privatization of various public sector jobs.[109]

While not all occupations are entirely male or entirely female, evidence suggests that where women are crowded into certain occupations the wages of that occupation are depressed.[110] Furthermore, these occupations often contain unskilled and low-paid grades, so that even if a woman is able to find a suitable man to compare her work with, she faces the further consequence of crowding: that in female-intensive occupations male earnings tend to be lower (even when controlled for factors such as skill) than in male-dominated occupations.[111] Thus crowding of women workers reduces the overall wage rate for these occupations and limits the extent to which women can achieve pay comparability with men in other occupations.

Comparability – Widening its Application?

The issue of comparability has often been taken as a starting point for explaining the structural limitations of the Equal Pay Act. Indeed the issue has received wide attention as various commentators have suggested ways in which the legislation might be amended.

One solution, favoured by the Equal Opportunities Commission, is the legal technique used in the Sex Discrimination Act of the woman comparing her work with that of a 'hypothetical male'.[112] The actual substantive and procedural process is not elaborated upon by the Equal Opportunities Commission. From the presentation of the issue in

Macarthys Ltd v. *Smith* we are left with the impression that this would be a limited comparison, the applicant in effect having to find a concrete example of how a man would have been treated differently. A more sophisticated statistical case could be feasible. The legal process would be for the applicant to allege and offer evidence that her pay would have been higher had a man been carrying out the job; the object of the claim being to achieve a measure of what the male would have earned in that job. Since these comparisons are hypothetical they are difficult to assess in any rigorous manner, and advocates of this type of claim have not offered any techniques. One possible solution is the approach used by economists, in which earnings differences are attributable to such factors as age, skill, education and experience by regression analysis.[113] Such analysis might be used to quantify what the 'hypothetical male' with identical characteristics to the claimant would have earned in a similar job. While such results are extensively published, a fair amount of economic and statistical expertise would be required to present and adjudicate upon this type of claim, and unlike their American counterparts British lawyers and judges seem reluctant to venture into this discipline. Indeed, as we see in chapter 4, the Employment Appeal Tribunal has explicitly committed itself to a 'common-sense', rather than 'elaborate', statistical approach to issues of indirect sex discrimination.

In addition to the practical problems there are conceptual flaws in this approach. Again it takes a stance of assimilation. A woman must be like a man in order to achieve equality. Thus differences in life-time participation in the labour market are overlooked. Factors which are seen as 'objective' by economists such as age and skill, are taken as given without any inquiry into the adverse impact they might have on women because of differences in labour market participation. Another weakness of the 'hypothetical male' claim is that it is unable to deal with earnings inequalities attributable to imperfections in the structure of the labour market, such as occupational crowding.

Nevertheless, on the positive side the claim offers potential, since it provides a way forward for a woman to establish that even though her work is not exactly comparable with a man's work her pay is disproportionately undervalued as a result of sex discrimination. The present requirement of treating like with like limits this type of claim. The use of the 'hypothetical male' formula would provide a legal mechanism for narrowing the earnings differential resulting from segregation in employment, and would also deal with attempts to deny an equal pay claim by technical and sometimes artificial arguments on differences within job classification schemes.

This type of claim also tackles the converse situation. Equal pay legislation tends to assume, often quite correctly, that the source of complaint is that a woman is receiving less pay than a man who is carrying out similar work. The absence of a male comparator or a valid, non-discriminatory job evaluation scheme leaves a woman without redress if her work is of a *greater* value than the only available male comparators who are carrying out work of a lesser value. Thus the use of the 'hypothetical male' comparison would allow a potential claim where a woman argues that her work has been undervalued because she is a woman, even though she is being paid more than a male worker.

In reality, however, there is little scope for the use of the 'hypothetical male' comparison in either British or European law. The European Court of Justice rejected the idea in *Macarthys Ltd* v. *Smith*. According to the Court, to allow such a comparison would require comparative studies of entire branches of industry, necessitating implementing measures at the European Community or national level. Comparisons were thus to be limited: 'to parallels which may be drawn on the basis of concrete appraisals of the work actually performed by employees of different sex within the same establishment or service' (para. 15). John Forman[114] suggests that this might not exclude the use of a 'hypothetical male' comparison in determining whether the work of actual comparators is of equal value, but this will still not help women in female-intensive sectors of employment where there is no actual male comparator.

Richard Plender[115] argues that, provided the court is not asked to engage in a 'comparative study of entire branches of industry', a woman should be able to ask for a hypothetical male comparison in situations where an employer maintains different salary scales for male and female employees. This could apply even though at the relevant time no males are engaged upon comparable work with the woman. To disallow such an approach would result in anomalies: 'Staff in small departments of a large enterprise might have no judicial relief against their employer's practice in discriminating, unlike those in larger departments, who are thus able to identify better paid employees engaged in identical work.' The spatial scope of Article 119 EEC is less precise than the detailed provisions of the Equal Pay Act, and there is some indication that wider comparisons may be necessary for the correct implementation of Directive 75/117/EEC. In the infringement action against the United Kingdom for failure to implement the equal value claim the EC Commission endorsed the Dutch system of review allowing for wider comparisons. The Netherlands Equal Wage Act 1975 s.3(2) states that: '[W]here no work of equal or approximately equal value is done by a worker of the other sex in the undertaking where the worker concerned is employed, the basis shall be the wage that a worker of the other sex normally receives, in an undertaking of as nearly as possible the same kind in the same section [of industry].' A similar endorsement of the Dutch law was found in the EC Commission's implementation review of the Directive.[116] Even with this system, however, few claims were initially brought, and this has been attributed to the consequences of occupational segregation *across* industries.[117] This indicates that, if any major gains are to be made, wider comparisons need to be drawn not only between similar industries but also across dissimilar industries. The spatial scope of comparisons under Directive 75/117/EEC has not been judicially determined, although some commentators have argued that it is limited in the same way as Article 119 EEC.[118]

Another solution would be to allow wider comparisons to be drawn across industries to identify and overcome the effects of crowding in wages structures. One can argue that it would technically be possible for a different kind of comparison to be made with *any* worker, male or female, in an industry where wages have not been depressed as a result of crowding. Again a fairly sophisticated knowledge of economics and statistics would be necessary to present and to adjudicate upon this type of claim, and despite the growing evidence that such knowledge is an essential part of understanding pay inequalities the British legal profession seems reluctant to admit it as part of the legal discourse.

A different solution, proposed by Rose Blumrosen[119] and endorsed by the American Equal Employment Opportunities Commission, is the alteration of the burden of proof. Since the same discriminatory factors which lead to job segregation also influence wage differentials between segregated jobs this might be a possible legal solution. If a woman can show that she occupies a traditionally segregated job, the onus should then be upon the employer to explain the wage structure by reference to non-discriminatory factors. While this type of claim tackles head-on the consequences of segregation and crowding, it would need a rigorous scrutiny of the 'defences' or explanations of the wages policy, particularly in the deconstruction of skill definitions, the acceptance and review of 'economic' factors and how far differences in female participation in the labour market are taken account of. Evidence to date, as we have seen in chapter 4 on indirect discrimination, and also in case law from the United States,[120] suggests that the judiciary is reluctant to embark upon such rigorous analysis.

The proposals put forward by Blumrosen bring to the fore one of the practical limitations of the present structure of equal pay legislation. She raises the issue of whether there is a way of using the concept of wage discrimination to challenge the segregation of a workforce and the use of a wage-setting process which utilizes no generally recognized system of wage determination, thus precluding a close analysis of an employer's intentions. This situation is most likely to occur where an employer with a small workforce is involved. American law can provide an illustration of a case which tackles the problems involved in systematic segregation of work resulting in discrimination in the pay structure. There is an example where the court was able to use a disparate treatment approach under Title VII of the Civil Rights Act 1964 to tackle an issue of wage discrimination. In *Taylor* v. *Charley Brothers Co.*[121] the employer segregated his workforce and then established a pay scale for the jobs in the 'female' health and beauty aids division that was 30 per cent lower than the jobs in the 'male' dry grocery division. For the most part the jobs undertaken by the two divisions of workers were identical in content, although it was argued that some of the work undertaken by the women required less effort. Despite the fact that there was no direct evidence to show how the employer had chosen the pay rates, or that he had intentionally acted to depress the female rates of pay, the court pieced together a 'mosaic of circumstantial evidence' to find discrimination.[122] This comprised the fact that no job evaluation of any kind had been undertaken, and the employer's 'pattern and practice of segregating women within a single department within the company; . . . its pattern and practice of only considering women job applicants for openings in that department; and [the] various discriminatory remarks made by company officials'.[123] This evidence was used to put the onus upon the employer to offer a rational explanation of the wage policy, and none was proffered.

While much attention has been focused on the spatial comparisons little empirical analysis has been undertaken to determine how useful they might be in eradicating pay differentials due to sex discrimination. Looking first at the 'hypothetical male' claim, we wonder how much further such a concept takes us? In reality it is merely saying to women: 'If you behave like a man in the labour market you can have equal pay.' The research evidence is that women do not behave like men in the labour market. This is one of the reasons why they receive unequal pay. The only value of this type of comparison lies in dealing with the situation where, by the unfortunate timing of the claim, there is no available male comparator.

In looking at the wider across-industry comparisons more recent work undertaken by economists in America in evaluating the utility of such comparisons for a 'comparable worth' concept has uncovered limitations in this approach. George Johnson and Gary Solon[124] find that, even when crowding has been taken into account in determining differences across occupations, it cannot explain the whole of the pay differential. A 'comparable worth' concept based on eliminating differences in pay attributable to industry and occupational specific characteristics would not be a great advantage to women. Johnson and Solon find that the narrowing of the male/female differential that would stem from eliminating the differences in wages attributable to industry and occupation-specific characteristics (presuming this to be the object of a comparable worth programme) is not substantial. Furthermore, Zabalza and Tzannatos,[125] working on the British labour market, show that the major source of the disparity between men and women's earnings is the difference in labour market experience, rather than crowding. For the most part these factors have been dealt with under the defence to the equal pay claim, although they may be relevant in determining if the work is comparable in the first place. It is to the operation of the defence that we now turn.

Defending Equal Pay Claims

In the chapters on direct and indirect discrimination it was suggested that an alternative way of analysing the structure of the legislation would be to focus upon the justification of inequalities of treatment by reference to what are seen as 'legitimate' differences between the sexes, or what are perceived of as legitimate 'objective' or 'economic' factors adduced by the employer for the operation of the business. In a similar vein we have already seen how an employer may explain away pay inequalities by showing that the jobs being compared are too dissimilar to warrant comparison. Employers may also prevent an equality clause from operating if they can show that the difference in pay is genuinely due to a material difference (other than the difference in sex) between the two jobs being compared.[126] For equal value claims the defence is worded slightly differently from the 'like work' claim in that reference is made to a 'genuine material factor'. The government spokesman introducing the equal value regulations in the House of Lords indicated that the different wording was attributable to the fact that since wider factors were to be taken into account in equal value claims the employer could legitimately draw on wider market forces arguments to defend the claim.[127] Since the judgment in *Rainey* v. *Greater Glasgow Health Authority*[128] it is unlikely that there will be a significant difference between 'like work' and 'equal value' claims, although there still remains a procedural difference in that with equal value claims employers are allowed two bites at the cherry – they may raise the defence once a *prima facie* case for equal value is shown, and again after the independent expert has submitted the report.

At first sight the ostensible reasoning behind the defence is to strike a balance between, on the one hand, justified differences in rates of compensation which stem from the working of the labour market, such as higher rates of pay for skill or experience or factors such as skill shortages or surplus labour and, on the other hand, the possibility of employers exploiting female labour by the systematic undervaluation of women's work. The operation of the defence is not as clear-cut.

Two issues stand out in relation to an appraisal of the working of the defence. The first relates to the question of how far 'economic' or 'market forces' defences are admissible. Secondly how closely will the defence be scrutinized for sex discrimination?

In Britain and America the notion of market forces was originally rejected. In *Corning Glass Works* v. *Brennan*[129] the Supreme Court stated:

> [A pay] differential [that] arose simply because men would not work at the
> low rates paid to women inspectors . . . reflected a job market in which

[the employer] could pay women less than men for the same work. That the company took advantage of such a situation may be understandable as a matter of economics, but its differential nevertheless became illegal once Congress enacted into law the principle of equal pay for equal work.[130]

There still remains controversy, however, as to whether a 'market forces' defence may be applied to a Title VII wage-discrimination case.[131]

In construing the original defence in equal pay claims the Court of Appeal in *Clay Cross (Quarry Services) Ltd* v. *Fletcher*[132] rejected the defence of paying a higher wage to a man 'because he would not come for less'. The Court went on to outline that a successful defence should relate to personal factors such as age, length of service, skill or productivity, and not to extrinsic or market forces. While such an approach made it difficult for employers to introduce market forces arguments, the concentration upon individual characteristics prevented equal pay claims from being seen as class issues and precluded an inquiry into the factors, economic, historical and societal, which perpetuate the differences between male and female participants in the labour market.

In taking some examples of labour market functioning and industrial relations practice we find the courts and tribunals have not always displayed an appreciation of gender issues when apply the defence – although not all tribunals and courts have seen fit to air their stereo-typed assumptions about women's participation in the labour market, as seen in Lord Denning's discussion of Lloyds Bank's motive for excluding female employees below the age of twenty-five from the occupational pension scheme:

> [T]here is a difference between the two pension schemes. These differences are due no doubt to natural causes. The young women under 25 are often birds of passage. They come for a short time and then fly off to get married and bring up their children. The men are usually long stayers. They make their careers in the bank until they retire.[133]

One of the earliest problems to confront the tribunals was the practice of 'red circling'. This is where an employer restructures the workforce but some employees are put in a protected pay category if the restructur-ing adversely affects their pay. The Employment Appeal Tribunal has been sensitive to how such practices may perpetuate sex discrimination, and in the consolidated decision of *Snoxell and Davies* v. *Vauxhall Motors Ltd and Charles Early and Marriott (Witney) Ltd* v. *Smith*[134] a general rule was established that an employer cannot rely upon the defence when it can be seen that past discrimination has contributed to the difference in pay. The employer had to show not only why it was necessary to protect a man's rate of pay, but also there must be a material and non-sexually based reason justifying the man's higher pay. The mere fact that the man had previously been paid more would not be sufficient.

In contrast, taking the issue of part-time work, we show elsewhere in this book[135] that the link between this form of labour market participation and women is significant, and why women have sought to use the sex discrimination legislation to fill the lacunae in the employment protection legislation. Conventional distinctions seemed to encourage the view that part-time work was qualitatively different from full-time work, implying that the former was a distinctive, marginal and supplementary workforce justifying lower rates of pay and less employment protection. In the context of the equal pay legislation the protection afforded to part-time workers has received a chequered history. While work carried out at different times has not led to an automatic refusal to admit a finding of 'like work', the differences in hours worked may give rise to a successful defence to an equal pay claim.[136] The first appellate decision bearing directly upon part-time work and equal pay was *Handley v. Mono*.[137] Here a claim was brought by a machinist who worked twenty-six hours per week and was paid sixpence less per hour than her chosen male comparator. Male employees were required to work a forty-hour week, whereas female employees had a choice: if they chose to work less than forty hours they were paid less per hour but if they worked forty hours they received the same rates of pay as male employees. The employer conceded employment on 'like work' but successfully pleaded that there was a genuine material difference explaining the disparity in pay. It was accepted that although the skill and output of women workers was equal to that of male workers the women contributed less to the company's total productivity because each worker was allocated his or her own machine and the employer had to cover overheads when the part-timers were not working. It was also pointed out that the part-time workers were at an advantage in that they were paid overtime rates once they worked above their shorter basic week. The idea that women were free to choose their hours of work without any constraints was not even commented upon in the legal discussion on the case. Similarly the employer's prerogative of having a preference as to how he organized the working time was accepted without questioning its impact upon women workers.

The defence was tightened up by the Employment Appeal Tribunal in *Jenkins v. Kingsgate (Clothing Productions) Ltd* (No. 2).[138] In order to evade the restrictions of the *Handley* decision a reference was made to the European Court of Justice asking whether paying part-time workers less than full-time workers was in breach of Article 119 EEC and Article 1 of Directive 75/117/EEC. The response from Europe was enigmatic. The Advocate-General rejected the idea of linking discrimination against part-time workers as *per se* sex discrimination. His view was followed by the European Court of Justice in ruling that a pay difference between full- and part-time workers is not prohibited under Article 119 EEC 'unless it is in reality an indirect way of reducing the pay of part-time workers, on the ground that that group of workers is composed exclusively or predominantly of women' (para. 15). Such reasoning, of course, ignores the considerable empirical evidence presented to the European Court of Justice that part-time work is predominantly female.

On the referral back to the Employment Appeal Tribunal a less restrictive stance was adopted. The Employment Appeal Tribunal chose to decide the issue under the Equal Pay Act and ruled that, at least in cases involving unintentional indirect discrimination, the employer must show a causal factor between the lower female rate of pay and a legitimate economic objective if the defence is to succeed. Although each case must be decided upon its own facts a set of guidelines was issued to the tribunals in order to identify the relevant issues. While such an approach introduced more rigour into the analysis of the defence it also opened the door for legitimizing economic justifications as overriding considerations of discriminatory impact of employment practices. The use of economic justifications was further reinforced by the decision in *Bilka-Kaufhaus*.[139]

Thus, as we saw in chapter 4, in discussing the concept of indirect discrimination, the focus of the discrimination model has switched attention away from the issue of the discriminatory impact of particular policies to a discourse on the management of the enterprise and economic priorities. From the cases decided so far little attention has been placed upon subjecting the defence to scrutiny of the discriminatory impact it may have upon female workers, or whether alternative, non-discriminatory means of organizing the business might be available. The limitations of an economic justifications approach are seen in the subsequent case of *Rainey* v. *Greater Glasgow Health Authority*.[140] The facts concerned the reorganization of the National Health Service prosthetic service. A change of policy involved the establishment of a prosthetic service within the National Health Service rather than using private contractors. The rates of pay offered by the National Health Service were too low to attract enough prosthetists and so, with the consent of the trade union, the ASTMS, the private contractors were invited to join the National Health Service as a block at their existing and higher rate of pay. All the private prosthetists were men, and all but one of the lower-paid existing National Health Service prosthetists were women. In their defence to the equal pay action the employers contended that the pay disparity related to the different methods of entry into the National Health Service. Lord MacDonald in the Scottish Employment Appeal Tribunal argued that the situation was similar to 'red circling', since the higher-paid prosthetists were in a protected class and all future entrants would be paid at the lower rate; it was purely coincidence that there were no women at the higher rates of pay and almost no men on the lower rate. Although the Employment Appeal Tribunal was prepared to accept that the practice amounted to indirect discrimination it felt obliged to conclude that the *Jenkins* defence could be upheld. The difference in pay was seen as reasonably necessary to achieve a result other than cheap female labour; indeed, the pay policy was considered essential in order to provide an adequate prosthetic service. The Court of Appeal dismissed an appeal from this finding, but by the time the case reached the House of Lords the European Court of Justice had refined the operation of the defence in the judgment in *Bilka-Kaufhaus GmbH* v. *Weber von Hartz*, where it laid down a threefold test for the national court to follow in adjudicating upon an equal pay claim:

> if the national court finds that the means chosen . . . meet a genuine need of the enterprise, that they are suitable for obtaining the objective pursued by the enterprise and are necessary for that purpose, the fact that the measures in question affect a much greater number of women than men is not sufficient to conclude that they involve a breach of Article 119 (para. 36).

The House of Lords was prepared to find that there were good and objectively justified grounds for paying the male prosthetist the higher rate of pay, and these were necessary to establish a prosthetic service.

In applying the *Jenkins* and *Bilka* rulings to a market forces defence the House of Lords has minimized any distinctions there may have been between equal pay for 'like work' claims and equal value claims. Several commentators have drawn favourable conclusions. The *Equal Opportunities Review*[141] argues that in replacing the personal factors equation of *Clay Cross* with an objectively justified standard the House of Lords has allowed employers to meet various market forces problems such as skill shortages by allowing male employees to be paid more than the value of their work, but it does not follow that this permits women's work to be undervalued because of market forces, since this would amount to sex discrimination.

The use of the *Bilka* test brings some uniformity to the approach taken towards indirect discrimination under the equal pay and sex discrimination legislation. The fact that indirect discrimination may be justified on economic grounds raise issues, so far undetermined, as to what these entail. The concept of reifying economic factors without questioning their discriminatory impact has already been challenged in chapter 4. The question remains as to how much prerogative will the courts and tribunals hold back for the employer? In particular are issues such as cost to the employer or profitability of the enterprise (particularly when these are raised as issues in relation to changing the discriminatory exercise) relevant considerations? In America such cost justifications have not been accepted. This is seen in the Supreme Court's rejection of such a defence in the decision of *City of Los Angeles Department of Water and Power* v. *Manhart*,[142] 'That argument might prevail if Title VII contained a cost justification defense. . . . But neither Congress nor the courts have recognised such a defence under Title VII.' Instead a narrower approach has been maintained, as seen in *Johnson* v. *Pike Corp. of America*:[143] 'The sole permissible reason for discriminating against actual or prospective employees involves the individual's capability to perform the job effectively. This approach leaves no room for arguments regarding inconvenience, annoyance or even expense to the employer.' The question arises, however, as to how far such personal characteristics can be carried through and applied to wages policy. In America the issue still remains controversial.[144]

While the more stringent test adopted by the European Court of Justice places the onus upon employers to explain the pay policy, and allows for greater scrutiny of indirectly discriminatory factors, nevertheless it takes a less critical view of why certain objectives are deemed necessary. From a discrimination perspective the approach avoids many of the issues fundamental to the different treatment of female labour. Examples of some of these issues can be seen in the *Rainey* case, such as why women were found predominantly in the public sector or whether women were given the same opportunities to practise in the private sector. Presumably a practice which perpetuated blatant discrimination would not be tolerated, but more subtle forms of indirect discrimination, particularly in the areas of part-time work, home-working and segregated workforces, might pass with less rigorous scrutiny.

Conclusions

In this chapter we have explained from a discrimination perspective the underlying premises of the equal pay legislation. In so doing we have argued that the concept of equality embraced by the legislation is influenced by historical factors and the prevailing philosophical consensus on the role of anti-discrimination legislation. At the outset we argued that equal pay for equal work or work of equal value was only one, and a very narrow, articulation of what the concept of pay equity might be. We have therefore elucidated the narrow focus of attention of the legislation and its subsequent interpretation, as well as its structural weaknesses.

Clearly the legislation has had some impact on the male/female wage differential, but the intervention of law is limited conceptually since it fails to take on board the multiplicity of factors which contribute to the explanations of the differences in pay between male and female workers. As Judith Mayhew commented, the legislation 'does little to remedy positively women's status as a worker. It leaves unaffected the social and economic policies which determine when, where, and how women will work.'[145] The major weakness is the failure to take on board a differences approach to discrimination. Indeed the legislation and its interpretation relies heavily upon differences arguments to uphold wages differentials. The specificity of women's position and participation in the labour market needs to be linked to wider issues such as the allocation of domestic responsibilities, construction of skills and the stereotyping of work. Until these factors are seen as issues of discrimination, and are brought into a wider legal discourse (which most likely will have to move beyond purely individualistic and contractual issues), any legal discussion of equality of pay will remain chained to a limited and unrealistic assimilationist ideal which pays deference to a model of individual justice based on the values of autonomy, achievement and merit.

Notes

1 For comment see Scorer, C. and Sedley, A., *Amending the Equality Laws* (London, National Council for Civil Liberties, 1983); Coote, A. and Campbell, B., *Sweet Freedom* (Oxford, Basil Blackwell, 1987); Coussins, J., *The Equality Report* (London, National Council for Civil Liberties, 1976); 'Equality for women: have the laws worked?', *Marxism Today*, January 1980, p. 6; Kahn, P., 'Unequal opportunities: women, employment and the law', in S. Edwards, (ed.), *Gender, Sex and Law* (London, Croom Helm, 1985); Millar, S. and Phillips, J., 'Evaluating anti-discrimination legislation in the U.K.: some issues and approaches', 11 *International Journal of the Sociology of Law*, 417 (1983); Atkins, S., 'The Sex Discrimination Act: the end of a decade', 24 *Feminist Review*, 57 (1986).

2 Department of Employment, 'Equal pay and sex discrimination', 91 *Employment Gazette* 165 (1983).

3 See 13 *Equal Opportunities Review* (1987).

4 See Chiplin, B., Curran, M. and Parsley, C., 'Relative female earnings in Great Britain and the impact of legislation', in P. Sloane, (ed.), *Women and Low Pay* (London and Basingstoke, Macmillan, 1980).

5 *Women and Equal Pay* (Cambridge, Cambridge University Press, 1985).

6 For an overview of these issues see Beechey, V., 'Women and employment in contemporary Britain', in V. Beechey and E. Whitelegg (eds), *Women in Britain Today* (Milton Keynes, Open University Press, 1986).

7 See the discussion by Pond, C., 'Wages councils, the unorganised and the low paid', in G. Bain (ed.), *Industrial Relations in Britain* (Oxford, Basil Blackwell, 1983); cf. with Metcalf, D., *Low Pay, Occupational Mobility and Minimum Wage Policy in Britain* (Washington and London, American Enterprise Institute for Public Policy Research, 1981). Since 1979 the wages inspectorate which polices Wages Council orders has fallen from 177 inspectors to seventy-one, and many employers are able to flout orders; see 'Low pay unit, the underpaid millions', *Low Pay Review* 30 (1987).

8 Section 12(2) of the Wages Act 1986 removed young people under the age of twenty-one from the scope of Wages Council regulation, and section 14 limited Wages Council orders to fixing a basic minimum hourly rate, overtime entitlement and a limit on deductions from pay that an employer can make for living accommodation. Several other procedural changes were

made, but total abolition as was originally envisaged was not implemented. For discussion of the Department of Employment's Consultative Paper on Wages Councils (March 1985) see Keevash, S., 'Wages councils: an examination of trade union and Conservative government misconceptions about the effect of statutory wage fixing', 14 *Industrial Law Journal* 217 (1985).

9   A general review of the issues can be found in Bazen, S., *Low Wages, Family Circumstances and Minimum Wage Legislation,* (London, Policy Studies Institute, No. 643, May 1985).

10   Hakim, C., 'Employer's use of homework, outwork and freelances', 92 *Employment Gazette* 7 (1984); Huws, U., *The New Homeworkers,* Research Report to the Equal Opportunities Commission (Manchester, 1983); 'New technology homeworkers', 92 *Employment Gazette* 13 (1984).

11   In figures taken from the (1985/86) *Low Pay Review,* 24, it is disclosed that 79.2 per cent of part-time women workers were earning less than £3 per hour compared with 52.7 per cent of full-time women and 21.8 per cent of full-time men.

12   This is an innovation used at Rank Xerox, whereby professionally qualified employees leave the company to start their own business and then contract to provide services to the company as well as seeking other clients. See 'In a net without a catch', *The Guardian,* 18 February 1987. For further details of new work patterns see C. Curson, (ed.), *Flexible Patterns of Work* (London, Institute of Personnel Management, 1986).

13   IFF Research Ltd, *Inquiry into the Employment of Women* (1980).

14   Section 6(6) Sex Discrimination Act 1975.

15   The drawbacks of this mutual exclusivity are clearly seen in the case of *Meeks* v. *National Union of Agricultural and Allied Workers,* [1976] IRLR 198, discussed earlier in chapter 4 on p. 101.

16   Case 80/70, *Defrenne* v. *Belgian State,* [1974] ECR 445; Case 12/81, *Garland* v. *British Railways Engineering,* [1982] 2 ECR 359. The interaction of Article 119 EEC with social security schemes remains problematic; see Atkins, S., Luckhaus, L. and Szyszczak, E., 'Pension schemes and European Community equality legislation', in C. McCrudden, (ed.), *Women, Employment and European Equality Law* (London, Eclipse Publications, 1988).

17   [1986] IRLR 287.

18   The Court of Appeal argues that this interpretation is consistent with European Community law. However, on the basis of jurisprudence so far the European Court of Justice has held that other benefits *may* fall within the scope of Article 119 EEC, but the Court has not ruled that the obligation contained in Article 119 EEC is met if the overall employment package is equal; see Case 12/81, *Garland* v. *British Railways Engineering,* [1982] 2 ECR 359.

19   Case 170/84, [1986] 2 CMLR 701.

20   For further discussion see Counter Information Service, *The New Technology,* CIS Anti-Report, No. 23; Bird, E., *Information Technology in the Office: the Impact On Women's Jobs* (Manchester, EOC, 1980); Faulkener, W. and Arnold, E., *Smothered by Invention: New Technology in Women's Lives* (London, Pluto Press, 1985).

21 See Meehan, E., *Women's Rights at Work* (London and Basingstoke, Macmillan, 1985).
22 *The Independent*, 2 February 1987. For further details see 13 *Equal Opportunities Review* 21 (1987).
23 Particular interest and controversy was sparked off by the application of Title VII of the Civil Rights Act 1964 to an issue of wage discrimination in the case of *County of Washington* v. *Gunther*, 25 FEP Cases 1521 (1981). The seminal article is considered to be R. Blumrosen, 'Wage discrimination, job segregation and Title VII of the Civil Rights Act of 1964', 12 *University of Michigan Journal of Law Reform* 399 (1979).
24 Equal pay for work of equal value was considered earlier in Britain but it was felt that the concept was too vague to translate into a legal process (see chapter 2). In America, beginning in 1945, gender-based wage discrimination was unsuccessfully proposed in every Congress for the next seventeen years with each of the proposals containing an equal pay for *comparable* work standard.
25 For a wide-ranging discussion see Weiler, P., 'The wages of sex: the uses and limits of comparable worth', 99 *Harvard Law Review* 1728 (1986).
26 Industrial Relations Services, 356 *Industrial Relations Review and Report* 2 (1987); 11 *Equal Opportunities Review* 10 (1987).
27 For example the long pay dispute at Ford and at Trimco.
28 A discussion of the possibility of contract compliance can be found in Carr, J., *New Roads to Equality: Contract Compliance for the UK?* (London, Fabian Society, No. 517, 1987).
29 Contrast the use of section 3 of the Equal Pay Act which allowed the parties to a collective agreement to refer an issue of equal pay to the Central Arbitration Committee. Initially the CAC interpreted its powers widely, reviewing collective agreements for anything amounting to sex discrimination. This process was abruptly halted by the Divisional Court in *R.* v. *CAC, ex parte Hy-Mac Ltd* [1979] IRLR 461, which restricted the role of the CAC to controlling explicit or overtly discriminatory pay differentials. However, in its last decision the CAC relied upon Article 119 EEC to amend a collective agreement which indirectly discriminated against women (Norwich Union Insurance Group, Award 87/2, 30.1.87). The Central Arbitration Committee has now been abolished by section 6 Sex Discrimination Act 1986, which declares void any discriminatory terms in a collective agreement. For a good discussion of the CAC's earlier work see Davies, P., 'The Central Arbitration Committee and equal pay', 33 *Current Legal Problems* 165 (1980). For a discussion of the role of class actions see Pannick, D., *Sex Discrimination Law* (Oxford, Oxford University Press, 1986) at pp. 272ff.; Widdison, R., 'Class actions: a survey', 133 *New Law Journal* 778 (1983); Bates, G., 'A case for the introduction of class actions into English law', 130 *New Law Journal* 560 (1980).
30 See *Wells* v. *F. Smales & Sons (Fish Merchants) Ltd*, discussed at page 138. Of the equal value applications to industrial tribunals only 150 employers are involved, and one employer, the National Coal Board, accounts for over half of the total number: 13 *Equal Opportunities Review* 13 (1987). Contrast the situation in *Electrolux Ltd* v. *Hutchinson*, [1977] ICR 252, which was one of 123 cases brought against the same employer by applicants doing the same

work. As Atkins, S. and Hoggett, B. point out in *Women and the Law* (Oxford, Basil Blackwell, 1984, p. 27): 'An obdurate employer can choose to fight each case on the individual characteristics of each worker'.

31 An average of less than £63,000 for the last eight years and less than £82,000 for the last four years has been available. Legal aid from the EOC has been crucial in assisting references to the European Court of Justice, but these references eat up a large proportion of the budget. For example, the legal costs incurred in Case 96/80, *Jenkins* v. *Kingsgate (Clothing Productions)*, [1981] ECR 911 amounted to £11,000. See A. Lestor, 'The uncertain trumpet' (mimeo). Surprisingly, unlike the Commission for Racial Equality, *Review of the Race Relations Act: Proposals for Change* (London, CRE, 1985), the EOC does not include the extension of legal aid for industrial tribunal claims in *Legislating for Change* (Manchester, EOC, 1986).

32 Leonard, A., *Judging Inequality*, (London, Cobden Trust, 1987)

33 Leonard, A., *The First Eight Years* (Manchester, EOC, 1986) pp. 22, 38.

34 For information on the trade union response see 11 *Equal Opportunities Review*, 10 (1987); for the management response see Wainwright, D., *Personnel Management* (August 1986) 3.

35 See Graham, C. and Lewis, N., *The Role of ACAS Conciliation in Equal Pay and Sex Discrimination Cases* (Manchester, EOC, 1985); cf. Gregory, J., 'Equal pay and sex discrimination: why women are giving up the fight', 10 *Feminist Review*, 75 (1982); Leonard, A., *Pyrrhic Victories* (London, HMSO, 1987).

36 Ministry of Labour's evidence to the Royal Commission on Trade Unions and Employer's Associations, 1965. See *Equality For Women* Cmnd. 5724 (1974), paras 82–92.

37 See Leonard, A., *The First Eight Years*, op. cit. note 33, ch. 1; Rubenstein, M., 'Why the EAT gets discrimination law wrong', 9 *Equal Opportunities Review*, (1986) p. 40; Hepple, B., 'The judicial process in claims for equal pay and equal treatment in the United Kingdom', in McCrudden, C. (ed.), supra note 16.

38 Lustgarten, L., *Legal Control of Racial Discrimination* (London and Basingstoke, Macmillan, 1980) at p. 195.

39 Rubenstein, M., op. cit. note 37.

40 Dickens, L., Jones, M., Weekes, B. and Hart, M., *Dismissed: A Study of Unfair Dismissal and the Industrial Tribunal System* (Oxford, Basil Blackwell, 1985).

41 Equal Opportunities Commission, *Tenth Annual Report* (Manchester, 1985).

42 Article 119 EEC provides: 'Each member state shall during the first stage ensure and subsequently maintain the application of the principle that men and women should receive equal pay for equal work. For the purpose of this article, "pay" means the ordinary basic or minimum wage or salary and any other consideration whether in cash or in kind which the worker receives, directly or indirectly, in respect of his employment from his employer. Equal pay without discrimination based on sex means: (a) that pay for the same work at piece rates shall be calculated on the same basis of the same unit of measurement; (b) that pay for the same work at time rates shall be the same for the same job.'

43 This is discussed in further detail on page 141.
44 [1981] IRLR 388.
45 Case 43/75, [1976] ECR 455.
46 Case 69/80, *Worringham and Humphreys* v. *Lloyds Bank,* [1981] ECR 767, para. 23.
47 Section 1(1)(1).
48 *Labour Law: Text and Materials* (London, Weidenfeld and Nicolson, 1984) at p. 372.
49 See Phillips, A. and Taylor, B., 'Sex and skill: notes towards a feminist economics', 6 *Feminist Review* (1980) p. 79; Cockburn, C., *Brothers: Male Dominance and Technological Change* (London, Pluto Press, 1983), and *The Machinery of Dominance* (London, Pluto Press, 1984).
50 Coote, A. and Campbell, B., *Sweet Freedom* (Oxford, Basil Blackwell, 1987) at p. 60.
51 MacKinnon, C., *Sexual Harassment of Working Women* (New Haven and London, Yale University Press, 1979) at pp. 40ff.
52 This issue may be tackled under the legal concept of indirect discrimination. For details of how such employment practices operate see Byre, A., *Indirect Discrimination* (Manchester, EOC, 1987).
53 *Capper Pass Ltd.* v. *Lawton*, [1976] IRLR 367.
54 Ibid. at p. 368.
55 supra note 51, at p. 135.
56 [1978] 1 WLR 1408.
57 *Peake* v. *Automotive Products Ltd*, [1977] 3 WLR 853, 858.
58 See, for example, *Electrolux Ltd* v. *Hutchinson*, [1977] ICR 252.
59 *The Equality Report*, p. 49.
60 *Dugdale* v. *Kraft Foods Ltd* [1977] ICR 48 (EAT); *National Coal Board* v. *Sherwin* [1978] ICR 700; *Thomas and Others* v. *National Coal Board, Barker* v. *National Coal Board*, [1987] IRLR 451.
61 [1978] IRLR 462.
62 *Waddington* v. *Leicester Council for Voluntary Service*, [1977] ICR 266 (EAT); *Eaton Ltd* v. *Nuttall*, [1977] ICR 272 (EAT); *Capper Pass Ltd* v. *Allan*, [1980] ICR 194 (EAT). This attitude may now be reversed using Article 119 EEC after the ruling of the ECJ in Case 157/86, *Murphy and Others* v. *Bord Telecom Eireann* unreported 4 February 1988 (reference from Irish High Court, [1987] 1 (MLR 559).
63 *O'Brien* v. *Sim-Chem Ltd*,[1980] ICR 573 (HL).
64 For a general discussion of job evaluation techniques see *Bromley and Others* v. *H. and J. Quick Ltd, The Independent Law Report*, 13 April 1988 and Bellace, J., 'Comparable worth: proving sex-based wage discrimination', 69 *Iowa Law Review* 655 (1984) 671ff.; Rubenstein, M., *Equal Pay for Work of Equal Value* (London and Basingstoke, Macmillan, 1984) pp. 75ff.; Income Data Services (Top Pay Unit), *Job Evaluation Review* (1983); Industrial Relations Services, *Staff Job Evaluation Survey* (March 1984).
65 Supra note 63, at p. 578.
66 Case 61/81, *EC Commission* v. *United Kingdom*, [1982] ECR 2061.
67 OJ L45/19.
    Evaluation, and in Equal Opportunities Commission, *Job Evaluation Schemes Free of Sex Bias* (1981); see also EC Commission, Ad Hoc Working

Group (Social Partners) on Equal Pay and Job Classification Schemes, *Indirect Discrimination by the Use of Job Classification Systems*, Working Paper V/660/80-EN, Brussels, 10 March 1981.

69 DC 21 FEP Cases 57 (1979).
70 Case 61/81, supra note 66.
71 Section 2A(3) Equal Pay Act 1970 (as amended).
72 See M. Rubenstein, 'Discriminatory job evaluation schemes and the equal pay (amendment) regulations', 133 *New Law Journal* 1021 (1983).
73 Case 170/84, [1986] 2 CMLR 701.
74 Case 237/84, [1987] IRLR 32.
75 In addition to that mode on the grounds of discrimination, a challenge may be made on the ground that there is a fundamental error on the face of the study (*Greene* v. *Broxtowe D.C.*, [1977] ICR 241 (EAT), or that it is unreasonable to regard the job evaluation study as governing the situation of the employees concerned (*England* v. *Bromley London Borough Council*, [1978] ICR 1 (EAT)).
76 *Equal Pay for Work of Equal Value*, supra note 64, at p. 99.
77 See the reluctance of the American court 'to open the Pandora's box' and inquire why mechanics and tree trimmers were paid more than nurses in a job evaluation system, in *Lemons* v. *City of Denver*, 17 Fair Empl. Prac. Case 906, 909 (1978).
78 Section 1(2)(c) Equal Pay Act 1970 (as amended).
79 *Pickstone and others* v. *Freemans plc*, [1987] IRLR 1.
80 46 HC 491 (20 July 1983).
81 HL Deb, vol. 445, cols 901–2.
82 20 October 1985, p. 5.
83 'Equal pay for work of comparable value: a new concept', *Labor Law Journal* (January 1981) p. 30.
84 Case 61/81, *EC Commission* v. *United Kingdom*, [1982] ECR 2061; Case 143/83, *EC Commission* v. *Denmark*, [1986] 1 CMLR 44.
85 For details of the procedure see Hepple, B., *Equal Pay and the Industrial Tribunals* (London, Sweet & Maxwell, 1984).
86 Bottomley, A., 'What is happening to family law?', in J. Brophy and C. Smart (eds), *Women in Law* (London, Routledge & Kegan Paul, 1985).
87 Section 1(2)(c) Equal Pay Act 1970 (as amended).
88 Rule 7A(3)(d) Industrial Tribunals (Rules of Procedure) (Equal Value Amendment) Regulations 1983, S.I. 1807/1983.
89 'Independent experts?', 6 *Equal Opportunities Review* 13 (1986).
90 [1986] IRLR 287.
91 2 *Equal Opportunities Review* 24 (1985).
92 6 *Equal Opportunities Review* 27 (1986).
93 7 *Equal Opportunities Review* 38 (1985).
94 *Ainsworth* v. *Glass Tubes and Components Ltd*, [1977] IRLR 74.
95 9 *Equal Opportunities Review* 32 (1986).
96 [1987] IRLR 218.
97 Case 129/79, *Macarthys Ltd* v. *Smith*, [1980] ECR 1275.
98 *Stankovitch* v. *Phillips Man Shops Ltd*, Ashford IT, 13.7.82, COIT 1302/113 (see Income Data Services Brief 239,16).
99 *Albion Shipping Agency* v. *Arnold*, [1982] ICR 22.
100 *Clwyd County Council* v. *Leverton*, [1985] IRLR 197.

101   *Hayward* v. *Cammell Laird Shipbuilders Ltd* [1986] IRLR 287.
102   This is defined in section 1(6) Equal Pay Act 1970 as 'If one is a company of which the other (directly or indirectly) has control or if both are companies of which a third person has control.'
103   *The Times Law Report*, 29 March 1988.
104   See the suggestion in 9 *Equal Opportunities Review* 36 (1986) that a proper construction should be whether or not the comparator would work under the same conditions and terms as he currently enjoys were he employed in the complainant's establishment and vice versa.
105   Snell, M., 'The Equal Pay and Sex Discrimination Acts: their impact on the workplace', 1 *Feminist Review* 37 (1979); Equal Opportunities Commission, *Annual Report* (1978).
106   Hakim, C., *Occupational Segregation*, Department of Employment Research Paper No. 9 (November 1979).
107   Supra note 13.
108   'How the S.D.A. has failed', *Legal Action Bulletin* (1984) 10. See also *The Times*, 1 May 1985. In introducing the code of practice aimed at eliminating discrimination the Equal Opportunities Commission report that a third of the people who went to the EOC for assistance were men: 'because of high unemployment more and more men are looking for jobs in what was previously regarded as women's work, and sometimes they run up against employer's assessments that they are unsuitable for the job, for example, that they do not have nimble enough fingers or would find the job monotonous'.
109   Coyle, A., 'Going private: the implications of privatisation for women's work', 21 *Feminist Review* 5 (1985).
110   Pike, M., 'Segregation by sex, earnings differentials and equal pay: an application of a job crowding model to U.K. data', 14 *Applied Economics* 503 (1982).
111   Woodward, N. and McNabb, R., 'Low pay in British manufacturing', 10 *Applied Economics* 49 (1978).
112   *Proposed Amendments to Sex Discrimination Act 1975 and the Equal Pay Act 1970* (Manchester, January 1981).
113   Greenhalgh, C., 'Male–female wage differentials in Great Britain: is marriage an equal opportunity?', 90 *Economic Journal* 751 (1980); Stewart, M., 'The determinants of earnings: a job specific model', London School of Economics (mimeo) (1976); Nickell, S., 'Trade unions and the position of women in the industrial wage structure', 15 *British Journal of Industrial Relations* 192 (1980).
114   *Legal Issues of European Integration* (1982) 17.
115   'Equal pay for men and women: two recent decisions of the European Court', 30 *American Journal of Comparative Law* 672 (1982).
116   Report of the Commission to the Council on the application as at 12 February 1978 on the principle of equal pay for men and women, COM (78) 711 Final, Brussels (16 January 1979) at p. 140.
117   Asscher-Vonk, I., 'The legal status of female labour in the Netherlands', 9 *Bulletin of Comparative Labour Relations* 271 (1978).
118   Steiner, J., 'Sex discrimination under UK and EEC law: two plus four equals one', 32 *International and Comparative Law Quarterly* 39 (1983).

119 Supra note 23.
120 Examples can be found in *Piva* v. *Xerox Corp.*, 654 F. 2d. 591 (9th Cir.1981); *Walker* v. *KFGO Radio*, 518 F. Supp. 1309 (DND) (1981). In discussing the use of a comparable worth theory some American commentators have even taken a restrictive view of the use of disparate impact discrimination to tackle wage discrimination under Title VII; see Seidenfeld, M., 'Sex-based wage discrimination under the Title VII disparate impact doctrine', 34 *Stanford Law Review* 1083 (1982).
121 25 FEP Cases (BNA) 602 (WD Pa. 1981).
122 Weiler, op. cit. note 25, at p. 1749.
123 Supra note 121, at p. 614.
124 'Pay differences between women's and men's jobs: the empirical foundations of comparable worth legislation', Working Paper No. 1473, National Bureau of Economic Research, Washington (September 1984).
125 See note 5. See also the book review by Disney, R., 24 *British Journal of Industrial Relations* 483 (1986).
126 Section 1(3).
127 HL Deb., vol. 445, col. 925 (5 December 1983). See McCrudden, C., 'Equal pay for work of equal value: the equal pay (amendment) regulations 1983', 12 *Industrial Law Journal* 4 (1983); 'Equal pay for work of equal value', 13 *Industrial Law Journal* 1 (1984).
128 [1987] IRLR 26.
129 417 US 188 (1974).
130 Ibid., at p. 205. Other courts have rejected market defences as a 'factor other than sex' under the Equal Pay Act 1963: *Laffey* v. *Northwest Airlines Inc.*, 567 F. 2d. 429 (1976); *Brennan* v. *Victoria Bank and Trust Co.*, 493 F. 2d. 896 (1974).
131 See the discussion in Weiler, supra note 25. Cf. Newman, W. and Owens, C., 'Race- and sex-based wage discrimination is illegal', in *Comparable Worth: Issue for the 80s*: A Consultation of the US Commission on Civil Rights, vol. 1, 6–7 June 1984, Washington.
132 [1979] ICR 1.
133 [1980] CMLR 292, 303.
134 [1977] IRLR 123.
135 Chapter 6.
136 It was held in *Capper Pass* v. *Lawton*, [1977] ICR 83 that the fact that a woman worked fewer hours than her male comparator was not a factor of 'practical importance'. The principle was albeit indirectly reinforced in *Dugdale* v. *Kraft Foods*, [1977] ICR 48.
137 [1979] ICR 147 (EAT).
138 [1981] IRLR 388.
139 Discussed above at p. 113.
140 [1987] IRLR 26.
141 (1987) No. 9, 35.
142 435 US 702 (1978).
143 DC Cal (1971) 3 PEP Cases 1025.
144 Compare Weiler, op. cit. note 25, at p. 1746 with the discussion in *Comparable Worth: An Analysis and Recommendations* (Washington, United States Commission on Civil Rights, June 1985), ch. 4.

145   'Women at work', in P. Carlen (ed.), *The Sociology of Law*, Sociological Review Monograph No. 23.

Chapter 6

Employment Protection and Social Security

Introduction – Gender Neutrality

In a book looking at the operation of equality and sex discrimination legislation it is appropriate to examine the protection afforded to women as workers under the general employment law provisions. This area of law is important, firstly, because the nature of protection available under the law has consequences for female workers. Secondly, its limitations explain why it is that, notwithstanding a system of employment protection, women turn to other areas of law, such as the Sex Discrimination Act 1975 and European Community law, to seek equality in treatment and protection from discrimination at work.

To understand employment protection legislation one also must consider the interrelationship with the operation of the social security scheme. For women employment protection and social security have much in common; not just because both areas are located in the public sphere and are regulated by the state through legislation, but also because employment protection and social security law purport to adopt a stance of gender-neutrality, but in reality contain legislative assumptions about women playing a role in the labour market which is conditioned by social norms as to marriage and the nuclear family. Consequently it can be argued that women's experience of both areas of law is not the same as men's experience, since differences between men and women's participation in the labour market are ignored by a set of gender-blind legal rules.

Throughout this book we have argued that women's experience of paid work is qualitatively and quantitatively different from men's experience of paid work, and this is the limiting factor in an equality model which insists that equality is satisfied by treating like alike. Evidence shows that many women have interrupted work histories, to bear and rear children and to perform other unpaid caring and domestic duties.[1] Where women have dependants, particularly young children, their participation in the labour market is often characterized by either temporary, casual or part-time work, or outwork. A further distinctive feature of women's participation is that women often work in different types of employment from men. They are often concentrated in distinctive 'female' work, particularly in the services sector.[2] Many of these distinctive or gender-specific aspects of female labour market participation are ignored in conventional analyses of employment law, which either obscure the specific characteristics of women's work or marginalize it by deploying a masculine conception of workforce participation.

We can point to some general examples of law in the area of employment protection and social security which, although gender-neutral in presentation, are far from gender-neutral in practice. In employment protection these include restrictions according to the number of hours worked, duration of labour market experience and size of firm. In social security law examples are found in the differential treatment of social security recipients according to the extent of labour market experience and value of lifetime earnings. Further examples are seen in the treatment of women as dependants, particularly in the area of pension provision, and their responsibility for the care of other adults, the infirm and children, without adequate recognition or payment for this kind of work.

Both popular and academic perceptions tend to see the social security and employment protection schemes as separate, almost polarized. A person is either in work and looks to the rights afforded by law through the contract of employment, collective bargaining and statutory employment protection or a person is not in work and looks to the protection offered through the social security scheme. Such a view mirrors some of the perceptions of the different roles men and women perform in society and the separate spheres they occupy: women are confined to the private role of domestic life and men are found in the public world of work.[3] However, as Erika Szyszczak argues, the situation is more complex; the interrelationship of employment protection and social security has implications for the labour market as a whole:

> it may affect the size of the labour market, determining how and when a person enters or leaves the labour market and how employers adjust to fluctuations in supply and demand, not only of labour, but also of the quantity of products or services produced. It may also determine how and when the state intervenes in the labour market in order to offset market failure.[4]

The interrelationship between employment protection and social security is not always neutral in operation, and this may have particular consequences for women. In relation to labour market participation the consequences can be seen in the fact that if an employee earns above the lower earnings limit the employer and employee become liable to pay National Insurance contributions on the whole amount of earnings.[5] There is therefore an incentive to avoid these payments, either by opting for self-employment, working on a casual basis or by working part-time.

By doing this the worker will not be eligible for any of the contributory social security benefits, and may not be able to satisfy the continuous-service requirements to qualify for the employment protection rights. As we shall see later in this chapter part-time work, temporary work and outwork are difficult to accommodate within the general employment protection structure.

The decision as to whether or not to leave the labour market may also be influenced by the interrelationship of employment protection and social security. Inadequate redundancy payments[6] or pension arrangements[7] may be a disincentive for many women (particularly those with interrupted work histories) to leave the labour market. For many of these women the choice as to whether or not to leave the labour market may not be as open as it is for many male workers. Women with limited labour market experience will not be eligible for redundancy payments, will not have adequate National Insurance contributions for unemployment benefit or a state pension, and most likely will not be members of occupational social security schemes or private insurance plans. For the employer, however, they are a cheap way of shedding excess labour.

There is also a disparity in the age of eligibility for the state pension between men and women, and this disparity is often mirrored in occupational pension arrangements.[8] The difference in pension age may result in different and discriminatory treatment between men and women. Of course in some ways men appear at a greater disadvantage since they have to work longer, and must also wait for benefits such as concessionary travel fares.[9] Nevertheless recent case law has shown that practices linked to the pension age may have discriminatory effects upon women, particularly in the situation where women wish to work beyond the state pension age in order to improve employment protection rights and pension entitlement.[10] The European Court of Justice has reduced some of these discriminatory effects by drawing a distinction between the state pension age and the retirement age.[11] Equality of treatment in retirement age is now extended to all employees by virtue of section 2 of the Sex Discrimination Act 1986, but the unequal provision of benefits, services and facilities connected with retirement is not covered.

Another important aspect of the interrelationship between employment protection and social security which has special consequences for women is seen in the provision of maternity rights. Previously maternity provision was divided in a complex way between the social security system and employment protection legislation.[12] In an attempt to cut back public expenditure in social security the government has 'streamlined' the maternity provisions, along with sickness provision, and transferred the administration of these benefits to employers.[13] The move is symbolic, particularly for women, since it reinforces the public/private dichotomy by creating an even closer nexus between these benefits and participation in the labour market, leaving the social security scheme to play a limited residual role.

Catharine MacKinnon argues that law, by positing a stance of neutrality, is in fact reflecting a particular conception of power: the power of men to define and objectify the subjects of law. She observes that:

> If objectivity is the epistemological stance of which women's sexual objectification is the social process, its imposition the paradigm of power in the male form, then the state will appear most relentless in imposing the male point of view when it comes closest to achieving its highest formal criterion of distanced aperspectivity. When it is most ruthlessly neutral, it will be most male; when it is most sex blind, it will be the most blind to the sex of the standard being applied. . . . Abstract rights will authorise the male experience of the world. [14]

Thus, she argues, women will receive little help from a legal system which sees and treats women the way men see and treat women. In the rest of this chapter we shall describe the attempts to introduce equality in the areas of employment protection and social security law, and examine how far MacKinnon's thesis is borne out by the operation of the two schemes.

Social Security

A feature of the social security system in Britain is the distinction between contributory and non-contributory social security benefits. The former are contingent upon National Insurance contributions (usually made through the employment relationship) and are sometimes of greater value than non-contributory benefits which are themselves often means-tested (a major exception being Child Benefit). Until pressure was put upon the British government by the European Community to conform with the Social Security Directive 79/7/EEC [15] social security was excluded from the ambit of sex discrimination law, leaving a system of discrimination which was complex and operating at different levels. Katherine O'Donovan identifies this discrimination as stemming from three sources: the common law obligation of a husband to maintain his wife, the Beveridge Report and the financial costs of implementing equality. [16]

The Beveridge Report in particular informed much of initial post-war thinking on provision for social security. Although history has proved otherwise, Beveridge believed that most married women would not engage in paid work: 'on marriage a woman gains a legal right to her husband as a first line of defence against the risks which fall directly on the solitary woman'. [17] This assumption led to three consequences. Firstly, wives were treated as dependants in social security legislation, receiving benefits through their husbands. Secondly, if they did engage in paid work they could elect to pay reduced National Insurance contributions. Thirdly, if married women decided to contribute to the National Insurance system they received reduced benefits. Thus married women had the option either to be insured through their husbands as dependants or to pay the full contribution but receive less benefit than a single person.

However, social perceptions on the one hand, and the requirements of the labour market on the other, are not unchanging. Women's participation in the labour market has not only increased but has also become more stable. Part-time married women workers in particular demonstrate this fact. In response to these changes, as well as the political and legal obligations imposed by the European Community, recent years have witnessed some radical changes to the social security system to accommodate the pressures for introducing equality of treatment.

Some of the moves to introduce equality into the social security scheme occurred alongside the measures to grant greater general employment protection rights in the mid-1970s. The phasing out of the married woman's reduced National Insurance contribution[18] was one such move, as was the introduction of the home responsibilities provisions in the pension scheme whereby a married woman was compensated for the years out of the labour market for looking after children or severely disabled family members in the calculation of contributions towards the state retirement pension.[19] Despite these changes certain discriminatory aspects remained in the social security scheme: for example, the withholding of adult and child dependency allowances from married women unless they could prove their husbands were incapable of self-support.[20] In relation to means-tested, non-contributory benefits married and cohabiting women were automatically excluded from entitlement to the means-tested supplementary benefit and the family income supplement. In addition, and paradoxically, the reform package of the 1970s also introduced two new non-contributory, non-means-tested benefits which specifically excluded married or cohabiting women from their entitlement. These were the Invalid Care Allowance, payable to those caring for people with severe disabilities,[21] and a non-contributory invalidity pension for the long-term disabled who did not qualify for a contributory invalidity pension. Married and cohabiting women were later able to claim a 'housewife's' version of this pension, but only if they could show that they were incapable of performing normal household duties.[22] These benefits therefore served to perpetuate an ideology that women's caring work within the domestic sphere was not of an economic value worthy of social security protection.

The areas of discrimination outstanding in the social security scheme were not tackled until the government reappraised the situation in relation to the obligations imposed by the European Community Social

Security Directive. Even this legal reform does not impose an overall standard of equality. Several areas are excluded from the equal treatment principle – for example, survivors' benefits,[23] certain wife's dependency benefits[24] and the determination of the pension age,[25] and the Directive is firmly located in the public sphere, explicitly seen in its application to the 'working population' in Article 2. Thus equality of treatment only applies to work-related risks. The Directive does not raise the issue of seeing caring and other domestic duties as social security risks to be covered,[26] or other discriminatory aspects of social security provision around which feminists have campaigned for reforms, such as the disaggregation of social security benefits.

A further limitation of the Directive is that member-states are given a discretion as to how to implement the obligations imposed by Directives, and as we have seen in the chapters on equal pay and sex discrimination the measures used to implement the equal treatment principle into British law are often tentative and piecemeal. In relation to social security, Susan Atkins and Linda Luckhaus argue that three distinctive approaches have been used to implement the obligations contained in the Social Security Directive.[27] The first approach was to equalize up – that is, to give married women the same rights as men. This is seen in allowing dependency additions to short-term contributory benefits to married women on an equal basis with married men,[28] allowing married and cohabiting women to claim Family Income Supplement[29] and supplementary benefit.[30] The latter amendment was introduced by complex means and married or cohabiting women may only claim the benefit if they can prove that they are the 'claiming partner'. It has been suggested that, in reality, all that has changed is that the *automatic* designation of the husband or male cohabitee has been abolished, but the continued use of a breadwinner and dependent model with the aggregation of the couple's income and needs will in practice result in men still being in a better position to make a claim on behalf of the couple.[31]

A second approach was to abolish a discriminatory benefit altogether, seen in the abolition of the child dependency addition to short-term contributory benefits[32] and the threatened abolition of the Invalid Care Allowance during the litigation surrounding the case of *Drake* v. *The Chief Adjudication Officer*.[33]

The third approach identified by Atkins and Luckhaus is described by them as 'less drastic but nonetheless consisted of giving with one hand while taking with the other'. This is where the government equalized access to benefits but at the same time introduced more restrictive conditions applicable to men and women. Examples of this are seen in the replacement of the long-term disability pensions by the Severe Disablement Allowance,[34] which imposed more onerous qualifying conditions, and by the introduction of a spouse's earning rule and the restriction of entitlement to the child dependency addition with long-term contributory benefits for male and female applicants. [35]

The foregoing analysis reveals that economic factors such as women's greater participation in the labour market, and political factors such as the obligations imposed by European Community law, have been influential in introducing the principle of equality of treatment into social security law. These reforms have been tempered by underlying historical influences, social assumptions and economic factors, particularly attempts to restrain public expenditure in this area. These factors continue to play a decisive role in deciding the kind of social security provision that will be available, and who will be a beneficiary of that provision.

The present reforms of the Conservative government [36] have placed little emphasis upon introducing equality into the social security system or breaking down the outmoded stereotyped assumptions on which it is based. Indeed several commentators have argued that the reforms will have an adverse impact upon women. [37] For example, the National Council for Civil Liberties described the proposals as depicting 'a Victorian view of women as subservient, dependent and unequal'. [38] The government argues that its 'twin-pillar' approach is intended to reduce public expenditure and to encourage a greater degree of private provision of social security through individual and occupational schemes. The emphasis upon greater personal autonomy and responsibility reflects a particular view of market society in which individuals are capable and free to make a rational choice. For many women, especially those with dependants to care for, the choice of private social security provision may be limited and often illusory. Despite its limitations the European Community Social Security Directive may play an important role in monitoring the changes to the social security system. The decisive factor may be how far European Community law is prepared to move beyond a concept of formal equal treatment, and how far it will develop a concept of indirect discrimination. These issues are discussed further in chapter 7. However, as Katherine O'Donovan argues, the Directive has had more than a substantive impact on social security provision, for 'Now national governments have to justify discriminatory policies; previously these were taken for granted.' [39]

Employment Protection

Generally, employment law in Britain has been characterized by the absence of legislative intervention. Only comparatively recently has the state intervened to introduce a minimum or 'floor' of basic employment rights. [40] In contrast to the comparability approach utilized by the equal pay and sex discrimination legislation, the basis of employment protection law is ostensibly neutral: the rights appear abstract and are available to all workers who satisfy the qualifying conditions.

The aim of employment protection law is not to achieve overall equality in workers' rights. The idea behind a 'floor of rights' approach is to facilitate the continued development of collective bargaining. The basic rights may be improved upon by either collective or individual negotiation, while at the same time giving minimum standards of protection for the weaker and poorly unionized workers. This reliance upon collective bargaining reflects a particular view of the organization of industrial life, since many women cannot automatically expect trade union support. As we argue in chapter 5, many women work in areas to which trade union coverage does not extend – for example, in small firms or in outwork or part-time work, or they work in segregated or disparate employment where unionization is difficult to organize. During the recent recession, however, as male membership of trade unions has declined some unions have actively attempted to recruit new members from the ranks of female, part-time employees.[41]

Even where women are represented in trade unions there is no guarantee that women's issues will be given a high priority on the bargaining agenda. The collective arena continues to be characterized by concerns of protecting (male) jobs or maintaining wage differentials. Issues which might improve the working lives of women, such as better provision of workplace nurseries, do not receive as much attention.[42] Women's employment issues are beginning to be addressed by some unions, particularly those with a high proportion of female members. In chapter 5 we referred to support for equal value claims, and some unions have negotiated improved rights for part-time workers and improved maternity (and in some cases, paternity) rights. The National and Local Government Officers Association (NALGO) has been particularly active in promoting policies on non-sexist language, workplace nurseries and sexual harassment.[43]

Without trade union intervention it is unlikely that the basic employment rights will be improved upon. Since legal aid is not available for industrial tribunal proceedings the absence of trade union backing may result in even the minimum rights being unenforced.[44] We have seen examples of trade unions colluding with management and utilizing the rules relating to qualification for employment protection rights in order to protect male jobs. This is in evidence in the case of selection of part-time workers for redundancy before the customary 'last-in–first-out' procedure in *Clarke and Powell* v. *Eley (IMI Kynoch).*[45]

Even where there is active trade union involvement in women's employment issues the statutory rights provide limited coverage of women's special employment problems. The rights appear neutral: rights to redundancy payments, unfair dismissal, trade union membership. Only the maternity provisions address women's specific needs of employment protection. Other aspects of women's experience of working life which might need protection, for example redress against sexual harassment, are not addressed by the legislation.[46]

The statutory framework does not provide universal protection in another sense. In order to qualify for the employment protection rights an employee must have worked under a contract of employment involving at least sixteen hours work per week, and the employee must have been continuously employed for a minimum period of two years.[47] It is possible for part-time employees to acquire employment protection rights if they work under a contract of employment involving more than eight hours work per week and they are continuously employed for five years. The Employment Protection (Consolidation) Act 1978 makes provision for 'legitimate' breaks in employment so that continuity is preserved,[48] and employees may not contract out of the basic rights except in limited circumstances.[49]

While the qualifying conditions appear neutral they are based upon a particular concept of labour market participation. The rights are only available to regular employees who have full-time and continuous participation in the labour market. Women, and especially women with young children, cannot always obtain or remain in full-time, regular employment. In order to reconcile domestic responsibilities with paid work many women undertake part-time, temporary, or casual work, or outwork. If we take a look at some of the distinctive forms of paid work undertaken by women some of the difficulties and consequences of applying the seemingly neutral rules to women's labour market participation are revealed.

Outwork

Outwork has traditionally been undertaken by female workers, particularly women from ethnic minority groups and women with young children. The range of outwork is wide, but is closely associated with traditional female skills such as child-minding, clerical work, packaging and sewing. Recent years have seen an increase in men working *from* home, but this form of work is distinctive and often, as in the case of networking,[50] is carried out by professionals who can provide private protection against social security and employment-related risks.[51] It is difficult to estimate the number of outworkers since they do not appear in official statistics.[52] There has, however, been recognition that outworkers are generally poorly paid and vulnerable because of lack of employment protection, and attempts have been made to extend employment rights to this 'hidden army'[53] of workers.[54]

Research by Sheila Allen and Carol Wolkowitz has been useful in shedding light upon the nature and organization of outwork.[55] Their research reveals that outworkers often work long hours under close regulation of the employer or person supplying the work. They argue that one of the most important factors in analysing women's experience of outwork is to undermine the 'romanticized notions of home-working, in which it is [seen] as akin to cottage industries.'[56]

In relation to employment protection outworkers are vulnerable because there may be a lack of formal commitments making employment status difficult to prove, and the work may be discontinuous, or the out-worker may work for several different employers, thus not acquiring sufficient continuity of employment with one employer to qualify for the employment protection rights. Outworkers have traditionally been treated as 'self-employed', and not working under a contract of employ-ment for the purposes of tax, social security and employment rights.[57] This has been justified by their job location and the perceived autonomy they have over how and when they work. The myth of autonomy is dispelled in the conclusions to Allen and Wolkowitz's study:

> Home-workers are thought to set their own hours of work, and combine home-working with all their other obligations within the home and outside it. It is true they do not have to clock in and do not have a supervisor leaning on their shoulder. In practice, however, their obligations to the supplier are those of an employee, and they are, if anything more con-strained than those who go out to work. The supplier establishes the hours of work through the times set for delivery and collection of work and the allocation of work with different piece-rates. Home-workers are not paid for work until it meets the supplier's specifications. Hours, pace and quality of work are so effectively controlled by the supplier that direct physical supervision is not required.[58]

The courts have adopted the common law approach to deciding if there is a contract of employment as the filter for deciding whether or not a worker falls within the scope of the employment protection legislation. Over time a variety of different tests have emerged to distinguish a contract of employment from self-employment. Initially the element of employer control was considered to be a decisive factor.[59] This was superseded by what was known as the 'integration' test: a contract of employment existed where the employee could be considered integrated into the employer's organization.[60] Later a more flexible 'multiple' test emerged. Under this the existence of a contract of employment depended upon the balancing of a number of factors such as the existence of control, ownership of machinery or tools, payment of wages, who bore the economic risk.[61]

The different common law tests were difficult to apply to the social and economic situation of outworking because of the divergence of the different forms of work and the different methods of organization. Two cases show the advantages of the now more flexible approach being taken towards determining the employment status of outwork. The facts of both reveal the difficulties of applying conventional working patterns to the situation of outwork.

In *Airfix Footwear Ltd* v. *Cope*[62] the outworker had worked regularly and full-time for seven years. She assembled shoe heels, for which she was paid a weekly wage based on the number of heels assembled. The employers provided the machinery, the shoes to be heeled, and gave directions as to performance and production targets. The Employment Appeal Tribunal held that there was an 'overall' or 'umbrella' contract of employment obliging the employers to continue to provide and pay for work, and the employees to continue to accept and perform the work provided. The employers 'decided the thing to be done, the manner of performance and in reality the time and place of performance.'[63] Thus the conditions of work were very similar to those of the factory. Once it was established that there was a contract of employment, the Employment Appeal Tribunal then went on to decide if continuity of employment had been maintained in order for Mrs Cope to qualify for the employment protection rights. In looking at the overall employment relationship the Employment Appeal Tribunal found there had 'by conduct been established a continuing relationship.' Thus the 'umbrella' contract was overriding; Mrs Cope did not merely have a series of short contracts which would have broken the continuity of employment.

While this decision reveals a willingness on the part of the judiciary to accept the economic reality of outwork the Employment Appeal Tribunal added a proviso which will limit the scope of the ruling. If Mrs Cope's employment had been less regular the conclusion might not have been the same. There was no general acceptance of outworkers being classified as employees. It was a question of fact to be determined in each case.

The legal status of outworkers appeared even more vulnerable after the Court of Appeal decision on *O'Kelly* v. *Trusthouse Forte plc.*[64] This case was concerned with the legal position of casual workers. Here, waiters who were described as 'regular casuals' attempted to bring a claim for unfair dismissal. Applying the 'multiple' test it was found that there was not sufficient 'mutuality of obligation' to allow for a finding of employee status. The employers were not obliged to offer work and the waiters were under no obligation to accept work when it was offered to them. Thus, neither side was under an obligation to carry forward the relationship. However, the Court of Appeal seemed to retreat from this ruling when dealing with a latter case concerning outwork. In *Nethermere (St Neots) Ltd* v. *Taverna and Gardiner*[65] an unfair dismissal claim was brought by two outworkers who had worked between five and seven hours per day for three years sewing pockets on children's trousers. There were some weeks when no work was carried out, and one of the women took twelve weeks break from outwork each year. Although the outworkers could choose how much work to do they had to 'make it worth his while for the delivery driver to call'. The employers provided the sewing machines. Tax and National Insurance contributions were not deducted from the outworkers' pay. The Court of Appeal held that the determining factor for employment status-was the 'irreducible minimum of obligation', and this could be found in this employment relationship.

In *Airfix* and *Nethermere* there was a fairly regular pattern of employment and a high degree of control over the outwork. In some cases of outworking such regularity and control may not be evident, and then it is likely that the outworker will be classified as either a casual worker or self-employed. It is to the legal position of temporary and casual work that we now turn.

Temporary and Casual Workers

Temporary and casual workers face the same double hurdle as outworkers. Again many women engage in casual work in a variety of ways and in a variety of jobs. At one end of the spectrum there may be the skilled worker, such as a nurse or secretary, who has a regular contract of employment with an agency. At the other end of the spectrum is the truly casual worker who works intermittently, often for different employers. For most of these workers employment is short-term, poorly paid and insecure. As with outwork, it is a question of fact as to whether a contract of employment exists,[66] and as we outlined above, the legal status of casual workers received a setback in the Court of Appeal ruling in *O'Kelly* v. *Trusthouse Forte plc*.[67] The 'mutuality of obligation' test is likely to pose a serious hurdle for casual employees since for many a formalized arrangement to supply and carry out work may not exist. Since many women rely upon flexible working arrangements in order to take time off in emergencies when children are ill, or at different times of the year for school holidays, the *O'Kelly* decision is likely to render their employment status even more vulnerable.

Even if a contract of employment is established temporary and casual workers are likely to have even greater difficulty than some outworkers in establishing the number of hours worked and length of service required to show continuity of employment. This will be particularly difficult where they are engaged in seasonal work or their hours of work are irregular. The case law relating to continuity of employment is discussed in the next section on part-time work.

Attempts have been made by the European Community to improve the legal position of temporary workers by greater regulation of their work and by establishing minimum legal rights.[68] These reforms, like most European Community measures, are not for altruistic reasons but are for economic considerations. They form part of the European Community's attempt to reorganize working time.[69] The EC Commission argues that if the forms of work which are vulnerable are given greater legal protection the work may appear more attractive, and will encourage workers to move from full-time work into this kind of work.

Part-Time Work

Part-time work is not easy to define. Even in official discourse the definition varies from working less than sixteen hours per week for employment protection purposes to working less than thirty hours per week for Department of Employment survey purposes.[70] Britain has one of the largest proportions of part-time workers in the European Community, and over 80 per cent of the part-time workers are female and concentrated in the services sector of employment.[71] Part-time employment has been viewed by employers and the law as a distinctive and marginal form of employment justifying lesser employment protection than full-time work.[72] However, Peter Elias and Brian Main, using evidence from the National Training Survey, show that a large proportion of women, particularly married women, now work for long periods of their lives in part-time jobs.[73] Furthermore, they argue that the stability of employment of many part-time workers is in many cases little different from full-time workers of either sex.

The growth in part-time work in Britain has been attributed to many factors. The need for flexibility in job structures has meant that part-time work is an attractive way for employers to respond to fluctuations in supply and demand. Careful organization of part-time work can reduce an employer's obligations to pay National Insurance contributions and liability for employment protection claims. Other factors include the growth of service sector employment, the increase in participation of married women in the labour market and the structure of the tax and social security system which, together with social pressures, still favour a model of dominant wage-earner and part-time working 'dependant'.

In contrast to outwork, casual and temporary work, part-time work is distinctive in that there is usually a recognized contract of employment. The legal issue is whether the employee works sufficient hours, and with sufficient regularity, to establish continuity of employment. Difficulties arise in that part-time work may be organized in a variety of ways, and problems occur in applying particular working patterns to the norm established in the employment protection legislation. A comparison of two cases reveals the limitations of the general approach for part-time employees. In *Corton House Ltd* v. *Skipper*[74] the contract of employment provided for four hours work every other evening, thus amounting to twelve hours work in one week and sixteen hours work in the following week. In practice the employee often worked more hours, but it was found that for three weeks the employee had worked below the sixteen-hour threshold for the qualification of employment protection rights.

This therefore broke the continuity of employment. In contrast, a decision of the Employment Appeal Tribunal shows the arbitrary working of the employment protection rules. In *Lloyds Bank* v. *Secretary of State for Employment*[75] an employee worked 'full-time', but only in alternate weeks. Nevertheless she could establish continuity of employment. This was because she could rely upon a part of the Employment Protection (Consolidation) Act 1978, which allows for the weeks in which the employee did not work as not being covered by the contract. So long as she worked in the weeks covered by the contract continuity was preserved.

Another way of organizing part-time work, which poses problems in fitting the working pattern into the continuity of employment provisions, is the situation where an employee is regarded as 'part-time' where laid off from work during slack periods and re-engaged when work resumes. A new contract may begin in the week when the old one ends, and continuity may be preserved. The employment protection legislation also makes provision for periods of work when there is no contract of employment in existence, but the time will nevertheless count towards continuity of employment. Such periods will cover illness, injury, pregnancy and confinement, or where there is a temporary cessation of work.[76] The latter category may prove helpful for part-time workers. The House of Lords has held that the question of whether there has been a temporary cessation of work must be answered in hindsight after the resumption of employment.[77] In a later decision, *Ford* v. *Warwickshire County Council*,[78] a teacher employed over a number of academic years but not during college vacations was able to establish continuity of employment. The House of Lords held that any cessation of work must be 'transient' and last for a relatively short time in contrast to the periods of continuous employment before and after it.

While it is possible to preserve continuity when there is a 'temporary cessation of work' for a few weeks a different legal problem may emerge where part-time workers continue to work week by week, but in order to respond to fluctuations in the availability of work their hours are reduced, causing them to fall below the relevant eight or sixteen hours employment necessary to qualify for employment protection. The question of whether such a variation broke continuity arose in *Secretary of State for Employment* v. *Deary*.[79] The case concerned school dinner supervisors employed under a 'variable hours contract'. There were a specified number of hours to be worked but these could be adjusted according to the number of meals served. The hours were then reduced to below eight hours per week and eventually some of the women were made redundant. The employer tried to argue that the reduction of hours broke the continuity of employment, thus preventing a claim for a redundancy payment. The Employment Appeal Tribunal held that the unilateral variation of hours was a breach of contract, and the number of hours the women were requested to work was always over eight. The Employment Appeal Tribunal seemed sensitive to the issue that flexibility to employers' demands should receive some legal recognition and the Tribunal was willing to look at the overall working of the contract rather than treating one dip below the statutory qualifying thresholds as automatically breaking continuity of employment.

Simon Deakin observes that: 'The standard or typical post-war model of full-time, regular and permanent employment has been eclipsed following a decline in the number of full-time jobs and the increase in the incidence of part-time working and various forms of out-work, temporary work and labour sub-contracting.'[80] The discussion of the qualifying conditions for employment protection suggests that the legal model for granting security of employment remains committed to a concept of rewarding only full-time and continuous workers in the labour market. Although in recent years the courts have gone some way in manipulating the legislation to fit the employment patterns of some female workers, the outcome of such an exercise depends very much upon the factual solution and so-called 'marginal' workers are not guaranteed the uniform and consistent protection afforded to full-time employees. It is not surprising, therefore, to see part-time workers looking towards the sex discrimination legislation as an alternative method of securing employment protection rights. But, as we have seen in chapters 3 and 4, the discrimination model presents its own limitations. The necessity of finding a comparable male, the procedural complexities of an indirect discrimination claim and the acceptance of an economic rationale to defend discrimination actions all combine to give a weaker standard of protection than the basic 'floor of rights' approach adopted in relation to full-time employees under the employment protection legislation.

As a result of the changes in the labour market and the limitations of the protection afforded to so-called 'marginal' workers, various suggestions have been made to alter the basis of employment protection. Bob Hepple, for example, has argued that a shift from rigid contractual models to a more flexible definition of employment relationships may be necessary.[81] Another solution has been to extend the employment protection rights to 'marginal' workers. The European Community has provided the impetus in this area, but the Conservative government has been particularly hostile to any proposals put forward by the EC Commission. The government argues that employment protection legislation, by adding to the fixed costs of labour, acts as a disincentive to recruitment. This is seen in the reaction to the proposed Directive on voluntary part-time work[82] by Michael Alison, the then Minister of State for Employment: 'Although its aim is to protect part-time workers, our assessment is that its effect would be the reverse. That is to say, it would increase labour costs and reduce flexibility, and would thus be likely to

increase female unemployment.'[83] An even more forthright condemnation of European Community intervention is seen in the Department
of Employment Press Release commenting upon the proposed Directive
on Temporary Work:

> [these] unnecessary proposals for legislation [which] have nothing to do
> with the creation of a common market and are, frankly, seen by a great
> many people in this country as an irrelevant piece of European
> busybodying. . . . By imposing new obligations on employers, by
> restricting use of temporary labour, it would probably introduce rigidities
> into the labour market, undermine competitiveness and actually reduce the
> number of jobs on offer.[84]

In contrast to the European Community proposals the Conservative
administration is committed to a policy of 'deregulation' of the labour
market.[85] Although the government does not intend to dismantle all the
employment protection and health and safety at work rights it has proposed higher qualifying thresholds. As the above discussion has shown,
any increase in the qualifying thresholds will not have neutral effects; it
will disproportionately affect women workers.

Maternity Provision

To conclude this chapter we now turn to look at how the legal system has
accommodated women's needs to bear and rear children and participate
in the paid labour market. For American feminist lawyers pregnancy has
occupied a central role in many feminist accounts of jurisprudence.
Lucinda Finley, for example, argues that 'The fact that women bear
children and men do not has been the major impediment to women
becoming fully integrated into the public world of the workplace.'[86]
Wendy Williams goes further in arguing that pregnancy is 'the final and
decisive battleground' in the struggle for the just treatment of both
sexes.[87] Pregnancy also occupies a central role in Anne Scales's account
'Towards a feminist jurisprudence', where she argues that 'The response
of the law to the issue of childbearing marks a pivotal point in the history
of the emergence of women as first class citizens.'[88] While pregnancy has
been identified as being of central importance to a feminist account of
jurisprudence, the handling of the issue has sparked off a serious debate
in America as to whether special treatment or equal treatment should be
accorded to pregnant women and working mothers.[89] In Britain the
debate has been informed less by theoretical issues, but has concentrated
more upon practical aspects of maternity provision and in particular the
need to protect established rights from erosion by the legal reforms
of the 1980s aimed at deregulating the labour market.[90] In chapter 3
we have already seen that the issue of pregnancy focuses sharply the
limitations of the equality model prescribed by the Sex Discrimination

Act. In this chapter attention will be focused upon the limitations of use of the gender-neutrality model of the employment protection legislation.

Historical Influences

It was the desire to protect the function of motherhood which influenced early attempts to regulate the work of pregnant women and mothers. This aim informed the protective legislation and the restrictions upon women returning to work within a specific period of giving birth.[91] Assumptions about women's child-bearing role and particular vulnerability are seen also in the legal discourse when challenges were made to the protective legislation. In *Muller* v. *Oregon*[92] the legislation limiting women to working only ten hours per day in laundries was subjected to judicial scrutiny. Although such a limitation on male workers was considered unconstitutional the American Supreme Court rationalized the disparity of treatment between male and female workers because 'women's physical structure and the performance of material functions place her at a disadvantage in the struggle for subsistence. . . . This is especially true when the burdens of motherhood are upon her.'[93] Even today reproductive issues, concentrating heavily upon female reproductive capacity, remain influential in denying claims to equality in employment.[94] This focus upon biological determinism continues to the present day in debates over protective legislation, maternity provision, and whether or not there should be a legal right to paternity leave and parental leave for adoptive parents.

It was not until the mid-1970s that the state intervened to provide a legal right to maternity leave and pay. This move was in response to the increased participation of women in the labour market, although the necessity of introducing efficiency in the operation of the labour market would seem to be the dominant reason for introducing a legal policy on maternity provision rather than altruistic concerns over women's rights. Crucial issues of who should bear the costs of maternity provision, and whether women should be given special or equal treatment, have been answered in a muddled fashion in British law. The social security and national insurance system has been used to finance some of the costs of maternity provision but in other areas, such as time off work for antenatal care, employers bear the cost. The maternity provisions comprise the right to time off work for antenatal care, the right not to be unfairly dismissed by reason of pregnancy, the right to maternity pay and the right to return to work after giving birth. These rights are moulded into the general structure of employment protection legislation, and therefore follow the same assumptions of the kind of labour market participation required to be considered worthy of receiving the benefit of these rights.

Time Off for Antenatal Care

The right of a pregnant employee to be given time off work to keep antenatal appointments is a social policy measure designed to reduce ill-health in pregnancy and infant mortality. All pregnant women, regardless of their length of service, are entitled not to be unreasonably refused paid time off work during working hours in order to receive antenatal care.[95] This right is conditional upon the woman producing for the employer's inspection (and on request) a medical certificate confirming that she is pregnant, plus an appointment card or other document showing that an antenatal appointment exists. These conditions do not apply to the first appointment. Once an employer has allowed a woman time off over several weeks payment of wages cannot be refused.[96] If the employer does refuse the request for time off work the employee has the right to complain to an industrial tribunal which may award compensation. Although there is no continuous-service qualification for this right some women may be reluctant to take advantage of it, for by disclosing their pregnancy they may run the risk of being dismissed or made redundant by their employer so that other maternity rights that are contingent upon a continuous service qualification can be avoided.

Protection from Unfair Dismissal

The law of unfair dismissal contains a special provision which provides that the dismissal of an employee because she is pregnant or for any other reason connected with pregnancy is automatically unfair.[97] There are two exclusions to this right. The first is where an employee is incapable of doing her job adequately because of her pregnancy, and the second is where continued employment of a pregnant woman would contravene a statutory restriction or duty. The pregnant woman may still claim that the dismissal is automatically unfair if a 'suitable vacancy' exists and the employer does not offer it to her. The 'suitable vacancy' must be suitable in relation to the employee and appropriate for her in the circumstances. The offer of such a vacancy must be in the form of a new contract of employment taking effect immediately, and the provisions of the contract as to the capacity, place and other terms and conditions must not be substantially less favourable than those of the previous contract of employment. The onus is upon the employer to show that no suitable vacancy existed, or that an offer of alternative employment was made but refused.

At one level, therefore, women are given some protection against arbitrary dismissal policies. A major limitation of the unfair dismissal legislation is that it is contingent upon the woman satisfying the minimum qualifying conditions for the employment protection rights.

As we have explained earlier in this chapter, this qualifying threshold debars many women who do not work under a contract of employment or who have limited labour market experience as a result of previous child-birth or other domestic commitments. As a result the kind of systematic discrimination against pregnant employees which has occupied the American courts[98] has not been fully discussed in British legal discourse, and therefore there has been little opportunity of discussing and challenging some of the stereotypical assumptions of women's mental and physical capabilities during pregnancy. The issue of dismissal is viewed in the light of the general principles of unfair dismissal law.[99] American case law, however, reveals that a fairly stringent appraisal of the employers' reasons for dismissal may be necessary, since many reasons relating to job capacity or safety may easily be utilized as a pretext to hide other prejudicial factors against employment of pregnant women. This is seen in the challenges that were made to the mandatory 'go when you know' policies employed against airline stewardesses.[100] As Lucinda Finley points out, such dismissals may have more to do with the perceived aesthetic tastes of the airline's customers than with any clear empirical evidence of the hazards of employing pregnant stewardesses.[101] Another limitation in the legal discourse in both Britain and America is the lack of stringent scrutiny of the exemptions to a claim of unfair dismissal because of the operation of the protective legislation. This area may be opened up in the future by resort to the Equal Treatment Directive of the European Community. At the moment, however, there is no recognition of a duty upon the employer to reorganize a pregnant employee's work to allow her to undertake work which will not produce risks to the unborn child.

As a response to the limited protection afforded by the unfair dismissal provisions some women have turned to the Sex Discrimination Act 1975 as an alternative legal mechanism to protect their jobs. Early attempts at using this legislation were frustrated by the Employment Appeal Tribunal decision in *Turley* v. *Allders Department Stores*,[102] where it was held that the appropriate comparisons under the Sex Discrimination Act 1975 were unavailable since there was no male equivalent of a pregnant woman. The later decision of the Employment Appeal Tribunal in *Hayes* v. *Malleable Working Men's Club* and *Maughan* v. *North East London Magistrates Court Committee*[103] has now allowed a comparison to be made between the treatment of the pregnant employee and the treatment of a sick male employee. While this decision opens up the basis of comparison, and has been used successfully in subsequent industrial tribunal hearings, certain misgivings in the approach being taken have been expressed. Nicola Lacey points to the fact that pregnancy is often associated with tiredness and a loss of concentration, leading to poor performance at work justifying a dismissal.[104] She argues that such general assumptions may be accepted by the industrial tribunals, and that differences between the comparators may be over-looked. For example, a sick man may be wholly or frequently absent from work, but this is not likely to be the case with a pregnant woman who is capable of discussing her future intentions with the employer, of training a replacement and even of being disciplined for any reduced performance. In addition to these disadvantages the remedies available under the Sex Discrimination Act 1975 (an award of damages and a recommendation for action to obviate or reduce the adverse effect on the complainant) are of a lesser value than the wider range of remedies available under the unfair dismissal provisions. The Equal Opportunities Commission has proposed that the protection afforded under section 60 Employment Protection (Consolidation) Act 1978 should be available without the qualifying period, and that further protection for a pregnant woman against discrimination on the ground of her pregnancy should be available by virtue of Article 2(1) of the Equal Treatment Directive.[105]

Maintenance of Income during Pregnancy, Child-birth and Child-rearing

Maternity pay was included in the wave of employment measures introduced in the mid-1970s to guarantee security of earnings in the contract of employment.[106] The maternity pay provisions operated alongside the social security payments of the maternity allowance (which was contingent upon a woman satisfying certain minimum National Insurance contributions) and a lump sum maternity grant of £25 which was payable irrespective of whether or not the woman had a National Insurance record. Maternity pay was paid by the employer at the rate of nine-tenths of the woman's gross weekly wage provided the woman remained at work until the eleventh week before the expected date of confinement, and she had at least two years continuous service with the employer. The maternity allowance was deducted from the woman's maternity pay irrespective of whether or not the woman received it.[107]

In order to prevent employers with a higher percentage of female workers from being at a disadvantage the financial costs of maternity pay were not borne directly by individual employers. A maternity fund was established, financed by National Insurance contributions, and employers were able to claim a rebate from this fund which was not experience-rated – that is employers were not penalized for drawing on the fund.

Anthony Ogus and Eric Barendt argued that 'the statutory right to maternity pay from the employer has to a large extent superseded in importance the social security allowance as an instrument of income maintenance'.[108] This assertion, however, is not corroborated by research undertaken by the Department of Health and Social Security, which showed that less than 16 per cent of women expecting a baby qualified for maternity pay;[109] the major impediment being the continuous service qualification which debarred women who work part-time or who had limited labour market experience.

Provision for the maintenance of income during pregnancy and child-birth was thus limited yet complex, involving employers, employees, the Department of Health and Social Security and the Department of Employment in an intricate relationship. For many women engaged in what is viewed as 'marginal' employment – outwork, part-time or temporary work – security of earnings was by no means guaranteed. The Department of Health and Social Security reviewed the provision of maternity benefits and suggested reforms aimed at simplifying the system of maternity payments in order to reduce administrative costs and to attempt 'a more equitable redistribution of resources'.[110] The new system of statutory maternity pay did not come into operation until 1987.[111] Now a much closer link is drawn between employment and rights to maternity pay. Employers now have the responsibility of assessing and administering a scheme of statutory maternity pay. In the Green Paper on Social Security this was described as 'a form of reward for continuous service with one employer for a period of years'.[112] Paradoxically, however, the employment protection aspect of maternity pay is diminished in that the Maternity Pay Fund has been wound up and the Department of Employment and the industrial tribunals are no longer concerned in disputes over maternity pay. Jurisdiction in these matters now lies with adjudication officers, social security appeal tribunals and social security commissioners. Although there is the close link with the employment relationship in the administration of statutory maternity pay, the definition of an 'employee' for the purposes of statutory maternity pay is different from the definition used to determine eligibility for the employment protection rights under the Employment Protection (Consolidation) Act 1978.[113] For statutory maternity pay purposes there is no requirement that the 'employee' be employed under a contract of employment. Thus some outworkers or agency workers who would otherwise be considered 'self-employed' may be eligible for statutory maternity pay if they are over sixteen years of age and treated as an 'employed earner' for social security purposes.[114]

There are now three layers to maternity payments, reflecting the degree of continuity of employment. A higher rate of statutory maternity pay is payable at 90 per cent of normal weekly earnings for six weeks and twelve weeks at a lower rate corresponding with the amount of statutory sick pay.[115] To qualify for this right a woman must have been continuously employed for at least two years before the fifteenth week of the expected date of confinement under a contract of employment involving at least sixteen hours work per week. In addition the woman's earnings in the eight weeks before the qualifying week must be above the lower earnings limit for paying National Insurance contributions.[116] A lower rate of statutory maternity pay may be payable for eighteen weeks to women who can show they have twenty-six weeks continuous employment. [117] Although the woman does not have to work a minimum number of hours to qualify for this right she must show that her average weekly earnings are at least equal to the lower earnings limit for paying National Insurance contributions. If an employee is not eligible for either the lower or the higher rate of statutory maternity pay she may be able to claim a maternity allowance from the Department of Health and Social Security. This is dependent upon the woman's National Insurance record, not continuous employment with one employer.

To conclude, the basic statutory provision for income maintenance still divides between more generous provision for women who have an attachment to the labour market and are rewarded as individuals for their ability to work in continuous employment and those who do not. Again a division is made between participation in the public world of paid work and the private domestic sphere. In terms of coverage and the level of maternity payment there has been little improvement of the maternity pay provisions, and certain benefits, such as the maternity grant, have been abolished altogether. Thus women are forced to choose between re-entering the public world quickly or becoming 'dependants' in the private sphere of either family support or social security benefits.

The Right to Return to Work

A woman has a right to return to work after pregnancy and giving birth provided she was employed continuously for at least two years by the beginning of the eleventh week before the expected week of confinement. The right to return to work has been complicated by extra and more stringent notice requirements imposed by the Employment Act 1980. Now a pregnant employee must give written notice that she intends to return to work at least three weeks before she commences maternity leave, and three weeks before she intends to return to work. [118] The employer may ask for additional written notice of the intention to return to work not earlier than forty-nine days from the expected date of birth. [119] A failure to comply with this request within fourteen days (or as soon as is reasonably practicable) will result in the loss of the right to return to work. [120] The employer may delay the return to work for up to one month and the woman may postpone her return for up to four weeks after the end of the statutory period of maternity leave if she can provide a medical certificate showing she is unfit to return to work. [121] The new and more stringent notice requirements create a number of pitfalls which may render the right to return to work vulnerable. Coping with the demands of a new baby is hardly the most appropriate time to be taking decisions, and remembering the complex bureaucratic requirements necessary to exercise the right to return to work. The application of the rules is rigid, and few allowances are made for women who do not conform to the statutory procedure. This is seen in the Court of Appeal decision of *Dowuona* v. *John Lewis plc.*[122] Here a woman gave birth prematurely to twins. One of the twins died, and the surviving baby and the mother were ill for some time after the birth. The mother added one week's contractual holiday to the end of the maternity leave and also sought to extend her leave by another four weeks by submitting a medical certificate. She remained unwell and submitted another medical certificate, whereupon the employer refused to take her back. She brought a claim for unfair dismissal, arguing that she had failed to return from holiday, not maternity leave, so that a claim could be brought under the unfair dismissal provisions of the Employment Protection (Consolidation) Act 1978. The Court of Appeal rejected these submissions. It was held that she was seeking to exercise a contractual right to return to work after maternity leave, and that she had not exercised this right correctly by giving the requisite notice requirements under section 47(1) Employment Protection (Consolidation) Act 1978.

In the 1975 package of maternity rights a woman was allowed to return to work in the job in which she was originally employed on terms and conditions not less favourable than those which would have been applicable to her if she had not been absent. Thus seniority, pension and other rights of employment would be preserved. If it is not practicable for the employer to permit an employee to return to work by reason of redundancy the employer must offer the woman alternative employment, which must be suitable in relation to her and appropriate in the circumstances. If the employer is unable to offer suitable alternative employment, and provided the employee exercises her right to return in accordance with section 47 Employment Protection (Consolidation) Act 1978, she is then treated as dismissed for the purposes of a redundancy claim. The nature of the right to return to work has been altered fundamentally by the Employment Act 1980, in that it no longer applies to employers who employ five or fewer employees and who can show that it is not reasonably practicable to permit the mother to return to the job or to offer her 'not less favourable' or 'alternative employment'.[123] Irrespective of the size of the firm, employers will also have a defence to an unfair dismissal claim if they can show it is not reasonably practicable to reinstate the mother in the original job (for a reason other than redundancy) and suitable alternative employment is offered, which is either accepted or unreasonably refused.[124] Even where the mother is able to bring a claim for unfair dismissal the Employment Act 1980 has removed the onus on the employer to defend the claim. Now the burden of proof is 'neutral' in that the industrial tribunal is directed to find

whether the dismissal was fair or unfair, having regard to the reason shown
by the employer, shall depend on whether in the circumstances (including

the size and administrative resources of the employer's undertaking) the employer would have been acting reasonably or unreasonably in treating it as a sufficient reason for dismissing the employee if she had not been absent from work; and that question shall be determined in accordance with equity and the substantial merit of the case. [125]

Thus attention is focused upon managerial requirements, and it would seem that a wide range of reasons may be used to justify a dismissal.

While the right to return to work remains protected for women who can satisfy the stringent qualifying provisions, the right appears inflexible in that it leaves mothers with little scope for rearranging their work to fit in with the demands of motherhood. Roy Lewis and Bob Simpson argue: 'The Act in effect encourages employers to make less effort to keep jobs open and entrenches (along with unfair dismissal changes) a two-tier status of employee rights with the inferior status attaching to employment in small firms.' [126] In a survey carried out by William Daniel it was found that only 10 per cent of all women employed during pregnancy gave notice of return to work with the same employer. This low rate of return is partly attributable to the fact that many women could not satisfy the continuous work requirements – in Daniel's study only 46 per cent of women qualified for the right to return. In addition lack of child-care facilities and the unresponsive nature of the workplace to parental needs amount to difficult hurdles for many women to overcome. It is not surprising therefore to see the Sex Discrimination Act 1975 again being used as a means to persuade employers to introduce more flexible working arrangements for mothers.

Although the applicant in *Home Office* v. *Holmes*[127] was successful in challenging a full-time work requirement of the employer, as we have seen in chapter 4, there is no guarantee that a complaint of indirect discrimination will be upheld in every case since the claim will focus predominantly on how far the employer can justify the organization of the labour force.

In addition to the limitations on how a woman returns to work after the birth of a child there is no legal right to insist upon breast-feeding or child-care facilities from the employer. These are for private arrangement. Similarly the public world of work would seem impervious to the demands of parenthood: the right to parental leave if, say, a child is ill, or the right to negotiate flexi-time to accommodate medical or dental appointments, to take and collect children from school, are not seen as suitable aspects of employment protection regulation.

Conclusion

The main themes of this chapter were outlined in the introduction and have been developed in the text. These themes may be summarized as

showing in the first place that the use of 'neutrality' in the legal framework of employment protection and social security legislation in reality
favours a particular kind of labour market participation, and by so doing
ignores sex differences in labour market participation. Secondly, provision for social security and employment protection to some extent
reflects the dichotomy of perceptions of a public world of work and a
private, domestic sphere and the refusal in legal provisions to see an
interconnectedness between these spheres. In recent years there has been
a shift in emphasis, seen in pressures for reform from the European
Community, to acknowledge the role played by women in the labour
market. But these 'reforms' have been offset against other economic
factors, particularly the desire to deregulate the labour market and to cut
public expenditure in social security provision. Thus by failing to tackle
underlying preconceptions of women's role there are serious limitations
in the scope of employment protection and social security provision for
women. This is seen in the way maternity provision has been moulded to
fit into the mainstream of employment protection legislation without
serious consideration of the specific needs of women.

Feminist responses to the problems posed by discrimination and
inequality in employment protection and social security have often fallen
into debates over whether equal or special treatment should be afforded
to women. While rejecting an equality analysis built upon an assimilation
approach which masks male bias, the question for feminists remains as
to how male-oriented ideas and values can be reworked to prevent the
marginalization of difference and to make the public world of the workplace responsive to women's needs and values. One way forward is that
suggested by Lucinda Finley, of accepting that work and family are the
two most important defining aspects of men and women. As a consequence she argues that:

> [The] idea that these two aspects of human existence occupy separate
> spheres must be replaced with legal policies and a framework for evaluating
> them that appreciates that public and private are a continuum, with each
> defining and affecting the other. If we supplement our existing conception
> of rights with a concept of responsibility to others arising out of our inter-
> connectedness, we can begin to move towards workplace policies that make
> it possible for both women and men to combine their work lives with
> involvement in the family.[128]

While such an approach may be complex and problematic in its practical
implementation we would argue that an appraisal of the operation of
employment protection and social security law reveals the necessity to
underpin the substantive legal provisions with a theoretical approach
which takes cognizance of these issues.

Notes

1 For an overview of the literature and commentary see Beechey, V., *Women and Employment in Contemporary Britain*, and Beechey, V. and Whitelegg, E. (eds), *Women in Britain Today* (Milton Keynes, Open University Press, 1986); see also Martin, J. and Roberts, C., *Women and Employment: A Life-time Perspective* (London, HMSO, 1984).

2 See Hakim, C., *Occupational Segregation: A Comparative Study of the Degree and Pattern of the Differentiation between Men and Women's Work in Britain, the United States and Other Countries*, Research Paper No. 9, Department of Employment, London, November 1979.

3 See the discussion of the public/private dichotomy in O'Donovan, K., *Sexual Divisions in Law* (London, Weidenfeld & Nicolson, 1985); Olsen, F., 'The family and the market: a study of ideology and legal reform', 96 *Harvard Law Review* 1497 (1983).

4 'Employment protection and social security', in R. Lewis (ed.), *Labour Law in Britain* (Oxford, Basil Blackwell, 1986) at p. 360.

5 At October 1987 this figure was £39 per week.

6 For discussion of the effect of redundancy provisions on women see Callendar, C., 'Gender inequality and social policy: women and the redundancy payments scheme', 14 *Journal of Social Policy*, 189 (1985); Coyle, A., *Redundant Women* (London, Women's Press, 1984); 'An investigation into the long-term impact of unemployment amongst women', *Equal Opportunities Commission Research Bulletin*, 68 (1983–4).

7 See Masson, J., 'Women's pensions', *Journal of Social Welfare Law* 319, 1986.

8 McGoldrick, A., *Equal Treatment in Occupational Pension Schemes: A Research Report* (Manchester, EOC, 1985).

9 See the claim brought in Case 12/81, *Garland* v. *British Rail Engineering Ltd*, [1982] 2 CMLR 174, and for further discussion see Equal Opportunities Commission, *Sex Equality and the Pension Age* (Manchester, EOC, 1977) and *Equalizing the Pension Age* (Manchester, EOC, 1978).

10 See the claim in Case 152/84, *Marshall* v. *South West Hampshire Area Health Authority (Teaching)*, [1986] 1 CMLR 688.

11 Ibid.

12 See the discussion in Szyszczak, op. cit., note 4.

13 Responsibility for sick pay was transferred to employers by the Social Security and Housing Benefits Act 1982, and the legal framework for maternity provision appeared later in the Social Security Act 1986.

14 'Feminism, Marxism, method, and the state: toward feminist jurisprudence', 8 *Signs* 635 (1983) at p. 658.

15 OJ 1979 L6/24.

16 'The impact of entry into the European Community on sex discrimination in British social security law', in J. Adams, (ed.), *Essays for Clive Schmitthoff* (Abingdon, Professional Books, 1983).

17 Beveridge, W., *Social Insurance and Allied Services*, Cmnd 6404 (London, HMSO, 1942) para. 108.

18 The Social Security Act 1975 laid down the basis for these changes which were phased in over a number of years. The married woman's option to pay

reduced contributions was not available for women starting to engage in employment after April 1977 (SI 1975/492).

19 For full details see Atkins, S., 'The home responsibilities provision in the new state pension scheme', *Journal of Social Welfare Law* 33 (1980).

20 Social Security Act 1975, ss. 44(3)(a), 47(1)(a), 66(1)(b), Schedule 20.

21 Section 7 Social Security Benefits Act 1975. See Equal Opportunities Commission, *Behind Closed Doors* (Manchester, EOC, 1981).

22 Section 6 Social Security Benefits Act 1975 introduced the benefit and the housewives' version is found in Social Security Act 1975 section 36(2) and SI 1978/1340). For discussion see Richards, M., 'A study of the non-contributory invalidity pension for married women', *Journal of Social Welfare Law* 66 (1978–9).

23 Article 3(2).

24 Article 7(c) and 7(d).

25 Article 7(a). Compare *Proposal for a Council Directive completing the implementation of the principle of equal treatment for men and women in statutory and occupational social security schemes*, COM (87) 494 Final.

26 See the discussion of Case 150/85 *Drake* v. *Chief Adjudication Officer*, [1986] 3 CMLR 43 by Luckhaus, L., 'Payment for caring: a European solution' *Public Law* 526 (1986).

27 'Social Security', in C. McCrudden (ed.), *Women, Employment and European Equality Law* (London, Eclipse Publications, 1988).

28 Section 44 Social Security Act 1975 as amended by the Social Security Act 1980. Schedule 1 brought into operation by SI 1983/1002.

29 Section 7 Social Security Act 1980.

30 Supplementary Benefit Act 1976 Schedule 1 para. 3(1) as amended by the Social Security Act 1980 Schedule 2 Part I and SI 1983/1004.

31 Land, H. and Ward, S., *Women Won't Benefit* (London, National Council for Civil Liberties, 1986).

32 Section 13 and Schedule 5 Health and Social Security Act 1984.

33 Op. cit., note 26. This case is discussed in greater detail in chapter 7.

34 For comment see Luckhaus, L., 'Severe disablement allowance: the old dressed up as new', *Journal of Social Welfare Law* 153 (1986).

35 Schedule 4, paras 3 and 4 Health and Social Security Act 1984.

36 Department of Health and Social Security, *Reform of Social Security*, Cmnd. 9517–9519 (London, HMSO, 1985); *Housing Benefit Review*, Cmnd. 9520 (London, HMSO, 1985); *Reform of Social Security: Programme for Action*, Cmnd. 9691 (London, HMSO, 1985).

37 See Land and Ward, op. cit. note 31; Land, H., 'Women and children last: *Reform* of Social Security?', in M. Brenton and C. Ungerson (eds), *The Year Book of Social Policy in Britain 1985–86* (London, Routledge & Kegan Paul, 1986); Equal Opportunities Commission, Green Paper: *Reform of Social Security, Response of the Equal Opportunities Commission* (Manchester, EOC, 1985).

38 Letter to *The Guardian*, 10 June 1985.

39 Supra note 16 at p. 98.

40 The phrase 'the floor of rights' was coined by Wedderburn, K., *The Worker and the Law* (Harmondsworth, Penguin, 1971).

41 Unions have also taken a greater interest in part-time workers' rights: see

A Fair Deal for Part-Time Workers (National Union of Public Employees, 20 Grand Depot Road, London SE18); *Less Than Full-Time Working* (Association of Professional, Executive, Clerical and Computer Staff, 22 Worple Road, London SW19 4DF).

42   For a discussion of trade union attitudes towards women's issues see Coote, A. and Campbell, B., *Sweet Freedom* (Oxford, Basil Blackwell, 1987), chapter 5; Coote, A. and Kellner, P. (eds), *Hear This, Brother: Women Workers and Union Power* (London, New Statesman, 1981); Stageman, J., *Women in Trade Unions* (Hull University, 1980); Ellis, V., *The Role of Trade Unions in the Promotion of Equal Opportunities* (Manchester, EOC, 1981); Equal Opportunities Commission, *Women and Trade Unions* (Manchester, EOC, 1983); Hunt, J., 'A woman's place is in her union', in J. West (ed.), *Work, Women and the Labour Market* (London, Routledge & Kegan Paul, 1982).

43   See the equal opportunity guides *Watch Your Language*; *Negotiating for Equality*; *Workplace Nurseries*; *Rights for Working Parents*; *Sexual Harassment is a Trade Union Issue*; *Positive Action for Women Workers*; *Organising for Equal Opportunity Adoption*; *The Right to Continue Working* (NALGO, 1 Mabledon Place, London WE1H 9AJ).

44   See the research by Leonard, A., *Judging Inequality* (London, Cobden Trust, 1987).

45   [1983] ICR 165, discussed in detail in chapter 4.

46   Some of these issues may be addressed because of the obligation in Article 1 of Council Directive 76/207/EEC (OJ 1976 L39/40) to introduce the principle of equality of treatment *inter alia* to working conditions. For example the EC Commission has commissioned a report on sexual harassment (Rubenstein, M., *The Dignity of Women at Work*, Brussels V/412/87 – EN Ong. EN, 1987).

47   For a table of the qualifying periods see Szyszczak, op. cit. note 4.

48   Schedule 13 Employment Protection (Consolidation) Act 1978. Difficulties arise when a worker has a contract to carry out a fixed task which is discharged by performance. Some 'task' contracts are ones of self-employment and if there is a contract of employment the employment protection legislation has little influence as the worker has not been dismissed: *Wiltshire County Council* v. *National Association of Teachers in Further and Higher Education*, [1980] ICR 455 (A); *Boyd Line Ltd* v. *Pitts*, [1986] ICR 244 (EAT); *Brown* v. *Knowsley Borough Council*, [1986] IRLR 102 (EAT).

49   Section 142 Employment Protection (Consolidation) Act 1978 allows an employee to waive rights to unfair dismissal and/or a redundancy payment on the expiration of a fixed-term contract. This must be done in writing during the currency of the contract, and the contract must be for a minimum of two years in the case of a redundancy payment and one year for an unfair dismissal waiver (section 8(2) Employment Act 1980).

50   This is where 'professional' employees leave a firm to start their own business and then contract to provide services for the firm as well as other clients. For details of other innovations in working see Curson, C. (ed.), *Flexible Patterns of Work* (London, Institute of Personnel Management, 1986).

51 See Hakim, C., 'Homeworking: some new evidence', 88 *Employment Gazette* 1105 (1980); 'Employers' use of homework, outwork and free-lances', 92 *Employment Gazette* 144 (1984); Huws, U., *The New Home-workers* (Manchester, Equal Opportunities Commission, 1983), 'The new technology homeworkers', 91 *Employment Gazette* 13 (1984).

52 Hakim, op. cit., note 51 estimates a number around 251,000.

53 Crine, S., *The Hidden Army* (London, Low Pay Unit, 1979).

54 See Ewing, K., 'Homeworking: a framework for reform', *Industrial Law Journal* 94 (1982).

55 Allen, S. and Wolkowitz, C., 'The control of women's labour: the case of home-working', 22 *Feminist Review* 25 (1986). A fuller discussion can be found in *Homeworking: Myths and Realities* (London, Macmillan, 1987).

56 Ibid., 22 *Feminist Review* (1986) at p. 26.

57 For discussion see Townshend-Smith, R., 'Law of employment: recognising a contract of employment – II', 119 *New Law Journal* 1022; (1970) Leighton, P., 'Employment and self-employment: some problems of law and practice', 91 *Employment Gazette* 197 (1983).

58 Op. cit., note 55, 22 *Feminist Review* at p. 46.

59 *Yewens* v. *Noakes*, (1880) 6 QBD 530; *Performing Rights Society Ltd* v. *Mitchell and Booker Ltd*, [1924] 1 KB 762.

60 *Stevenson Jordan and Harrison Ltd* v. *MacDonald and Evans*, [1952] TLR 101.

61 *Ready Mixed Concrete (South East) Ltd* v. *Minister of Pensions and National Insurance*, [1968] 2QB 497.

62 [1978] ICR 1210.

63 Ibid., at p. 1215.

64 [1983] IRLR 369.

65 [1984] IRLR 240.

66 See *Wickens* v. *Champion Employment*, [1984] ICR 365.

67 Op. cit., note 64.

68 OJ C128/82 and as amended, OJ C133/84. For a discussion of the legal position see Hepple, B. and Napier, B., 'Temporary workers and the law', 7 *Industrial Law Journal* 84 (1978).

69 For discussion of this see Hepple, B., 'The crisis in EEC labour law', 16 *Industrial Law Journal* 77 (1987).

70 On the difficulties of using survey data on part-time work see Robertson, J. and Briggs, J., 'Part-time working in Great Britain', 87 *Department of Employment Gazette* 671 (1979).

71 A useful source of information on part-time work is the House of Lords Select Committee on the European Communities (1982), *Voluntary Part-Time Work*, session 1981–82, 19th Report. See also Beechey, V. and Perkins, T., *A Matter of Hours: Women in Part-Time Work and the Labour Market* (Oxford, Polity Press, 1987).

72 See Disney, R. and Szyszczak, E., 'Protective legislation and part-time employment in Britain', 22 *British Journal of Industrial Relations* 78 (1984); Hunt, A., *Management Attitudes and Practices towards Women at Work* (London, HMSO, 1975); Robinson, O. and Wallace, J., *Part-Time Employ-ment and Sex Discrimination Legislation in Great Britain*, Research Paper No. 43 (London, Department of Employment, 1984); Sedley, A., *Part-Time*

Workers Need Full-Time Rights (London, National Council for Civil Liberties, 1980); Labour Research Department, *Part-Time Workers* (London, Labour Research Department, 1986).

73   *Patterns of Work* (Institute of Employment Research, University of Warwick, 1982).

74   [1981] ICR 307.

75   [1979] ICR 258.

76   Schedule 13 Employment Protection (Consolidation) Act 1978.

77   *Fitzgerald* v. *Hall, Russell and Co. Ltd*, [1970] AC 984.

78   [1983] IRLR 126.

79   [1984] IRLR 180.

80   'Labour law and the developing employment relationship in the UK', 10 *Cambridge Journal of Economics* 225 (1986).

81   'Restructuring employment rights', 15 *Industrial Law Journal* 69 (1986).

82   OJ 1982 C62/82; COM 830 Final (1982).

83   Supra note 71, at p. 32. For a critique of this assertion see Disney and Szyszczak, op. cit.

84   Department of Employment, Press Notice, 1984.

85   See, *inter alia*, Department of Employment, *The Challenge for the Nation* (Cmnd. 9474, London, HMSO, 1985); *Building Businesses . . . Not Barriers* (Cmnd. 9794, HMSO, 1986); Department of Trade and Industry, *Burdens on Business: Report of a Scrutiny of Administrative and Legislative Requirements* (London, HMSO, 1985), *Lifting the Burden* (Cmnd. 9571, London, HMSO, 1985). For a comparison with the position in other member states of the European Community see Vranken, M., 'Deregulating the employment relationship', 7 *Comparative Labour Law* 143 (1986).

86   'Transcending equality theory: a way out of the maternity and workplace debate', 86 *Columbia Law Review*, 1118 (1986) at p. 1119.

87   Legislation to Prohibit Sex Discrimination on the Basis of Pregnancy: Hearings Before the Sub-Committee on Employment Opportunities of the House Committee on Education and Labour, 95th Congress, 1st Session 21 (1977).

88   56 *Indiana Law Journal* 375 (1981) at p. 376.

89   See Williams, op. cit. note 87, and 'Equality's riddle: pregnancy and the equal treatment/special treatment debate', 13 *New York University Law Review of Law and Social Change* 325 (1985).

90   See Mayhew, J., 'Pregnancy and employment law', in S. Edwards, (ed.), *Gender, Sex and Law* (London, Croom Helm, 1985); Winch, F., 'Maternity rights provisions – a new approach', *Journal of Social Welfare Law* 321 (1981); Ellis, E., 'Parents and employment: an opportunity for progress', *Industrial Law Journal* 97 (1986); Apex, R. and Morris, A., 'Maternity rights – illusion or reality?', *Industrial Law Journal* 218 (1981).

91   See Creighton, W., *Working Women and the Law* (London, Mansell, 1979) pp. 37ff.

92   208 US 412 (1908).

93   Ibid., at p. 421.

94   See Kenny, S., 'Reproductive hazards in the workplace: the law and sexual difference', *International Journal of the Sociology of Law* 393 (1986); Williams, W., 'Firing the woman to protect the fetus: the reconciliation of

fetal protection with employment opportunity goals under Title VII', 69 *Georgia Law Journal* 641 (1981).

95 Section 13 Employment Act 1980.

96 *Gregory* v. *Tudsbury Ltd*, [1982] IRLR 267.

97 Section 60 Employment Protection (Consolidation) Act 1978 (as amended). Note *Brown* v. *Stockton-on-Tees Borough Council*, [1987] IRLR 230, where a woman succeeded in a claim for unfair dismissal when her post was made redundant and she was not selected for an alternative post when it was discovered that she was pregnant and would need maternity leave.

98 For discussion see Erickson, N., 'Pregnancy discrimination: an analytical approach', 7 *Women's Rights Law Reporter* 11 (1981).

99 For comment upon the development of unfair dismissal case law see Collins, H., 'Capitalist discipline and corporatist law', *Industrial Law Journal* 78 (1982).

100 See *Levin* v. *Delta Air Lines*, 730 F. 2d. 994 (5th Cir. 1984); *Burwell* v. *Eastern Airlines*, 633 F. 2d. 361 (4th Cir. 1980); *Harriss* v. *Pan Am. World Airways*, 649 F. 2d. 670 (9th Cir. 1980).

101 Op. cit. note 86 at p. 1134.

102 [1980] ICR 66.

103 [1985] ICR 703.

104 'The law relating to sex discrimination' 15 *Industrial Law Journal* 43 (1986).

105 Council Directive 76/207/EEC OJ 1976 L39/40. Article 2(1) states 'For the purpose of the following provisions, the principle of equal treatment shall mean that there shall be no discrimination whatsoever on grounds of sex either directly or indirectly by reference in particular to marital or family status.' See *Legislating for Change* (Manchester, EOC, 1986).

106 Sections 34–35 Employment Protection (Consolidation) Act 1978. If employers paid a more beneficial rate of maternity pay under the contract of employment this was offset against the statutory rights.

107 Problems also arose if the woman worked for two employers, in that each employer was bound to deduct the maternity allowance from the maternity pay. Thus in *Cullen* v. *Creasey Hotels (Limbury) Ltd*, [1980] IRLR 59 the woman's earnings from her two part-time jobs were so low that she received no maternity pay from either employer.

108 *The Law of Social Security* (London, Butterworths, 1982) at p. 249.

109 *A Fresh Look at Maternity Benefit* (London, HMSO, 1980).

110 Department of Health and Social Security, *Reform of Social Security*, vol. 2: Cmnd. 9518 (London, HMSO, 1985).

111 The legal framework for the new system is set out in Part V; supplemented by Schedule 4 of the Social Security Act 1986. The detailed regulation of statutory maternity pay is to be found in the Statutory Maternity Pay (General) Regulations 1986 SI 1986/1960.

112 Op. cit. note 111, at para. 5.22.

113 See the discussion earlier on page 170.

114 Regulation 17(1) SI 1986/1960. For statutory maternity pay purposes an 'employee' is a woman over the age of sixteen who is treated as an 'employed earner' for social security purposes – that is a person whose earnings attract a liability for employer's Class 1 National Insurance contributions.

115   At present the lower rate of statutory maternity pay is £32.65, but this is liable to be changed annually at the start of the financial year in April (Regulation 6 SI 1986/1960).

116   Sections 48(4) and (5) Social Security Act 1986.

117   Section 46(2)(a) Social Security Act 1986.

118   Section 33 Employment Protection (Consolidation) Act 1978.

119   Section 11 Employment Act 1980 amending section 33 Employment Protection (Consolidation) Act 1978.

120   Section 33(3B) Employment Protection (Consolidation) Act 1978.

121   Section 47(2)(3) Employment Protection (Consolidation) Act 1978.

122   [1987] IRLR 310.

123   Section 86 Employment Protection (Consolidation) Act 1978.

124   Section 56A(2)–(4) Employment Protection (Consolidation) Act 1978.

125   Section 57(3) Employment Protection (Consolidation) Act 1978 as amended by the Employment Act 1980 Schedule 1 para. 23. Lewis, R. and Simpson, B. argue that 'A woman who is not permitted to return to her original job can rarely be certain whether or not her return was not reasonably practicable and if so whether her refusal of any alternative employment offered will result in the loss of a potential remedy for being denied the right to return', *Striking A Balance?* (Oxford, Martin Robertson, 1981) at p. 53. See also the comment 'Maternity leave: do mothers have rights?', *The Independent*, 31 July 1987.

126   Op. cit., note 125 at p. 56.

127   [1984] IRLR 299.

128   Op. cit., note 86 at p. 1182.

Chapter 7

The European Community and Equality Legislation

Background

In recent years the major impetus for introducing equality of treatment into British law has come from membership of the European Community. As we saw in chapter 2, the Equal Pay Act 1970 was implemented with a view to future membership of the European Community and the consequent need to fulfil the commitment to equal pay contained in Article 119 of the Treaty of Rome 1957. Subsequent European Community secondary legislation, and the developing jurisprudence of the European Court of Justice, has introduced to British law new methods of interpretation of equality legislation as well as expanding the forms of discrimination capable of legal challenge.[1] In particular the power of British courts and tribunals to refer questions of interpretation of European law to the European Court of Justice through the preliminary ruling procedure has added a legal and political space for applicants to circumvent the limitations of British precedent and the scope of domestic law. The use of infringement actions against the British government for failure to implement European Community obligations has also provided a higher, supra-national standard against which the domestic concept of equality may be measured.

Although there have been only two infringement actions against the British government for failure to comply with the Treaty of Rome, the effects on British law have been far-reaching. One infringement action led to amendments to the Equal Pay Act 1970 in order to introduce the wider claim of equal pay for work of equal value.[2] The other resulted in amendments to the Sex Discrimination Act 1975, removing the exemption of small businesses from the scope of the Act and also providing for any provisions contrary to the principle of equal treatment contained in collective agreements, individual contracts and the rules governing the professions to be null and void.[3] In addition the jurisprudence of the European Court of Justice has widened the ambit of the domestic legislation, and details of this have been outlined earlier, particularly in chapter 5. The supra-national standards have also provided a useful benchmark against which to measure the legality of the Conservative government's attempts to reform social security.[4] Finally they have provided a longstop in the present climate of introducing 'deregulation' in the labour market through the reduction of collective and individual employment rights.[5]

Development of the European Community Role

In chapter 1 we argued that the intervention of the European Community into the realm of equality law can be explained by Weber's analysis of a rationalization of the market. The link between economic motivations and equality legislation is not disguised, but is instead fully articulated in European Community policy. Indeed employment issues, and what are termed 'social' issues, were not a high priority on the political agenda of the framers of the Treaty of Rome 1957. The aspiration to improve working conditions and raise the living standards of the peoples of Europe contained in the Preamble, Articles 2 and 117 of the Treaty was seen as an automatic by-product of the creation of a free market in goods, services, labour and capital. Part III of the Treaty contained various *ad hoc*, general aspirations to developing aspects of social policy, but these merely supplemented the basic economic aims by concentrating upon aspects of employment policy.[6]

Only one provision, Article 119 EEC, stands out in imposing a firm legal obligation to implement a policy of 'equal pay for equal work'. But this was added on economic grounds, as a compromise to France to protect her from unfair competition from other member-states where such legislation was not in existence. Even this legal obligation remained dormant[7] until a series of test cases referred to the European Court of Justice from the Belgian courts[8] in the 1970s established the legal scope of the obligation.

The 1970s saw further involvement of the European Community in developing an embryonic social policy, beginning in 1974 with the Council Resolution establishing a Social Action Programme.[9] The legal basis of the programme was tenuous and the focus of the social programme has been mainly concerned with employment issues to further the economic aims of the European Community. The promotion of women's rights, however, has been a central tenet of much of the European Community social policy; Article 119 EEC has been complemented with directives on equal pay,[10] equal treatment,[11] equal treatment in state[12] and occupational[13] social security schemes. A directive for equal treatment for the self-employed has also been introduced.[14] Aspects of women's employment issues have also been singled out for special consideration in the new wave of proposals designed to combat unemployment through the adaptation of working time programme.[15]

Various explanations for this interest in equality legislation can be put forward. Clearly the economic motive is predominant. By the 1970s most of the member-states of the European Community had enacted some form of concurrent equality legislation as a response to women's increased participation in the labour market. The European Community therefore had an interest in ensuring some degree of harmony between the various national provisions in order to prevent the distortion of competition within the labour market. The economic recession of the 1970s, sparked off by the oil crisis, provided the impetus for the European Community to rationalize a greater degree of economic planning to deal with increasing unemployment throughout the European Community. The notion of a 'Social Action' programme was perhaps an attempt to paint a 'human' face over bare economic priorities. The shift in emphasis from purely economic priorities to encompassing social priorities, even if symbolic, was at any rate short-lived. This is seen particularly in the attitude of the member-states towards new policy proposals in this area,[16] as well as in some of the decisions of the European Court of Justice and the policy-making institutions. For example, in a recent Communication from the Commission to the Council on the problems of social security in times of economic recession, policies geared towards economic expansion are to be accorded priority over policies involving increases in expenditure on social security.[17]

In addition to the economic rationale there is also a political motive. Many of the member-states had experienced political and social unrest in the late 1960s, and while formal equality measures for minority groups had been implemented it was increasingly clear that further measures beyond token equality would be necessary if any further gains were to be made. This is seen particularly in the feminist movements in Europe, which espoused a 'differences' approach to civil rights and sought to organize separately in alternative structures.[18] National and supra-national governments were compelled to take note; not only to respond to the political demands of such movements but also to attempt to incor-porate them back into 'mainstream' politics. These groups in turn provided a convenient vehicle for the weaker European institutions such as the European Parliament and EC Commission to conduct their own internal power struggle with the 'executive' arm of the European Community, the Council of Ministers.[19] While both these institutions have kept the issue of equality legislation alive, the impact on the nature of the decision-making process within the European Community, and the content of the legislation, has been limited.

The result has been what Ruth Nielsen terms 'state feminism', that is, equality laws which are neither mobilized for, nor implemented by, women, and which create rights only on an individual basis.[20] As a result the European Community decision-making process appears remote and inaccessible, and results in law which Catherine Hoskyns describes as 'complex, technical and abstract and confers rights on individuals without opening up effective means of enforcement'.[21] The interest of the European Community in equality legislation has, however, resulted in the establishment of both official and unofficial networks of European women, and has encouraged pressure groups to be interested in the proposals. Official bodies such as the European Parliament have organized formal committees to discuss women's issues, and a women's bureau has been established in the EC Commission. But all these remain outside direct contact of the EC Commission–EC Council dialogue where the real power lies. As Hoskyns argues, 'The European legislation . . . was not fought for in any direct sense by women, and remains virtually unknown to those who are supposed to be its beneficiaries.'[22]

Equality within the European Community

The Scope of the Legislation

In addition to the limitations inherent in the political process for adopting European Community equality legislation a further criticism that can be levelled against the European Community is that the legislation does not relate to the total situation of women in society. In particular it does not invade the 'private' sphere around which much of the political motivation of the European women's movement has organized.[23] The issue of 'body politics' – issues of reproduction, abortion, male violence or redressing the balance in domestic responsibilities, lie outside the scope of the law. The European Parliament has attempted to address some of these issues in its debates but there has been no positive intervention at the legislative level. While the EC Commission recognizes what it terms 'true equality'[24] the legal argument put forward is that the equality programme is circumscribed by the Treaty of Rome. This means it only addresses issues essentially located in the 'public' sphere – in particular women's access to, and participation in, the labour market. Some of the more recent proposals begin to bridge the public/private divide – for example, the directives on parental leave and part-time work cross over – but these are limited measures and are concerned only with the terms of labour market participation.

This emphasis upon the 'public' world is seen in the scope of the directives, their subject-matter and the limitations of their coverage. A notable example is the Directive on social security, which limits the personal scope to the 'working population'. In one sense this is defined widely to include the self-employed, people seeking employment as well as those whose employment is interrupted by accident, sickness or involuntary unemployment, retired and invalided workers.[25] The limitations of this definition are seen in Britain in the attitude taken towards two particular social security benefits which discriminated against women. Although several changes were made to the British social security system in the 1970s in order to bring the social security scheme into line with the Directive,[26] two non-contributory non-means-tested benefits which discriminated against married and cohabiting women were omitted from the reforms.[27] These were the Invalid Care Allowance (available for those caring for people with severe disabilities) and a non-contributory invalidity pension for the long-term incapacitated who had insufficient contributions to qualify them for the contributory invalidity pension. In 1977 a 'housewives' version of non-contributory invalidity pension was introduced, and married or cohabiting women could subsequently gain entitlement if they could show they were incapable of performing normal household duties.[28] The British government argued that the benefits were not within the scope of the Social Security Directive, and although discrimination existed in these benefits, married or cohabiting women were not within the definition of the 'working population'. Following the EC Commission's interim report on the implementation of the Directive,[29] the government accepted that the Housewife's Non-Contributory Pension fell within the scope of the Directive and the whole system of contributory pensions for the disabled has been replaced by a new Severe Disablement Allowance from November 1984. Linda Luckhaus, however, argues that many of the vestiges of the old discriminatory benefit have now been replaced by indirectly discriminatory provisions.[30] One of the transitional arrangements[31] has already been subject to scrutiny from the European Court of Justice, suggesting that vestiges of discrimination may still be tackled. In *Borrie-Clarke* v. *Chief Adjudication Officer*[32] a disabled woman suffering from Menière's disease[33] challenged the refusal of a disability pension. Her claim fell within the transitional arrangements which allowed people entitled to a non-contributory pension in the two months preceding the coming into force of the Severe Disablement Allowance to be transferred on to the new benefit without having to comply with the more stringent 80 per cent severe disablement test. While in one sense this was a more generous provision, in another it perpetuated discrimination in that married women applicants still had to satisfy a discriminatory test since the normal household duties test was imposed only upon married women. The Court found discrimination, and following its earlier ruling in *The Netherlands* v. *Federatie Nederlandse Vakbeweging*[34] applied a formal definition of equal treatment: 'as from 23 December 1984 . . . women are entitled to be treated in the same manner, and to have the same rules applied to them, as men who are in the same situation. . . .'

The government persisted with the view that the Invalid Care Allowance fell outside the scope of the Directive. Caring responsibilities were obviously seen as part of women's 'natural' functions of wife and mother.[35] As we argued in chapter 6, benefits for those engaged in caring have not traditionally been perceived of as an employment-related risk.

A case was taken to the European Court of Justice to test the validity of such distinctions in social security provision.[36] The European Court of Justice, in somewhat tortuous reasoning, was careful not to confront the issue as to whether or not a benefit paid for caring was within the scope of the Directive – that is perceiving caring as an aspect of paid work. Instead the Court focused upon the aspect of invalidity. The claimant had given up work to care for her disabled mother. The issue of whether the fact that the benefit was paid to a third person rather than the invalid was presented by the Court as being the *legal* issue. The Court went on to define the term 'working population' to include *inter alia* 'workers . . . whose activity is interrupted by illness, accident . . .'. The Court, almost by a sleight of hand, was able to include a person whose work had been interrupted by one of the risks covered in the Directive as part of the 'working population'.[37] There was 'a clear economic link between the benefit and the disabled person since the disabled person derived an advantage from the fact that the allowance was paid to the person caring for him'.[38]

In the discourse of equality the European Community has failed to take on board debates within the women's movement, and to discuss how far differences between men and women should be acknowledged in pursuing the ideal of equality.[39] Indeed, as with the British legislation, the resort to biological difference is seen as a justification in several of the provisions for exclusion of the concept of equality rather than coming to terms with accommodating a differences approach. The limitations of the discourse are seen, for example, in provisions relating to maternity and pregnancy which are excluded from the Equal Treatment Directive and the Social Security Directives. Furthermore the European Court of Justice has displayed a cautious approach to these issues.[40] In *Hofmann* v. *Barmer Ersatzkasse*[41] a father arranged unpaid paternity leave with his employer for the period following the eight-week 'protective period' granted to mothers by German law after the birth of a child. For four months after the 'protective period' German law allowed mothers to receive an allowance, paid from public funds, equivalent to their normal remuneration. Hofmann's application for the maternity allowance from the state was refused despite his argument that the leave after the eight-week period was not for biological or medical reasons but was concerned only with the care of the child. The German government successfully argued that the leave represented an uninterrupted extension of the 'protective period' for mothers. Drawing upon the maternity exemptions of the Equal Treatment Directive the European Court of Justice argued that an analysis of the wording indicated that the Directive was only concerned with the employment sphere and was not intended to deal with matters of family organization or to 'alter the division of responsibility between parents'.[42]

In contrast, at least on the face of it, the derogations permitted under the Equal Treatment Directive were given a narrow construction in the case of *Johnston* v. *Chief Constable of the Royal Ulster Constabulary.*[43] A complaint was brought by a woman officer in the full-time reserve of the Royal Ulster Constabulary against the practice of not allowing female officers to carry firearms. This hindered women's career chances within the Royal Ulster Constabulary and the complaint was based upon Articles 2 and 6 of the Equal Treatment Directive 76/207/EEC. The principal issue of the case was the justifications which member states could raise to exclude claims of sex discrimination on the grounds of national interest.[44] Of wider significance is the debate on the nature of protective legislation which we discussed in chapter 3. The Court held that the derogation contained in Article 2(3), which provides that the Directive is 'without prejudice to provisions concerning the protection of women, particularly as regards pregnancy and maternity', must be interpreted strictly. Any derogation from this principle must be justified according to the principle of proportionality:

> That principle requires that derogations remain within the limits of what is appropriate and necessary for achieving the aim in view and requires the principle of equal treatment to be reconciled as far as possible with the requirements of public safety which constitute the decisive factor as regards the context of the activity in question.[45]

The Court was keen to point out that women should not be excluded from a particular employment 'on the ground that public opinion demands that women be given greater protection than men against risks which affect women and men in the same way and which are distinct from women's specific needs of protection'.[46] While section 7 of the Sex Discrimination Act 1986 has removed the statutory restrictions on women's hours of work, the ruling in *Johnston* may still be significant for other restrictions based on reproductive hazards or other biological *and physiological restrictions.* The reasoning in the *Johnston* case suggests that the decision of the Employment Appeal Tribunal in *Page* v. *Freight Hire (Tank Haulage) Ltd*[47] that the employer need only show that his actions were 'reasonable', has been refined by the principle of proportionality. It would seem that employers now have the burden of actually showing that jobs cannot be reasonably organized to minimize or avoid reproductive hazards. In one sense the ruling is a liberal one, particularly if it is read in the light of the *Bilka-Kaufhaus* v. *Weber von Hartz* ruling.[48] In rejecting unsubstantiated notions of stereotyping women for certain work it may be moving closer to the American equal opportunity concept. In the United States, instead of accepting discriminatory and unsubstantiated 'play-safe' policies of employers of excluding women automatically from certain jobs, the burden of proof is upon the employer to show the necessity for women to be excluded by objectively justified scientific evidence, or by showing a considerable body of opinion that the risk is confined to women workers, and that there is no acceptable alternative which would achieve the required protection in a less discriminatory way.[49] However, even this analysis is limited. It fails to take on board the effects of reproductive hazards upon male workers, thus confining women to a special sphere and reinforcing gender hierarchies. Moreover, it subjects the employment policy to a 'business necessity' approach. Thus many women may be excluded from the higher-paid and traditionally male jobs by cost factors, and economic justifications may be given priority at the expense of equality. As with the arguments reproduced in relation to wage discrimination in chapter 5 it is still controversial in America as to how far the so-called 'business necessity' test should be limited to an examination of the capabilities for fulfilling a particular job, and under what conditions the test can be transposed to a justification of other employment practices.[50]

A further development in the scope of the European Community involvement with equality is the tendency not only to treat the legal provisions as mutually exclusive, but also to read restrictively into separate areas of law exemptions to the principle of equality of treatment from other areas. In particular the EC Commission and the member states have attempted to narrow down the scope of Article 119 EEC. But as Erika Szyszczak argues, Article 119 EEC is the fundamental and underlying constitutional basis for the principle of equal treatment, and the subsequent secondary legislation is intended to expand and clarify the legal obligation not narrow its scope.[51]

An example of how this legal technique has been used to preclude certain areas of law from the ambit of equality legislation is seen in the economically sensitive area of provision for old age.[52] As we saw earlier in chapters 3 and 5 a major limitation of the scope of the British legislation on equal pay and sex discrimination is the blanket exclusion of provisions relating to death or retirement. Mirroring the inequalities which continue to exist in the member states, European Community law also excludes aspects of old age provision from its scope. For example, under the Social Security Directive member-states may continue to operate different state retirement ages for men and women. Member-states may also exclude such things as the derived entitlement of a wife to an old age pension or invalidity pension based on the husband's employment record.[53] In addition Article 9 of the Occupational Social Security Directive allows the member-states to defer the compulsory application of equal treatment in the determination of pension age, survivor's pensions and the use of certain actuarial data.[54]

The European Court of Justice has added to this list of exclusions by ruling that the fixing of certain conditions of employment such as special age limits which have pecuniary consequences, for example access to a pension scheme, are not within the scope of Article 119 EEC.[55] The

Court has, however, drawn up a distinction between the upper age limit for leaving paid work (retirement age) and the qualifying age for the receipt of a retirement pension (pension age). Following the decision in *Marshall* v. *South West Hampshire Area Health Authority (Teaching)*[56] state employees are entitled to an equal retirement age, and this has been extended to all employees by section 2 of the Sex Discrimination Act 1986.

The complexities of the rules relating to provision for old age have been increased by the scope of the Equal Treatment Directive. Initially uncertainty as to the scope of the Directive was created by the ruling in *Burton* v. *British Railways Board*.[57] Here discrimination was alleged by a male employee in a voluntary redundancy scheme in which a collective agreement determined that the minimum age a worker could volunteer for redundancy was five years before the state pension age. Mr Burton was aged fifty-eight when his application for voluntary redundancy was refused. He claimed that a female employee aged fifty-eight would have received the benefit of applying for voluntary redundancy. The case was brought under Article 119 EEC and the Equal Treatment Directive, although the European Court of Justice held the issue only concerned the latter. The Court decided that Article 5(1)[58] of the Directive could be given a broad construction to cover the termination of the employment relationship but 'read' into the Directive the exclusion relating to the maintenance of differences in state retirement ages found in Article 7 of the Social Security Directive 79/7/EEC. As the voluntary redundancy scheme was linked to the state retirement age a breach of the principle of equal treatment was found not to occur.

A different aspect of alleged discrimination occurred in *Roberts* v. *Tate and Lyle Industries Ltd.*[59] The occupational pension scheme provided for different retirement ages of sixty for women and sixty-five for men. The employers agreed with the trade union that employees made redundant should receive an immediate occupational pension at the age of fifty-five. This resulted in unequal treatment in that male employees received the pension ten years prior to normal retirement age, whereas women received their pension only five years prior to retirement. The European Court of Justice was prepared to hold that the issue fell within Article 5(1) of the Equal Treatment Directive – the termination of employment in connection with a mass redundancy. *Prima facie* the scheme did not discriminate between men and women since it applied the same age limit to both, but looking at the consequences of the difference in the statutory and occupational pension ages the Court argued that benefits linked to a national scheme which adopted different minimum pension ages for men and women may lie outside the Equal Treatment Directive by virtue of the exemption contained in Article 7 of the Equal Treatment Directive 76/207/EEC. The Court then went on to hold that, in view of the fundamental importance of the principle of equality of treatment, Article 1(2) of Directive 76/207/EEC (which excludes matters of social security from the scope of the Directive) must be interpreted strictly. Thus as a consequence Article 7 of Directive 79/7/EEC would apply only to the determination of pensionable age for the purposes of granting old age and retirement pensions, and to the consequences this may have for other social security benefits.

In *Roberts*, however, the issue concerned a contractual provision dealing with redundancy, and since the age for dismissal was the same for both women and men there was no discrimination despite the consequences of the dismissal in relation to access to the occupational pension. However, if different ages for the dismissal of men and women had been chosen in relation to a difference in retirement age then this would fall within the scope of discrimination outlawed by the Directive as the Court confirmed in *Beets-Proper* v. *F. Van Lanschot Bankiers NV.*[60]

One of the more problematic legal issues has been the area of social security schemes and the interrelationship with Article 119 EEC. Pension contributions have been the main focus of legal attention but, as chapter 5 indicates, the whole notion of 'pay' is becoming increasingly complex, especially since social security schemes are establishing closer links with the employment relationship. The major stumbling-block has been the judgment in the first *Defrenne* case, where the European Court of Justice drew a distinction between general social security schemes which did not form a sufficiently close nexus with the employment relationship to be included within the scope of pay and schemes that could be considered a part of an employee's pay.[61] The Court has subsequently held that the employer's share of financing occupational schemes may form part of an employee's pay, particularly where they have pecuniary consequences for other employment-related benefits.[62] In a later case the contractual employment nexus was upheld in the context of a supplementary occupational pension scheme.[63] A setback in these developments has occurred however, in *Newstead* v. *Department of Transport and HM Treasury.*[64] This was a complaint brought by a male civil servant who declared himself to be a confirmed bachelor, and who objected to the compulsory deduction of 1½ per cent of his gross salary by way of a contribution to a fund for widow's pensions. Female employees were not subject to this deduction, and although the deductions were refunded with interest (either on retirement or death of the male employee) Mr Newstead contended that discrimination occurred contrary to Article 119 EEC and Articles 1(1), 2(1) and 5(1) of Directive 76/207/EEC by virtue of the fact that he was denied immediate access to part of his salary. The Court of Justice and Advocate-General Darmon have concluded that the issue falls within Articles 117 and 118 EEC, not Article 119 EEC. The distinction has been made between a case involving the obligation to *make* a contribution and a case involving inequality in the *amount* of contribution. Where the amount was included in gross salary for the purposes of determining other benefits, as in the *Worringham* and *Liefting* cases, Article 119 EEC could apply. Where the obligation to contribute was unequal, the Equal Treatment Directive and Social Security Directive would apply except in cases like *Newstead*, which involved matters specifically excluded from their scope.

In spite of the way in which the *Newstead* case has been handled in terms of substantive law, the rulings discussing provision for death or old age are particularly important, given the attempts by the government to encourage greater individualization of pensions. Already the government has reduced the state benefits available, particularly to widows, in order to reduce the burden on public expenditure of the state scheme in the future. Such developments may open up the issue of provision for old age which is not presently subject to scrutiny for sex discrimination by virtue of section 51 and other exemptions contained in Sex Discrimination and Equal Pay Acts.[65] However, as in other areas considered by the European Court of Justice, we find the focus of legal attention is limited by the consideration of the legal issues in a way which concentrates upon procedural and technical matters. By so doing a wider analysis of the scope of the concept of equal treatment, particularly where it might challenge accepted social and legal practices, is precluded. It is to this issue we now turn.

Concepts of Discrimination

The European Community equality legislation adopts a gender-neutral or assimilation approach. The principle of equal treatment is taken as the generic standard, and issues of direct and indirect discrimination are seen as examples of practices which infringe the principle. Positive action is hardly addressed except in a permissive sense,[66] and the member-states ultimately chose to adopt only a Recommendation on positive action.[67] While this binds the member-states it does not give individuals directly enforceable rights in the same way that Article 119 EEC may be used against employers and the state,[68] and in the same way that parts of Directives may be enforced against the state either acting in its capacity as employer[69] or in a welfare capacity in social security provision.[70]

The legislation is based upon the concept of equality and is aimed primarily at tackling issues of overt discrimination within the labour market. There is no guarantee that equality must be achieved by levelling up – that is, raising women's rights to the standard of the male comparator – or that the policy be implemented in a way that benefits women. The European Court of Justice in *Defrenne* v. *Sabena SA* (No. 2)[71] argued that, in order to achieve the principle of equal pay as set out in Article 119 EEC, women's salaries should be raised to a level comparable with that of the male salary. In times of recession, however, this principle has been challenged by the member states, particularly in the area of social security where economic pressures have been used by the governments of the member states to justify cutbacks in public expenditure.[72] Catherine Hoskyns sums up the position:

> Community provisions on women's rights treat equality in a formal way and are much concerned with agreements, written provisions and the text of the law. They have little to say about implementation and, apart from requiring the availability of recourse to law, do not insist that resources be made available to assist women either to lobby on these proposals or enforce their rights.[73]

Direct Discrimination

Direct discrimination is identified as being the situation where like cases are treated differently. In the second *Defrenne* case the European Court of Justice defined direct discrimination as being the situation where discrimination 'may be identified solely with the aid of the criteria based on equal work and equal pay' referred to in Article 119 EEC. The narrowness of this concept is seen in the reluctance of the European Court of Justice to widen the basis of comparison in *Macarthys Ltd* v. *Smith*[74] to include hypothetical comparisons.

Other than enforcing the notion that equal treatment means 'no discrimination whatsoever on the grounds of sex'[75] the concept of direct discrimination is not fleshed out in any of the subsequent secondary legislation. In particular the use of, say, the Equal Treatment Directive to identify and sustain issues of gender discrimination has not been put forward in case law as a means of furthering the idea or developing the concept of 'discrimination based on sex'.[76]

As we argued earlier in chapters 3 and 4 there is a tendency to treat direct discrimination as unproblematic, although in practice we find that employers and the state are wise to the practice and will find a multitude of pretexts other than sex on which to justify discriminatory behaviour. In relation to social security provision, however, the European Court of Justice has been prepared to find infringements of the Social Security Directive on the grounds of direct sex discrimination. In particular the Court has cut through complex arguments of economic costs and the acceptance of discriminatory systems of benefits based upon stereotyped notions of married women's role in the family and the labour market. This example could be followed in other areas of law.

Unemployment provision has provided the main benefit in which sex-stereotyped attitudes have been questioned. For example, in the Netherlands two unemployment benefits existed. One was a contributory benefit payable to the unemployed for six months. After this period unemployment assistance was payable for a two-year period. This was not available to a worker 'who, being a married woman could not be regarded as a wage-earner'. The Netherlands government attempted to eradicate this discriminatory provision by a 'levelling down' solution, which proved unacceptable to the legislature.[77] New legislation finally repealed the discriminatory rule but transitional measures reduced the amount of unemployment assistance for people aged under thirty-five. This exclusionary rule applied to workers unemployed before 23 December 1984, the date on which the Social Security Directive came into force. Thus the measures had the effect of perpetuating discrimination for married women. On the date the equal treatment in Social Security Directive came into force the Netherlands Trade Union Federation (FNV) sought an order against the Netherlands government to suspend the discriminatory rules, relying upon Article 4 of Directive 79/7/EEC.[78] While the discriminatory nature of the rules was not in dispute the Court provided useful guidelines on how transitional measures which apply retrospectively, and which perpetuate discrimination, may be brought within the direct effect of European Community law: 'In the absence of measures for the implementation of that article, women had the right to be treated in the same manner and to have the same system applied to them as men in the same situation, a system which remained, failing execution of that Directive, the only valid system of reference.' [para 22] As we saw earlier (page 197) these criteria proved useful in the *Borrie-Clarke* case against the British government. It would also seem that they introduce, by default, a 'levelling up' solution to equality, which runs counter to the prevailing economic climate of reducing public expenditure.

This approach is seen also in the Irish case of *McDermott and Cotter*.[79] Again the applicants relied upon Article 4 of the Social Security Directive to challenge provision for unemployment benefit under which married women received less benefit, and for a shorter period, than men and single women, despite having paid the same contributions. The Irish government, in the face of this reference to the European Court of Justice, subsequently repealed the discriminatory provisions although it did not make the measures fully retrospective to 23 December 1984.

While this method of interpretation has been successful in tackling broad issues of direct discrimination, and in a way which cuts through the complexities of different social security provisions and economic constraints, it goes no further. The mechanism of harmonization through the use of directives leaves a fair measure of discretion to the member states as to the implementation of the equal treatment principle. The tasks of leaving issues of fact to be determined by the national courts, and the ability to look at the wider issues of social security provision, do not have a place in the concept of equal treatment.

Indirect Discrimination

The concept of indirect discrimination is utilized in the secondary European Community legislation, although no substantive definition of what the concept entails is given.[80] A full definition remains to be fleshed out in the jurisprudence of the European Court of Justice. From the case law indirect discrimination would seem to have two meanings. As first defined in the second *Defrenne* case, in relation to Article 119 EEC, it constitutes 'indirect and disguised discrimination which can only be identified by reference to more explicit implementing provisions of a Community or national character'.[81] This definition was refined in the later ruling of *Jenkins* v. *Kingsgate (Clothing Productions) Ltd*,[82] where the words 'indirect and disguised' were dropped.

The second definition is best articulated in Advocate-General Mancini's Opinion in *Teuling-Worms* v. *Bedrijfsvereniging*. Indirect discrimination

> may be presumed here where a measure which is apparently neutral in fact predominantly affects workers of one sex, without it being necessary to establish that discrimination was intended. On the contrary, it is for the person applying the measure . . . to provide proof that it was objectively justified and did not involve any intention to discriminate.[83]

This latter definition is closer to the disparate impact doctrine borrowed from American law and utilized in the Sex Discrimination Act 1975.

In *Jenkins* v. *Kingsgate (Clothing Productions) Ltd* the European Court of Justice held that a difference in pay between full-time and part-time workers would not constitute discrimination 'unless it is in reality merely an indirect way of reducing the level of pay of part-time workers on the ground that that group of workers is composed exclusively or predominantly of women'.[84] In *Bilka-Kaufhaus GmbH* v. *Weber von Hartz* the Court held that

> if it were found that a considerably smaller percentage of women than men work full-time, the exclusion of part-time workers from the occupational pension scheme would be contrary to Article 119 of the Treaty if, taking account of the difficulties encountered by women in arranging matters so as to be able to work full-time this measure cannot be explained by factors excluding discrimination based on sex.[85]

In this ruling the European Court of Justice further elucidated the criteria to be used in determining an objective justification of discriminatory treatment: 'the means [must] meet a genuine need of the enterprise, that they are suitable for attaining the objective pursued by the enterprise and are necessary for that purpose'.[86] The limitations of this concept were discussed in chapter 5, where it was suggested that the focus of attention upon the justifications for the discrimination seem to prevail over an inquiry into the discriminatory consequences of the policies being challenged.

One of the more difficult problems raised by European Community involvement in equality legislation is that it subjects the activities of the state to judicial scrutiny. The new economic-factors defence to indirect discrimination (discussed in chapter 5) claims is therefore much harder to apply in areas where the state is making the decisions, particularly in the area of social security. The concept of indirect discrimination, however, has been used to challenge state policy. In *Teuling-Worms* v. *Bedrijfsvereniging*[87] the issue concerned a contributory invalidity benefit established in the Netherlands in 1966, which entitled a worker injured at work, and rendered incapable of work for over a year, to a benefit based on the degree of incapacity and the last salary before the accident. Although this benefit as earnings-related and not means-tested there was a minimum level based on the minimum wage. In 1982 the formula for calculating the benefit was changed, and the base date for calculating the benefit became the date when the benefit was payable (that is one year after the accident). Since most workers would have suffered a reduction in entitlement as a result the Netherlands government took con-temporaneous measures using a means-tested benefit to prevent injured workers from falling below the poverty line, by incorporating a formula used for calculating a lower invalidity benefit which had previously been overtly discriminatory, but had been changed in 1979 in order to conform with the Social Security Directive. The link with the last salary was retained only for claimants who would have qualified for the highest level of non-contributory benefit. The means-tested supplementary regulations were alleged to be discriminatory; despite an appearance of sex-neutrality the reforms disadvantaged twice as many women as men. While the European Court of Justice and the Advocate General accepted that indirect discrimination had occurred the issue focused upon the defence – the objective justification of the measures. The Court accepted that the governments of the member states were the sole competent authorities to assess the situation, and accepted the Netherlands government argument that payments paid to people with no other source of revenue could be justified if they are given to cover extra costs of having dependants and if the aim was to ensure that their income did not fall below the legal minimum.

Finally the European Community has drawn upon the concept of human rights as part of its equality strategy. In *Defrenne* v. *Sabena SA* (No. 3) the European Court of Justice held that 'respect for fundamental personal human rights is one of the general principles of Community law, the observance of which it has a duty to ensure. There can be no doubt that the elimination of discrimination based on sex forms part of those fundamental rights.'[88] Generally the European Community is pursuing a policy of developing a human rights doctrine independently of that found in the European Convention on Human Rights and Fundamental Freedoms and the national constitutions of the member states. However, only rarely has the European Court of Justice found an infringement of human rights. Furthermore there are few procedural mechanisms for pursuing a human rights claim at either national or European Community level.[89] The exact scope of the human rights concept in relation to equal treatment is to be determined by jurisprudence, and in some respects it stands as a symbolic rather than substantive ideal. For the most part this concept has been used to fill lacunae in European Community law to achieve a 'just' result.[90] This is particularly noticeable in employment issues relating to the staff of the European Community institutions. A significant judgment, however, is that of *Razzouk and Beydoun* v. *EC Commission*,[91] where two widowers of Community employees were denied a survivor's pension because the staff regulations did not provide for widower's pensions although widows are entitled to a substantial survivor's pension. The claimants argued that Article 119 EEC should apply by analogy to Community officials and, in the alternative, that there was an underlying principle that officials should be treated equally in like or comparable situations. On the ground that there was an infringement of the fundamental right of equal treatment of the sexes the European Court of Justice annulled the EC Commission decision, denying the survivor's pension on the ground of the fundamental right of the equal treatment of the sexes. It is interesting to note that the Court went out of its way to state that the principle of equal treatment of the sexes was by no means limited to the obligations arising under Article 119 EEC and the subsequent secondary legislation, at least in the employment relationship of the EC institutions and its employees. It remains to be seen how far the Court might extend the principle beyond this sphere, particularly given the virtual standstill in the adoption of legislation in the equal treatment field. A major limitation will be how far the doctrine of human rights is limited to a formal principle of equal treatment.

To sum up, the European Community has played an important strategic role in widening the substantive scope of sex discrimination and equality legislation. By placing women's employment issues firmly on the legal and political agenda the Community has encouraged new member states such as Greece, Spain and Portugal to adopt new forms of equality legislation, while in times of recession the supra-national safeguards have prevented any back-sliding and erosion of women's rights in states where those rights have already been implemented. Despite this the European Community focus upon equality has many conceptual limitations. Some of this is self-imposed through a narrow interpretation of legal powers and by the adoption of a limited notion of formal equal treatment. On the one hand straightforward issues such as stereotypical assumptions of women's roles are acknowledged as issues of discrimination, particularly in the pursuit of an equality of opportunity goal seen, for example, in the *Johnston* case. On the other hand the more problematic 'differences' arguments are not fully addressed or resolved, and this is evidenced in the cases dealing with the maternity exemptions and the issues of pension entitlements. In addition the underlying economic rationale for the legislation continues to motivate the legal discourse. This is evidenced, as we have shown, in the reluctance to include sensitive issues such as positive action or provision for old age fully into the equal treatment principle. Perhaps an even greater articulation of the over-reaching economic considerations is the way in which the concept of indirect discrimination has been introduced into the legal discourse, somewhat reluctantly, and with the acceptance of a certain amount of leeway for economic priorities (both in the public and private sector) to have the final consideration.

Notes

1 An overview of the scope of European Community law in the area of equality legislation can be found in McCrudden, C. (ed.), *Women, Employment and European Equality Law* (London, Eclipse Publications, 1988); Verwilghen, M., *Equality in Law between Men and Women in the European Community* (Louvain-la-Neuve, Presses Universitaires de Louvain, 1987).
2 Case 61/81, *EC Commission* v. *United Kingdom*, [1982] ECR 2061.
3 Case 165/82, *EC Commission* v. *United Kingdom*, [1983] ECR 3431.
4 *Reform of Social Security*, Cmnd. 9517–9520 (1985); *Reform of Social Security: Programme for Action*, Cmnd. 9691 (1985).
5 Some measures have already been introduced in the Employment Acts of 1980 and 1982 and the Trade Union Act of 1984. Further 'deregulatory' measures are envisaged in *Employment: the Challenge for the Nation* Cmnd. 9474 (1985); *Lifting the Burden* Cmnd. 9571 (1985); *Trade Unions and their Members* Cmnd. 95 (1987).
6 For discussion see James, E., 'The role of the European Community in social policy', in C. Jones and J. Stevenson (eds), *The Year Book of Social Policy in Britain 1980–81*, (London, Routledge & Kegan Paul, 1982); Shanks, M., 'The social policy of the European Communities', 14 *Common Market Law Review* 357 (1977).
7 For details of the history see Forman, J., 'The equal pay principle under Community law: a commentary on Article 119 EEC', 1 *Legal Issues of European Integration* 17 (1982); McCrudden, C., 'Comparable worth: a common dilemma', 11 *Yale Journal of International Law* 396 (1986).
8 Case 80/70, *Defrenne* v. *Belgian State*, [1974] ECR 445; Case 43/75, *Defrenne* v. *Sabena SA (No. 2)*, [1976] ECR 455; Case 149/77, *Defrenne* v. *Sabena SA ((No. 3)*, [1978] ECR 1365.
9 OJ 1974 C13/1.
10 Council Directive 75/117/EEC OJ 1975 L45/19.
11 Council Directive 76/207/EEC OJ 1976 L39/40.

12   Council Directive 79/7/EEC OJ 1979 L6/24.

13   Council Directive 86/378/EEC OJ 1986 L225/40.

14   Council Directive 86/378/EEC OJ 1986 225/40.

15   See for example the draft directives on voluntary part-time work (COM (83) 543 Final) and temporary work (OJ 1982 C 128).

16   The British government has frequently used the veto to block new proposals; for example, the draft directive on parental leave (COM (84) 631 Final). For discussion of the future of European Community labour law see Hepple, B., 'The crisis in EEC labour law', 16 *Industrial Law Journal* 77 (1987); Szyszczak, E., 'Responses to vulnerability: the European Community dimension', *Employee Relations*, 41 (1987).

17   *Problems of Social Security – Areas of Common Interest*, COM (86) 410 Final, Brussels, 24 July 1986.

18   For further discussion see Lovenduski, J., *Women in European Politics* (London, Harvester, 1986); Hoskyns, C., 'Women's equality and the European Community', 20 *Feminist Review* 70 (1985) and 'Women, European law and transnational politics', 14 *International Journal of the Sociology of Law* (1986) 299.

19   See Wickham, A., 'Engendering social policy in the EEC', p. 4, 5 (1980); Vallance, E. and Davies, E., *Women of Europe: Women MEPs and Equality Policy* (Cambridge, Cambridge University Press, 1986).

20   *Equality Legislation in a Comparative Perspective – Towards State Feminism* (Copenhagen, Kvinderidenskabelight Forlag, 1983).

21   'Women, European law and transnational politics', *International Journal of the Sociology of Law* 299 (1986) at p. 14.

22   'Women's equality and the European Community', 20 *Feminist Review*, 70 (1985) at p. 72.

23   The literature on how law has operated differently within the public and private spheres, and how it legitimates and maintains such a divide, can be found in O'Donovan, K., *Sexual Divisions in Law* (London, Weidenfeld & Nicolson, 1985); Olsen, F., 'The family and the market: a study of ideology and legal reform', 96 *Harvard Law Review*, 1497 (1983); Polan, D., 'Toward a theory of law and patriarchy', in D. Kairys, (ed.), *The Politics of Law* (New York, Pantheon Books, 1982).

24   *Equal Opportunities for Women – Medium Term Community Programme 1986–1990*, COM (85) 801 Final, Brussels, 19 December 1985 at p. 5.

25   Article 2, Council Directive 79/7/EEC.

26   For details see Atkins, S., 'The EEC Directive on equal treatment in social security benefits', *Journal of Social Welfare Law* 244 (1978–79); 'Social Security Act 1980 and the EEC Directive on equal treatment in social security benefits', *Journal of Social Welfare Law* 16 (1981); O'Donovan, K., 'The impact of entry into the European Community on sex discrimination in British social security law', in J. Adams (ed.), *Essays for Clive Schmitthof* (Abingdon, Professional Books, 1983); Luckhaus, L., 'Social security: the equal treatment reforms', *Journal of Social Welfare Law* 153 (1983).

27   See Equal Opportunities Commission, *Behind Closed Doors* (Manchester, EOC, 1981).

28   Richards, M., 'A study of the non-contributory invalidity pension for married women', *Journal of Social Welfare Law* 66 (1978).

29 COM (83) 793 (Final).
30 'Severe disablement allowance: the old dressed up as new', *Journal of Social Welfare Law* 325 (1986).
31 SI 1984/1303, Regulation 20.
32 Case 384/85, [1987] 3 CMLR 277.
33 This disease results in dizziness when the victim is subject to loud noises. As a result Mrs Borrie-Clarke was forced to give up her school cleaning job in January 1983.
34 [1987] 3 CMLR 767, para. 21–2.
35 See Groves, D. and Finch, J., 'Natural selection: perspectives on entitlement to the Invalid Care Allowance', in J. Finch, and D. Groves (eds), *A Labour of Love: Women, Work and Caring* (London, Routledge & Kegan Paul, 1983).
36 Case 150/85, *Drake* v. *Chief Adjudication Officer*, [1986] 3 CMLR 43. See the discussion by Luckhaus, L., 'Payment for caring: a European solution', *Public Law* 526 (1986).
37 Ibid., para. 22.
38 Ibid., para. 24.
39 For further discussion see Piva, P. and Ingrao, C., 'Women's subjectivity, union power and the problem of work', 16 *Feminist Review*, 51 (1984); O'Donovan, K., *Sexual Divisions in Law* (London, Weidenfeld & Nicolson, 1985) at pp. 160ff.
40 See, for example, Case 163/82, *Re Italian Sex Equality Laws: EC Commission* v. *Italy*, [1984] 3 CMLR 169.
41 Case 184/83, [1984] ECR 3047.
42 Ibid., para. 24.
43 Case 222/84, [1986] 3 CMLR 240. For details of the background to the case see 'Police lose sex bias case', *The Independent*, 10 March 1987.
44 For discussion see Rubenstein, M., 8 *Equal Opportunities Review* 31 (1986).
45 Para. 38.
46 Para. 44.
47 [1981] IRLR 13.
48 Case 170/84, [1986] 2 CMLR 701.
49 *Wright* v. *Olin Corporation*, 697 F. 2d. 1172, 1182–83 (4th Cir. 1982).
50 For discussion see Williams, W., 'Firing the woman to protect the fetus: the reconciliation of fetal protection with equal employment opportunity goals under Title VII', 69 *Georgia Law Journal* 641 (1981); Note, 'Getting beyond discrimination: a regulatory solution to the problem of fetal hazards at the workplace', 95 *Yale Law Journal* 577 (1986). The issue of the scope of protective legislation may be subject to even closer judicial scrutiny in the future as the EC Commission has commenced infringement actions against eight member-states because of their failure to repeal laws on protective legislation. See Centre for Research on European Women Reports, August/September 1987, vol. 7, no. 8/9.
51 'The equal pay directive and United Kingdom law', in C. McCrudden (ed.), *Women, Employment and European Equality Law* (London, Eclipse Publications, 1988).
52 For a fuller discussion of the legal issues see Atkins, S., Luckhaus, L. and Szyszczak, E., 'Pensions and the European Community equality legislation',

in C. McCrudden (ed.), op. cit. note 51; Curtin, D., 'Occupational pension schemes and Article 119 EEC: beyond the fringe?', 24 *Common Market Law Review* 215 (1987).

53   Article 7.
54   At the time of writing the EC Commission is considering a draft Directive covering issues of a flexible retirement age and equality in survivor's pensions and family benefits. See Centre for Research on European Women Reports, August/September (1987) vol. 7, no. 8/9. A proposal has been published OJ C 309/10, 19 November 1987.
55   *Defrenne* v. *Sabena SA (No. 3)* note 8.
56   Case 152/84, [1986] 1 CMLR 688.
57   Case 19/81, [1982] 2 ECR 555.
58   Article 5(1) provides that 'Application of the principle of equal treatment with regard to working conditions, including the conditions governing dismissal, means that men and women shall be guaranteed the same conditions without discrimination on the grounds of sex.'
59   Case 151/84, [1986] IRLR 150.
60   Case 152/84, [1986] ICR 706.
61   Supra note 8.
62   Case 69/80, *Worringham and Humphreys* v. *Lloyds Bank*, [1981] ECR 767; Case 23/83, *Liefting* v. *Directive van het Academish Zienkenhuis*, [1984] ECR 3225. See also the Opinion of Advocate-General Slynn in Cases 75/82 and 117/82, *Razzouk and Beydoun* v. *EC Commission*, [1984] 3 CMLR 470.
63   Case 170/84, *Bilka-Kaufhaus GmbH* v. *Weber von Hartz*, [1986] 2 CMLR 701.
64   Case 192/85 [1988] 1 CMLR 219.
65   For a full discussion of the issues of discrimination in this area see Masson, J., 'Women's pensions', *Journal of Social Welfare Law* 319 (1986).
66   Article 2(4) Directive 76/207/EEC. See Hoskyns, C., supra note 18.
67   OJ 1984 L331/84.
68   Case 43/75, *Defrenne* v. *Sabena (No 2)*, [1976] ECR 445; Case 248/83, *EC Commission* v. *Germany*, [1982] 2 CMLR 588.
69   Case 152/84, *Marshall* v. *South West Hampshire Area Health Authority (Teaching)*, [1986] 1 CMLR 688.
70   See the discussion on p. 204.
71   Supra note 8.
72   Case 126/86, *Fernando Roberto Gimenez Zaera* v. *Instituto Nacional de la Seguridad Social*, unreported.
73   Supra note 18, (1986) at p. 305.
74   Case 129/79, [1980] ECR 1275, discussed in greater detail in chapter 5.
75   See, for example, Article 2, Directive 76/207/EEC.
76   M. Rubenstein, puts forward a case for seeing wage discrimination as an issue of gender discrimination under the Equal Treatment Directive in 'The Equal Treatment Directive and UK Law', in McCrudden, C., op. cit. note 51.
77   The phrase 'levelling down' means to reduce the preferential benefit (or even to abolish it altogether) so that men and women are treated equally, rather than raising women's entitlement to a level comparable with that of a male.
78   Case 71/85, *The Netherlands* v. *Federatie Nederlandse Vakbeweging*, [1987] 3 CMLR 767.

79 Case 286/85, *McDermott and Cotter* v. *Minister for Social Welfare*, [1986] 2 CMLR 607.

80 A report was prepared identifying and seeking to draw up a firm legal definition of indirect discrimination. The report has remained unpublished, and no action has been taken to define the legal concept of indirect discrimination through European Community legislation: Byre, A., *First Report of the Network of Experts Set Up to Monitor the Application of Community Equal Treatment Legislation*, V/1035/84–EN, Brussels (1984). This author has also prepared a report for the Equal Opportunities Commission (*Indirect Discrimination*, Manchester, 1987) setting out the practical and legal problems of the concept.

81 Supra note 8, at para. 18.

82 Case 96/80, [1981] ECR 911.

83 Case 30/85, unreported. Noted in 13 *European Law Review* 52 (1988).

84 Case 96/80, [1981] ECR 911, para. 15.

85 Case 170/84, [1986] 2 CMLR 701, para. 29.

86 Ibid., at paras 36 and 37.

87 Supra note 83.

88 Case 149/77, [1978] ECR 1365, paras 25 and 26.

89 See Schermers, H., 'Human rights in Europe', 6 *Legal Studies*, 170 (1986); Dauses, M., 'The protection of human rights in the Community legal order', *European Law Review* 398 (1985).

90 See for example, Case 20/71, *Sabbatini* v. *European Parliament*, [1972] ECR 345.

91 Supra note 62.

Chapter 8
Enforcement

Enforcement of the equality legislation depends largely on individual complaint. It is for the person who feels that sex was the reason for perceived unequal treatment to take the case to an industrial tribunal or county court. Although the Equal Opportunities Commission has a role in helping tribunal applicants in certain cases, it is primarily for the individual to act. This is a deliberate policy. The legislative history shows that, at the time of the passing of the Equal Pay Act, the Secretary of State, Barbara Castle, was determined to provide individual remedies. Under the then existing anti-discrimination legislation, the Race Relations Act 1968, the individual could not complain directly to a court or tribunal. A complaint had to go to the Race Relations Board, which investigated and 'formed an opinion' as to whether the law had been broken. If that was the conclusion conciliation and settlement were attempted. It was only where these efforts failed that the case went to court, and then only at the initiative of the Board. There was no appeal from the discretionary decision of the Board on legal action.[1]

There was dissatisfaction with this system because of the denial of direct access to legal remedies, because of the inadequacies of settlements accepted by the Board, and because of the discretionary decision on legal action. Mrs Castle decided to provide a right of individual complaint to a court under the Equal Pay Act: 'One of the points on which I insisted was that the law should be easily enforceable by the women themselves.'[2]

There was one major advantage of the system under the Race Relations Act 1968 (which was altered to an individual complaint system in 1976). As Laurence Lustgarten points out, it 'enabled the victim of discrimination to acquire, without cost, the services of the Board's staff, who over the years developed a substantial expertise in tunnelling beneath the surface of denials and pleas of ignorance'.[3] Few applicants have the time, energy, money and legal competence to undertake these types of investigations and negotiations. It seems that some form of compromise between public investigation and individual legal action is necessary for the enforcement of anti-discrimination legislation. This chapter considers whether this has been achieved.

Four of the main criticisms of enforcement procedures are examined. The first criticism is that too great a burden is placed on the individual because of lack of structural support in terms of legal assistance and the class action. The second criticism is that the procedures of tribunals have not lived up to their promises of informality, speed and simplicity. The third criticism is that the Equal Opportunities Commission has failed in its law enforcement role in relation to equal opportunities. The fourth criticism is that the remedies available under the legislation are inadequate and sometimes unenforced. In assessing the validity of these criticisms this chapter analyses possible reforms. In the final section an alternative approach outside the scope of the legislation, that of affirmative action, is examined.

Being a Complainant

The Equal Opportunities Commission receive about 6,000 inquiries a year concerning sex discrimination. This has grown from about 3,000 at the end of the 1970s. Yet the number of applications to tribunals and the County Courts is declining. As Bob Hepple points out:

> In 1976, the first year of operation of the Equal Pay Act there were 1,742 applications to industrial tribunals; by 1981 this had declined to 54 (39 in 1982 and 26 in 1983). Yet in 1981 women were no better off, relative to men, than they were in 1976. Women's hourly earnings were 76.1 per cent of men's in 1981 compared with 76.3 per cent in 1976. There has been a marginal increase in the number of applications to tribunals under the Sex Discrimination Act from 229 in 1977 to 256 in 1981. . . . In view of the overwhelming social survey evidence of continuing occupational segregation of women, . . . these applications obviously represent only the tip of the iceberg. In the County Courts in the five years 1976–80 there were only 34 proceedings under the Sex Discrimination Act.[4]

The disparity between the numbers of inquiries received by the Equal Opportunities Commission and the numbers making a formal complaint under the Acts can be explained in part by normal wastage,[5] and in part by the conciliation process undertaken by the Advisory, Conciliation, and Arbitration Service.[6] However, it seems that a low rate of success and minimal damages serve to discourage applicants from seeking redress at law.[7] There is evidence to suggest that men have used the legislation more successfully than women.[8]

Conciliation is a major method of dealing with complaints of unequal treatment on grounds of sex. Of the 1,742 applications in 1976 under the Equal Pay Act 55 per cent were settled by conciliation or withdrawn. In 1980 there were ninety-one equal pay applications, of which 71 per cent were settled by conciliation or withdrawn. In 1984 of seventy complaints sixty-four resulted in withdrawal or conciliated settlement.[9] However, it should not be concluded that conciliation necessarily means a satisfied applicant. Research by Graham and Lewis identifies dissatisfaction and discouragement because of lack of advice, lack of resources, lack of access to information resulting in a high rate of settlement and withdrawal of cases.[10] For complaints under the Sex Discrimination Act the comparable figures are 243 applications in 1976 of which 51 per cent were settled or withdrawn; 180 applications in 1980 of which 62 per cent were settled or withdrawn; and 310 applications in 1984 of which 61 per cent were settled or withdrawn.[11]

Research by Alice Leonard highlights the low rate of success of those applicants who proceed with their complaint before a tribunal or court. From 1976 to 1983 of 2,147 equal pay claims heard by tribunals only one-fifth were successful; of 717 sex discrimination claims only one-fourth were successful. 'Put differently, under both Acts only about 10% of all applications filed were ultimately upheld by a tribunal', concludes Leonard.[12] There is considerable evidence to show that applicants with legal representation are twice as likely to succeed either in getting a settlement or at tribunal hearing.[13] This leads successful applicants, interviewed in a major study, to recommend to others that they 'obtain informed advice and representation'.[14] Yet many of those who succeeded reported considerable difficulties in obtaining help.

The issue of help to applicants raises other issues. The Royal Commission Report on Legal Services (1979) recognized that representation by a lawyer, or qualified person, makes a considerable difference to the success rate before tribunals. The Report recommended that where legal representation is needed 'legal aid should be available unless legal aid is specifically prohibited by statute'.[15] At present legal aid for representation is not available for tribunal cases. Some preparatory assistance at public expense can be obtained under the legal advice scheme. This is extremely limited because of the cost of a solicitor's time. Empirical studies which have interviewed tribunal applicants report that the Advisory, Conciliation, and Arbitration Service was said to be unhelpful and discouraging. Trade unions will not always assist their members. The overall picture is of frustration because of lack of access to information and bewilderment at the complexity of the law.[16] There is also evidence that legal advisors may not be of much help unless they are experienced in this branch of the law.[17]

The individualization and isolation of applicants which results from the structure of the legislation and British legal procedures has already been discussed in chapter 3. American anti-discrimination law is predicated on the class action which has been significant in the judicial development of Title VII.[18] The class action allows the plaintiff to bring suit on behalf of the members of a class, and common questions of fact or law between the defendant and each member of the class can be determined in one action. Evidence of discrimination against any member of the class is admissible and there are wide powers of discovery. Any member of the class may intervene. If the pattern or practice of alleged discrimination is proved the burden of proof shifts to defendants to show that they did not discriminate unlawfully. Remedies are broad. This leads Bob Hepple to conclude that the class action 'was a general procedural development particularly well-suited to cases of indirect discrimination. The evidence of disproportionate impact "inevitably is evidence that an entire class has suffered from a violation." The substantive development of the judicial doctrine of disparate effect was nurtured in the procedure of the class action.'[19]

By contrast the British approach to enforcement leaves the victim to fight unsupported by other members of the same class. It is true that there is an analogical action in English law – the representative action – but this is vastly inferior, and not available in industrial tribunals. Thus an American concept of equal rights was transplanted into British law, but without the procedural methods by which to cultivate it. The Equal Opportunities Commission has a role under section 75 of the Sex Discrimination Act in assisting applicants. But this is limited to cases which raise questions of principle; or where it is unreasonable, given the complexity of the matter, to expect the applicant to proceed with the case unaided. It is not the Commission's primary role to assist applicants; it does so in a small, but growing, number of cases; it apportions a limited amount of its resources to legal services.[20] Thus complainants are doubly isolated: through lack of a class action and through lack of legal advice and assistance.

Tribunal Procedures

The complainant of discrimination who proceeds to a tribunal hearing still faces difficulties. If accompanied by an experienced legal representative, the chances of success are greater than for the unrepresented. However, procedural complexities and issues of the burden of proof, combined with lack of knowledge or inexperience of legal representatives or tribunal members, may add up to difficulties for all applicants.

Problems of proof and procedure have already been discussed at the end of chapter 3. Solicitors, tribunal chairs and academic writers have expressed doubt as to the suitability of the present tribunal system for the development of the law. There are doubts also as to whether tribunals are designed to cope with the presentation of the complex and novel legal and factual issues often involved in equal pay and discrimination cases.[21] Tribunals were originally intended to be an inexpensive, informal and speedy alternative forum to courts.[22] It was assumed that tribunals would deal with simple matters free from the constraints of lengthy legal procedures; that tribunal members would elicit the facts through informal questioning; that applicants would be put at their ease. [23] But the complexities of anti-discrimination law may be too great for such a forum.

The applicant may feel bewildered and lost in the law. All the empirical studies of discrimination applications confirm the importance of legal advice and assistance, yet legal aid is not available for tribunal cases. The vast majority of cases which go for adjudication are employment-related and therefore heard by tribunals. [24] Other cases relating to education or the provision of goods, facilities and services go to County Courts, or in Scotland to Sheriff Courts. [25] According to the Equal Opportunities Commission very few of the thousands of complaints concerning education and consumer services have reached the County Courts. It seems that complainants are deterred by delays, formality, procedure and cost. [26]

Leonard's study of applicants who won their cases at an industrial tribunal documents the winners' views that legal representation is crucial. Eighty-two per cent were represented by a barrister and/or a solicitor. Of those who received help from their trade union the great majority reported favourably on this. [27] This finding has to be tempered by the fact that these people won their cases, and by the disillusion of those whose trade unions refused to help. The findings of the Advisory, Arbitration and Conciliation Services in Leonard's study and in that of Graham and Lewis were that applicants found the services negative and unhelpful. [28] The general view of the successful applicants on assistance from the Equal Opportunities Commission was positive.

Criticism of the handling of discrimination cases by industrial tribunals is supported by two empirical studies. Leonard, in a detailed analysis of cases heard at tribunal in 1980–2, concluded that there were serious deficiencies, inconsistencies and errors in the handling of discrimination cases. A number of tribunals misunderstood the legislation, were unaware of its provisions or misapplied it. This study particularly identifies the misapplication of the standard of 'reasonableness' and 'fairness' which applies in unfair dismissal cases, to discrimination cases. [29] The standard in discrimination cases is unequal treatment on grounds of sex, or marital status. A study of tribunal decisions on cases of sex discrimination in dismissal from employment also arrives at the conclusion that the wrong standard was often applied by the tribunal. [30] This can be largely explained by inexperience and lack of training of tribunal members. But whether the complexities of indirect discrimination, for example, will ever be easily understood by tribunal members drawn at random from panels of trade unionists and employers may be open to doubt. Furthermore the under-representation of women on tribunal panels may preclude the emergence of women's perspectives. This might seem a trivial matter. But in 1984 women made up 7 per cent of chairs of industrial tribunals and 21 per cent of members. [31] Research on sex discrimination cases suggests that the presence of a woman on the panel increases applicants' chances of success.[32] And the majority of applicants are women.

The Equal Opportunities Commission[33]

The Equal Opportunities Commission is charged with the promotion of equal opportunity for the sexes; in reality this means for women. The Commission has two other duties: to work towards the elimination of discrimination, and to keep the equality legislation under review and submit proposals for amendment. As part of its role in the elimination of discrimination the Commission can advise individuals, assist them under section 75, conduct formal investigations under sections 57–61 and issue a non-discrimination notice under section 67 backed up by the injunction procedure of section 71. Proceedings on a limited range of matters not open to individual complaint, can be initiated in cases of discriminatory practices and advertisements, and instructions to, or pressure on, another person to discriminate.[34] There is also a procedure under section 73 in relation to actions contrary to the employment provisions of the legislation.

Assessment of the success or failure of the Equal Opportunities Commission in its law enforcement capacity must be made in the context of institutional constraints on a public body. The government appoints the Commissioners and funds activities, and although the Commission is theoretically responsible to Parliament through the Annual Report,[35] there is evidence of an uneasy relationship with government.[36] Not only that, but there is also evidence of tension amongst the Commissioners, drawn to represent various interests,[37] and between the Commissioners and management.[38] According to Vera Sacks, this leads to lack of strategic planning and failure on the part of the Commission to evaluate its work.[39]

The advice and assistance that the Commission affords individuals, and its limited nature and quality, has already been discussed. Formal investigations may be initiated by the Commission at its own discretion, or under order of the Secretary of State.[40] This power has been used in relation to the allocation of places to girls in comprehensive schools, equal pay at Electrolux Ltd,[41] appointment and promotion of teachers at two institutions, membership of the Society of Graphical and Allied Trades, equal opportunities in employment of the Leeds Permanent Building Society, of Dan Air Services, and of Barclays Bank; redundancy provisions at British Steel and courses in colleges of further education. There have also been joint reviews of retail credit procedures, and applications for mortgages with the institutions involved.[42]

Critics of the Commission's record on formal investigations argue that there is no evidence of coherent strategy or ability to plan and conduct investigations. A distinction should be drawn between cases appropriate for formal investigation with the sanction of a non-discrimination notice,[43] and cases appropriate for individual complaint with individual remedy. The Commission may find it more effective to provide assistance for the latter, and to reserve the formal investigation to cases involving a large number of victims where an important principle is at stake.[44] To some extent this is analogous to Polonius's advice to Laertes. Appleby and Ellis indict the Commission with poor judgment in the choice of the topic for its first investigation and the methodology applied. This was the investigation into Thameside comprehensive schools' allocation of places to girls. The second investigation into Electrolux Ltd had to be partially discontinued because it proved too large and cumbersome. 'The overall picture of investigations launched reveals no coherent policy as to what might be regarded as key targets in terms of dismantling traditional strongholds of sex discrimination.'[45]

The major sanction that the Commission can apply on conclusion of a formal investigation is to issue a non-discrimination notice to which no penalty is attached, except the threat of an injunction. This can be done after the observance of due procedural safeguards for the respondent. Only once has the Commission used this power – against Electrolux Ltd. This is disappointing, as the Commission's own annual reports testify to the continued widespread discrimination in employment, particularly in recruitment. A commissioned study has revealed that women, and especially mothers of small children, are the subjects of discriminatory treatment in job applications.[46] It is clear that the Commission has an important role in enforcing the law, that it has the legal powers to do so, and that a better use of its legal powers would be a fulfilment of both the letter and the spirit of the legislation.

The Commission could spend more of its budget on legal services. At present only about 5 per cent of the total budget is allocated to this.[47] Therefore neither the assistance and legal representation of applicants to tribunals under section 75, nor the powers under sections 37–40, has been used as extensively as the legislation permits. For example, in 1984 there were more inquiries on advertising than on any other topic, yet the Commission has very rarely litigated in respect of an advertisement.[48]

The internal tensions within the Commission, and the consequent failure to develop a coherent strategy, have already been discussed. There are also problems arising both from the structure of the Sex Discrimination Act and the powers it gives the Commission. These have been increased by judicial interpretation which has imposed stringent conditions for investigations. Thus the terms of reference of a formal investigation must specify the grounds for suspicion of unlawful discrimination which then limit the inquiries, which are also limited by the principles of natural justice.[49] Investigations therefore are confined to the narrow factual issues raised initially, and cannot be broadened even where new evidence is unearthed. The requirement of natural justice has led to delay as the Commission feels obliged to seek respondents' response every time a finding is made.

In *Science Research Council* v. *Nassé* Lord Denning M.R. said of the powers of the Commission that: 'they were immense . . . you might think that we were back in the days of the Inquisition. . . . They demand to see documents made in confidence, and to compel breaches of good faith – which is owed to persons who are not parties to the proceedings at all. You might think that we were back in the days of the General Warrants.'[50] But in fact, as indicated above, the machinery is far from effective, due to a variety of factors, and at a later date Lord Denning described it as 'in danger of grinding to a halt'.[51] The hostility of investigatees who have used delaying tactics and legalistic challenges to investigations has also hampered enforcement.

Remedies

The major remedy available for those who bring an individual action for sex discrimination is an award of damages. There is a consensus amongst those who practise or write in the area of discrimination law that awards of compensation are low. Atkins and Hoggett give the following figures for the cases in which awards of damages for sex discrimination were made by tribunals in 1982. There were seventeen such cases out of a total of 150 complaints to industrial tribunals. Five cases received awards over £1,000; two were between £500 and £750; one was between £300 and £500; three were between £150 and £300; and six were under £49.[52] The figures for thirty-nine cases in the same year settled with the help of the Advisory, Conciliation and Arbitration Service are that all but three were under £1,000 and twenty-four were under £300.[53]

Other remedies, such as forcing the employer to give a job to a woman discriminated against, or to promote a woman who was passed over, are not available. There is a power to make recommendations of action by the respondent/employer. Failure to comply is sanctioned by an increased compensation award subject to a maximum figure. However, this has been the subject of restrictive judicial interpretation. In *Prestcold Ltd* v. *Irvine* the tribunal made a finding of sex discrimination where a woman did not get promoted and a man was brought in over her head. The tribunal recommended that the employers pay her the promoted rate until she received the actual promotion. This was compensation for lost earnings in the future as the employer could not, as a practical matter, promote her immediately. The Court of Appeal held that the tribunal had no power to make such an award.[54] Yet this type of 'front pay' award is well established in American case law as a remedy for precisely this type of case. The reasoning of the Court was that it was not open to the tribunal to make recommendations on wages. That is the province of the Equal Pay Act. Action recommendations concern non-monetary matters. This is an argument for bringing pay and equal opportunities together under one Act. A claim under the Equal Pay Act is limited to two years' back pay. There is a specific financial limit (at present £8,000) under section 65(2) of the Sex Discrimination Act.

Leonard has established that of ninety-nine tribunal awards recorded by the Department of Employment between 1976 and 1983 the median figure was £299.[55] The Departmental statistics show another ninety-three successful applications in these years, and it is likely that these cases were the subject of an action recommendation or a declaration of rights under section 65. These may bring practical benefits to the applicant.

A detailed study of some successful applicants to industrial tribunals shows that only 27 per cent felt that they had been fully compensated by the award of compensation for the discrimination they had suffered.[56] Where the victim had lost her job the monetary amounts were insufficient. There is a ceiling on what the tribunal can award.[57] Awards for injury to feelings were so low as to be described as an insult. The case law on the legislation shows that the courts do not recognize how close the analogy between defamation and discrimination can be. Awards for feelings are kept small.[58] Bringing a tribunal action is stressful. Those particularly affected were women who continued in their jobs while bringing a case against the employer. Where the awards were low it was felt that this would not deter the employer in a future case.

Once an award has been made there are problems of collection. In England and Wales, if the compensation is not paid voluntarily, the applicant has to start new proceedings at the County Court for enforcement. There is evidence from victims of delays in payment of money and of difficulty in collecting the award. In Leonard's study 46 per cent of applicants stated that they had experienced difficulty or delay in getting the employer to pay the award, or to take the action recommended by the tribunal. Of the sixty-one cases detailed, four actually had to go to the County Court for enforcement, with some or no success.[59]

Where there is victimization of those involved in a complaint of sex discrimination section 4(1) makes such victimization unlawful discrimination in itself. The idea is that if conduct in relation to the exposure of unlawful discrimination leads to victimization by the discriminator, then he or she can be the subject of a complaint on grounds of victimization.[60] However, there is little evidence to show that discriminators take this provision seriously, or that it protects those who complain of discrimination. Applicants studied by Leonard most frequently responded that relationships had deteriorated in the workplace. Several left the job because of this; several believed they had been made redundant because of their applications under the legislation. No victim of sex discrimination, successful in her application to a tribunal, felt that her employment situation had improved as a result of bringing the action.[61] Perhaps this is the most telling criticism of the legislation yet made. Nevertheless the great majority of the successful applicants studied stated that bringing the claim had been worthwhile. The major reason for this was 'a matter of principle'. In other words, these victims had values other than personal advancement or financial gain, and they were pleased to see these values upheld by the tribunal, a public body. The principles involved were those of sexual equality and respect for law. There was also a more personal response of the restoration of self-confidence and a more altruistic response of helping other women in a similar position.

Some of the problems of enforcement outlined above are susceptible of solution by changing the law. For example, it should not be necessary to go to the County Courts to enforce the tribunal award. More disturbing, however, is the report by applicants that taking legal action did not improve their work situation. Yet the outcome seems to have had some beneficial effects, in so far as these victims felt vindicated.

Reform of the Law

Four criticisms of enforcement procedures of the equality legislation have been examined in this chapter. These are the burden on the individual complainant, tribunal procedures which are defective, the failure of the Equal Opportunities Commission to enforce the law effectively and the inadequacy of remedies. Various proposals for reform to deal with some of these criticisms have been made. Of these the most wide-ranging proposals have come from the Equal Opportunities Commission. In a consultative document *Legislating for Change* the Commission has proposed a simplification of the complexities of the legislation through consolidation into a single statute under which individuals would be able to complain to tribunals. It is further proposed that the requirements of European law be incorporated.[62] This proposal, if enacted, should simplify matters for applicants. However, without provision for greater legal aid and assistance the unrepresented claimant will continue to be at a disadvantage, unless tribunals are reformed.

Tribunals have not proved to be the flexible, informal, non-legal institution that was hoped for when they were brought in to deal with employment matters. Indeed, the justification for not providing legal aid for tribunal hearings was that the unrepresented claimant would have access to such an informal institution. This hope has not been realized. Research on unfair dismissal cases, including discrimination cases, reveals the weaknesses of industrial tribunals as institutions for safeguarding workers' rights.[63] How does the Equal Opportunities Commission propose to deal with this problem? Tribunals are to become more specialized in discrimination cases, and chairmen are to be given special training.[64] The burden of proof in discrimination cases is to be altered so that, once the applicant has made out a *prima facie* case, a presumption of discrimination will arise requiring the respondent to prove non-sexual or non-victimization grounds for unequal treatment.[65]

In relation to its powers of formal investigation and the issue of a non-discrimination notice the Commission recognizes that the provision in section 58(3A) of the Sex Discrimination Act for pre-investigation representation by the proposed investigatee delays and hampers the investigation. The right under section 67(5) of representation by a person on whom the Commission is minded to serve a non-discrimination notice may also delay the process. It is proposed to repeal these provisions while safeguarding the investigatee's right to answer allegations and to appeal. The content of the non-discrimination notice is to be enlarged to enable the Commission to order changes to the practices or procedures of the person on whom it is served. In addition it is proposed that the Commission be free to by-pass the formal investigation procedure and issue a complaint in an industrial tribunal alleging unlawful discrimination. The object is to create a speedy and simple procedure whereby an authoritative ruling can be obtained on a specific act, practice or procedure. In some cases this would relieve individuals of the responsibility of making their own complaints.[66] The Commission admits that the legislation has not been effective against systemic discrimination – that is, against the effects of practices and systems on a group or class defined by reference to sex or marital status. Indeed, in some indirect discrimination cases tribunals have been concerned to emphasize the individual nature of the finding of discrimination, and to assert that other cases involving the same condition or requirement might produce an entirely different result. Yet the nature of an indirect discrimination claim is that it concerns groups. To counter this it is proposed that tribunals be given the power to make a finding of general discrimination.[67]

On the issue of remedies the Commission recognizes that the present level of awards is too low, and that this reflects a failure to take discrimination seriously. One way of dealing with this would be to increase the maximum awards payable, to specify minimum awards both for a finding of discrimination and for injury to feelings and to incorporate specific guidelines governing compensation into the legislation. In relation to victimization, where there have been few and small awards, the Commission proposes a prescribed minimum substantial level of compensation. Since the enforcement of awards is a major problem, it is also proposed that an enforcement mechanism be introduced to enable tribunals to recover the awards.

These proposals, if enacted, will improve the operation of the equality legislation. However, they represent reforms within the present structure which is taken as satisfactory. It is doubtful whether they meet all the criticisms already outlined. In particular the accessibility of tribunals to claimants without legal representation must be open to question. Furthermore, given the Commission's acceptance that widespread discrimination in employment against women continues to exist,[68] the question of what reformed legislation might achieve remains open. Allied to this is the question whether a more positive approach to discrimination against women could be implemented.

Positive Action

The idea of 'positive' or 'affirmative' action has attracted much attention and some hostility.[69] It is contentious topic. Some of the controversy arises from misunderstanding of what the idea and its practice are about. In the United States the idea of affirmative action, which was written into Title VII of the Civil Rights Act 1964, is used 'to refer to actions taken to identify and replace discriminatory employment practices, and to develop practices which result in the greater inclusion and participation in the work force of women and minorities'.[70] Positive action is the term used in the United Kingdom for a similar idea. Its statutory form is to be found in sections 47 and 48 of the Sex Discrimination Act.[71]

The positive action aspects of the Act are limited to the provision of single-sex training where it can be shown that one sex is under-represented in a certain type of work, or to provide training for those returning to work after a break due to domestic responsibilities. However, although training courses may be held for existing employees which may aid their promotion at work, there is no provision for the positive recruitment of those trained. The Equal Opportunities Commission is opposed to such a policy, believing 'that it is better to adhere to the general principle that all recruitment must be non-discriminatory'.[72] The Commission for Racial Equality, however, favours a greater degree of positive action in the field of employment.[73]

The whole tenor of the equality legislation is to prohibit discrimination on grounds of sex in certain areas of public life. Therefore positive action provisions which permit single-sex activities in relation to employment, or otherwise, are exceptional.[74] Whether or not these positive action provisions should be extended is the question which will now be examined.

The case for positive action is based on dissatisfaction with the equality legislation as a means of achieving the goals it set itself, as discussed in chapter 2. Pessimism about existing methods of tackling sex discrimination leads to a search for alternatives. It is appropriate to examine the case for positive action in a broader context than the existing limited provisions of the law. Before this can be done further definitional clarification must take place. A distinction must be drawn between policies, such as those contained in British law, which reach out to members of a previously under-represented group without giving them preferential treatment, and policies which prefer members of the under-represented group over others.

Opponents of positive policies argue that there is no clear boundary between preferential treatment and action to reach under-represented groups. 'Positive discrimination and positive action lie . . . on a continuum where anodyne positive action merges into "soft" positive discrimination and the latter into "hard" positive discrimination', according to John Edwards.[75] However, Christopher McCrudden, looking at the use of the term 'positive action' in common parlance, distinguishes five different types of action.[76] The first involves identifying and replacing discriminatory practices. In so far as these practices are unlawful such action, through Codes of Practice for example, is a form of law enforcement. The second sense of positive active covers policies which attempt to increase the proportion of the under-represented group through apparently neutral policies, which nevertheless are likely to reach the hitherto under-represented. For example, if it is known that women are more likely to have taken a break from employment than men, then an employment policy which stipulates that the job is open only to returnees from employment breaks is facially neutral. The problem is that such a condition may be held to be indirect discrimination.

The third sense of positive action is the outreach programmes, lawful under sections 47 and 48 of the Sex Discrimination Act. The fourth sense is preferential treatment, where being a woman or a black is an advantage, although not a job-related qualification. Within the idea of preferential treatment there is a broad range of possibilities between making membership of the minority group trumps where the candidates are otherwise equal, and reserving a certain number of places for minorities. The fifth sense is where group membership is a job-related qualification; for example, where being a midwife is reserved for women, which is not the case under the present law. The idea is that, by identifying with the woman in labour, the woman midwife may do a better job.

The object of this review is to show how limited present positive action under the law is. This can be reinforced by reference to empirical studies of practices in employment which, although not obviously discriminatory, are exclusive. In a study of the North Sea oil industry, Moore and Wybrow found that the club-type environment of the male world of geology excluded women, who it was considered would not fit in.

Furthermore the informal network which existed, and which advised others on job vacancies and opportunities, operated to maintain the club.[77] Margaret Curran's study of the retail and clerical job market established that 'personal qualities' were of major importance in the decision to hire. This can lead to sex discrimination, 'since in our society it is extremely difficult to disentangle notions of personality from gender'.[78] This also leads to the segregated workforce that exists at present.

Wider use of policies such as outreach, and the introduction of preferential treatment, could help combat this sort of segregation. But for this to happen the law would have to change to permit broader positive action. Using sex or race as a positive factor in employment decisions in order to make the workforce more representative of society as a whole would have to become lawful. At present this is unlawful under anti-discrimination legislation. Is this the right road to follow? To answer this question we must first consider possible justifications for preferential policies, and the counter-arguments. There are three main arguments in favour. These are compensation, distributive justice and social utility.[79]

Arguments based on compensation are rarely used in relation to sex discrimination, except in so far as individuals are compensated by tribunals or courts for individual acts against them. The idea that women should be preferred to men in the granting of benefits such as jobs or education places, as compensation for the preference for men in the past, has not found general favour. Counter-arguments refer to the penalizing of those who were not responsible for past discrimination,[80] and to the benefiting of those already most privileged in the minority group.[81]

Arguments based on distributive justice refer to inequalities in society which it is proposed to reduce through positive action. The redistribution of benefits such as jobs or education is justified by reference to the needs of minorities. Policies which seek to meet these needs through preference for members of the group rely on the idea of 'special needs'. Thus Lord Scarman argues that 'given the special problems of the ethnic minorities . . . justice requires that special programmes should be adopted in areas of acute deprivation. In this respect, the ethnic minorities can be compared with any other group with special needs, such as the elderly or one-parent families.'[82] However, the counter-argument is that there is an insufficient correlation between need and membership of the beneficiary group to make the latter a proxy for need. In other words, if positive policies are to be directed at need, then the needy should be identified economically and not by race or sex. This is an empirical argument and its proponent concedes that if 'the *relative* position of some ethnic minorities were significantly to worsen as a whole, then positive discrimination might turn out to be the best or most efficient means of meeting their needs'.[83]

The third common justification is based on social utility. This is not a rights-based justification, but rather a felicific calculus, 'the great happiness of the greatest number'. Here preferences 'are not based on the idea that those who are aided are entitled to aid, but only on the strategic hypothesis that helping them is an effective way of attacking a national problem'.[84] This is the sort of language which was used in Parliament to justify the passing of the equality legislation.

Economic arguments concerning the labour market, widening the pool of talent available, and rationalizing structure are based on social utility. But if it can be shown that, for example, a sexually segregated workforce is to the advantage of the national economy, the argument based on rationalization may fail. Other utilitarian arguments refer to the enrichment of society generally through the presence of minorities in decision-making positions; to the provision of role models for young women to whom they can look in planning their own lives;[85] to the inclusion of the under-represented to prevent social disorder.[86]

It has already been argued in chapter 1 that a major motivation for the United Kingdom and European legislation on sex discrimination is the rationalization of the labour market and the promotion of fair competition. It is worth noting that, as women form the majority of the British population, utilitarian arguments have a certain resonance. In this respect, although it is common to include women in arguments referring to 'minorities', the terminology is not strictly correct. Women are a minority in so far as the group referred to constitutes the labour force or full-time workers, but not where the reference is to society as a whole. This may give rise to suspicion where the application of arguments concerning ethnic minorities is carried over to women's position.

Conclusion

It is clear that the equality legislation has not achieved the goals it set itself. This conclusion has been arrived at after a review of the legislation, its structure and the empirical studies that have been made. Some improvements can be made by reform of the legislation. But it is doubtful whether this will have far-reaching effects. It is tempting to conclude that this experiment in social engineering is a failure. This chapter on enforcement must certainly contribute to such a conclusion. It is disappointing to find the legislation so full of defects. Very worrying is the dismal picture painted by those who actually won tribunal cases. Victimization, deterioration in workplace relationships, dismissal or redundancy as a result of bringing a case, or forced departure from the job because the situation was untenable, was the experience of the vast majority. This led in turn to further difficulties when seeking new employment. Not one winner found that success at tribunal hearing had improved her working conditions and prospects. This is indeed an indictment.

There is another way of looking at the achievement of the equality legislation. It is significant that the despondent winners whose personal experience was so disappointing nevertheless viewed their experiences positively. These women would prefer that the legislation continued to exist and be used. Their major reasons related to their expectations of justice and of vindication, to the value they placed on public statements about equality, and to solidarity with other women also victims of discrimination. When we view the legislation in these terms rather a different picture emerges.

The statement contained in anti-discrimination legislation is of symbolic significance to women, notwithstanding its qualifications and limitations. Discriminatory laws, policies, actions and practices can be challenged. Even where it is established that these are lawful a process of explanation and justification is required. This calls for a practical reason for the action or practice, and the reason can in turn be challenged. In other words, practical reason involves dialogue. The dialectical process gives women an opening in which to express their viewpoint, how they see things. The legislation also helps to create a language, a vocabulary in which to express an alternative viewpoint from that which is taken for granted.

It is this opening up of dialogue that is valuable. This is also what we learn when we examine the history of women's challenges through law to their exclusion from the public world in the nineteenth and early twentieth centuries. This is not to claim that the equality legislation is satisfactory, or that a symbolic gesture is sufficient to deal with discrimination and victimization. From what has gone before it is clear that this is not so. This dialogue must be seen as part of a larger dialectical process in which women are reaching out to (re)claim their part of the societies in which they live.

Notes

1 Lustgarten, L., *Legal Control of Racial Discrimination* (London, Macmillan, 1980) ch. 10.
2 Castle B., *The Castle Diaries 1964–1970* (London, Weidenfeld & Nicolson 1984) p. 704.
3 Lustgarten, supra note 1, at p. 190.
4 Hepple, B., 'Judging equal rights', [1983] *Current Legal Problems* 71 at p. 72 (footnotes omitted).
5 The EOC speculates that about 70 per cent of inquiries disappear. In other cases the EOC negotiates for the inquirer and a small number request assistance. The figures for requests are: 1980, 145; 1981, 245; 1982, 236; 1983, 246; 1984, 390. See Sacks, V., 'The Equal Opportunities Commission – ten years on', 49 *Modern Law Review* 560 (1986) at p. 572.
6 See Graham, C. and Lewis, N., *The Role of ACAS Conciliation in Equal Pay and Sex Discrimination Cases* (Manchester, EOC, 1985).

7   Sacks, supra note 5 at p. 573.
8   Hutton, J. 'How the SDA has failed', *Legal Action* (April 1984).
9   'Industrial tribunals – discrimination cases', *Employment Gazette* 52 (February 1986).
10 Graham and Lewis, supra note 6. See also Gregory, J., 'Equal pay and sex discrimination: why women are giving up the fight', 10 *Feminist Review* (February 1982).
11 *Employment Gazette*, supra note 6, at p. 54.
12 Leonard, A., *The First Eight Years* (Manchester, EOC, 1986) p. 5.
13 Leonard, A., *Judging Inequality* (London, The Cobden Trust, 1987).
14 Leonard A., *Pyrrhic Victories: Winning Sex Discrimination and Equal Pay Cases in the Industrial Tribunal, 1980–84* (London, EOC, 1987) p. 50.
15 *Report of the Royal Commission on Legal Services*, Cmnd. 7648 (London, HMSO, 1979) at p. 172.
16 Graham and Lewis, supra note 6. Gregory, supra note 10.
17 Leonard, supra note 13.
18 On the class action see Chayes, A., 'The role of the judge in public law litigation', 89 *Harvard Law Review* 1281 (1976); Pannick, D., *Sex Discrimination Law* (Oxford, Clarendon Press, 1985) pp. 284–300; 'Developments in the law – class actions', 89 *Harvard Law Review* 1318 (1976); 'Antidiscrimination class actions', 88 *Yale Law Journal* 868 (1979); Rutherglen, G., 'Title VII class actions', 47 *University of Chicago Law Review* 688 (1980).
19 Hepple, supra note 4, at p. 77, citing Rutherglen, G., 'Title VII class actions', 47 *University of Chicago Law Review* 688 (1980) at p. 713.
20 Sacks, supra note 5.
21 Hepple, supra note 4; Bindman, G., 'Proving discrimination: the importance of discovery', *Law Society Gazette* (26 March 1980); Lustgarten, L., 'Problems of proof in employment discrimination cases', *Industrial Law Journal* 212 (1977).
22 Report of the Committee on Administrative Tribunals (the Franks Committee), Cmd. 218 (London, HMSO, 1957).
23 See also the speech by the Secretary of State, Mrs Castle, in introducing the Equal Pay Bill in Parliament. Parliamentary Debates, House of Commons, vol. 795, col. 918 (London, HMSO, 1970).
24 Leonard, supra notes 12 and 13.
25 Sex Discrimination Act, s.63.
26 EOC, *Legislating for Change* (1986) para. 4.2.12.
27 Leonard, supra note 14, pp. 9–13.
28 Graham and Lewis, supra note 6.
29 Leonard, note 13, pp. 34–7.
30 Earnshaw, J., *Sex Discrimination and Dismissal: a Review of Recent Case Law* (UMIST, Department of Management Sciences, Occasional Paper No. 8505, 1985).
31 EOC, *Legislating for Change* (1986) para. 4.12.14.
32 Leonard, supra note 13, p. 70.
33 The Sex Discrimination Act, s.53 created the Equal Opportunities Commission. S.54 gives power to the Commission to undertake or assist research and educational activities.

34 Sex Discrimination Act, ss.37–40. If, in the course of formal investigation, the Commission becomes satisfied that there has been an unlawful discriminatory act, or a contravention of ss.37–40, or a breach of an equality clause in an employment contract, the Commission may issue a non-discrimination notice under s.67. For a general account of enforcement machinery see Jowell, J., 'The administrative enforcement of laws against discrimination', [1985] *Public Law* 119.

35 Sex Discrimination Act, s.56 requires the making by the Commission of an annual report to the Secretary of State, who shall lay a copy before Parliament.

36 For example, the Annual Reports published by the EOC are carefully drafted to avoid any direct criticism of government policy.

37 The Trades Union Council and the Confederation of British Industry nominate three Commissioners each. There is a Scottish representative, a Welsh representative, a media representative, a chairperson and three others.

38 Byrne, E. and Lovenduski, J., 'The Equal Opportunities Commission', 2 *Women's Studies International Quarterly* 131 (1978).

39 Sacks, supra note 5, pp. 562–7.

40 For a full account of the background to formal investigation, in the context of racial discrimination, see McCrudden, C., 'Institutional discrimination', 2 *Oxford Journal of Legal Studies* 303 (1982).

41 See *Electrolux Ltd* v. *Hutchinson*, [1977] ICR 252, where the then President of the EAT, Phillips J., suggested that the EOC might intervene because there was a possibility of over 600 equal pay claims to industrial tribunals.

42 See Appleby, G. and Ellis, E., 'Formal investigations: the Commission for Racial Equality and the Equal Opportunities Commission as law enforcement agencies', [1984] *Public Law* 236, on which this section has drawn. See also EOC, *Tenth Annual Report* (Manchester, EOC, 1986) ch. 7.

43 Sex Discrimination Act s.67 requires three procedural safeguards following on a formal investigation. These are: (a) a letter to the respondent giving warning of the Commission's 'mindedness' to issue a notice, specifying the grounds; (b) the offer of the opportunity within a period of 28 days or more of representations; (c) such representations must be taken into account before the notice is issued. The purpose of the notice is to prevent further unlawful acts. See *Commission for Racial Equality* v. *Amari Plastics Ltd*, [1982] 1 QB 1194.

44 Appleby and Ellis, supra note 42.

45 Ibid., at p. 260.

46 Curran, M., *Stereotypes and Selection: Gender and Family in the Recruitment Process* (London, HMSO, 1986).

47 Supra note 42.

48 *EOC* v. *C. M. Robertson and others*, [1980] IRLR 44.

49 Sacks, V. and Maxwell, J., 'Unnatural justice for discriminators', 47 *Modern Law Review* 334 (1984).

50 *Science Research Council* v. *Nassé*, [1979] 1 QB 144 at p. 172.

51 *CRE* v. *Amari Plastics Ltd*, [1982] ICR 304, a case concerned with the comparable powers of the Commission for Racial Equality.

52 Atkins, S. and Hoggett, B., *Women and the Law* (Oxford, Blackwell, 1984) p. 37.

53 Ibid.
54 *Prestcold Ltd* v. *Irvine*, [1981] ICR 777.
55 Leonard, A., *The First Eight Years* (Manchester, EOC, 1986) p. 49.
56 Leonard, supra note 14, pp. 34–7.
57 Two years' back pay in cases under the Equal Pay Act.
58 *Hurley* v. *Mustoe* (No. 2), [1983] ICR 422.
59 Leonard, supra note 14, p. 17.
60 *Cornelius* v. *University College of Swansea*, [1987] IRLR 141 (CA). See also *Chadwick* v. *Lancashire County Council*, EOC Information Leaflet No. 13 (1985).
61 Leonard, supra note 14, pp. 22–5.
62 EOC, supra note 26, paras 2.14 and 2.21.
63 Dickens, L., Jones, M., Weekes, B. and Hart, M., *Dismissed: A Study of Unfair Dismissal and the Industrial Tribunal System* (Oxford, Blackwell, 1985).
64 EOC, supra note 26, paras 4.2.10 and 4.2.15.
65 Ibid., para. 4.2.26.
66 Ibid., paras 4.1.13 to 4.1.17.
67 Ibid., paras 4.2.5 and 4.2.6.
68 EOC, *Tenth Annual Report*, supra note 42, p. 5.
69 See, e.g., *Hughes* v. *London Borough of Hackney*, 8 *Equal Opportunities Review* 27 (1986).
70 McCrudden, C., 'Rethinking positive action', 16 *Industrial Law Journal* 219 [1987] at p. 220. US Executive Order 11, 246 uses the term 'affirmative action' to describe the obligations of a federal government contractor in a situation where minority or women workers are under-represented in the workforce of the contractor.
71 Section 47 of the 1975 Act has been amended by section 4 of the Sex Discrimination Act 1986. Section 48 permits an employer to provide single-sex training for existing employees and for recruits for that training. It is proposed by the EOC that 'training' in sections 47 and 48 be extended to include apprenticeships in the hope of breaking down job segregation.
72 EOC, supra note 26, para. 5.1.7.
73 CRE, *Review of the Race Relations Act 1976: Proposals for Change* (1985) recc. 23(1).
74 Christopher McCrudden is of the opinion that the effect of the amendment of section 47 of the 1975 Act by section 4 of the 1986 Act (supra note 71) is to reduce the potential for positive action. McCrudden, supra note 70, at p. 235.
75 Edwards, J., *Positive Discrimination, Social Justice and Social Policy* (London, Tavistock, 1987) p. 209.
76 McCrudden, supra note 70, pp. 223–5. What follows draws on McCrudden's typology.
77 Moore, R. and Wybrow, P., *Women in the North Sea Oil Industry* (EOC Report, 1984) p. 47.
78 Curran, M., *Stereotypes and Selection: Gender and Family in the Recruitment Process*, EOC Research Series (London, HMSO, 1985) p. 30.
79 Duncan, M. L., 'The future of affirmative action', 17 *Harvard Civil Rights – Civil Liberties Law Review* 503 (1982).

80 Edwards, supra note 75.
81 Radcliffe-Richards, J., *The Sceptical Feminist* (Harmondsworth, Penguin, 1982) p. 239.
82 Scarman Report, *The Brixton Disorders, 10–12 April 1981,* Cmnd. 8427 (London, HMSO, 1981).
83 Edwards, J., supra note 75, p. 200.
84 Dworkin, R., *A Matter of Principle* (Oxford, Clarendon Press, 1985) p. 296.
85 O'Donovan, K., 'Affirmative action', in A. Milne and S. Guest (eds), *Equality and Discrimination – Essays in Freedom and Justice* (Wiesbaden, F. Steiner Verlag, 1985).
86 Scarman Report, supra note 82, p. 135.

Afterword

At the outset of this book varying conceptions of equality were discussed as a framework for the work as a whole. We have seen how the equality legislation is based primarily on a concept of equal opportunity limited to fitting women into work patterns already created by and for men. This is disappointing, because this model of equality cannot accommodate women where they are different from men. However, when the notion of equal opportunity is pushed to encompass the idea of an equal starting point it has greater potential than may have been appreciated hitherto. For it then involves alterations in existing work practices to take account of persons in their existing life patterns.

The concept of indirect discrimination goes further than equal opportunity in looking to the impact of practices and rules. Even where practices are ostensibly neutral they can be held to be unlawful if their impact is inegalitarian between the sexes. Here the law goes beyond formal equality to consider outcome. Thus where a greater proportion of one sex cannot fulfil a requirement this raises suspicion of discrimination. The possibilities of using this concept have not yet been fully realized.

This book shows the conceptions of equality contained in the legislation as limited. There can be no expectation of a transformative effect on society through law. Market-place activities dominate the legislation and its implementation. The Law does not reach into domestic lives, so crucial to women. Courts and tribunals do not always understand the goal articulated in Parliament. Yet the picture is not one of total gloom. There is, within the narrowly drafted provisions, room to broaden scope.

A recent case in the Court of Appeal illustrates this point. A single parent challenged the rules of a pension scheme which made automatic provision for spouses but not for children. The applicant argued that this was sex discriminatory as the majority of single parents are women. A majority of the court held the application to be misguided and the scheme to be lawful. Lord Justice Lawton explained his view as follows:

> The fact that more single women than single men look after dependent children has nothing to do with the pension scheme. It is derived from the way society is organised nowadays. The pension scheme gives married

members better value for their subscriptions than single members, be they male or female.[1]

Yet if the 'posture and condition' of a single mother is taken into account, as required by law, the application has merit, as recognized by the dissenting judge.

What is particularly interesting is the statement concerning 'the ways society is organised nowadays'. The challenge posed by the concept of indirect discrimination is to existing organizational arrangements. Although the court in this case failed to understand the point of the application, nevertheless we see how challenging discrimination law might be to the status quo, if properly understood.

Challenging existing organizational arrangements through anti-discrimination law opens the way for women's voices to speak. It is true that women may have to learn a new language, that of legal claims. This language is embedded within current ways of seeing. It expresses and reflects a particular structure of practices and organizations; perhaps those very institutions which are being challenged. Whether these forms of speech are adequate to convey women's experiences, whether legal institutions can encourage and legitimate them, may be doubted by those who read this book. Yet the attempt to do so can serve in the unmasking of power.

Classical liberalism's belief in equality before the law leads to attacks on inequality. It is for women to raise their voices where their point of view is ignored. Non-recognition of difference, whether it be a difference of perspectives, of life-patterns or of biology, gives legitimacy to an apparent neutrality. But this apparent neutrality advances the dominant and penalizes those who are different. Recognition of difference is not without dangers for the different. It opens the possibility for domination based on the trait of difference. But in such cases it is out in the open, and can be held up as violating the canons of equality before the law, whereas ignoring difference reinforces the dominant. Acknowledgement of difference is a first step to enlarging conceptions of equality to accommodate diversity.

Entering into the language and the world of legal claims implies an acceptance of a particular structure. For this reason some feminists do not wish to be involved. Entering into law can be perceived as legitimating anti-discrimination legislation, with all its limitations. This book has shown how extensive these limitations are. Use of this law can be argued to be another form of accommodation to the power of men. It is a stark choice: participation in a public world in which the discourse and rules are made by and for the dominant group, or relegation to a private world in which the discourse of subordination can take place.

The experience of women who have used anti-discrimination legislation to speak of the unlawful treatment they received because of their womanhood is not encouraging for those who advocate participation.

Yet these women have spoken of a vindication by law of their perspectives on the unequal treatment to which they were subjected. Furthermore their desire to help other women, within their own workplaces and generally, by being test cases, is instructive. This is not a discourse of bureaucracy and legal claims, but of relationships to others. Feminist scholarship has identified concern for others, recognition of our essential connection to one another as human beings, as major elements in women's discourses. The concern for others expressed by women applicants under the equality laws is an example of the introduction of a new discourse placed alongside legal discourse. If this discourse of connection with and concern for others can be further introduced into legal discourse this will create space for women's voices to speak and be heard. It might be possible for the legal vision of persons as separate, isolated, individualistic selves to be displaced by a vision of persons as connected to one another by relationships of care and concern.

Women are not satisfied with their relegation to a private world in which they are subordinated. There are satisfactions and pleasures to be gained in such a world, and these are reflected in a discourse of altruism and care for others. But it is through the merging of the legal discourse with a discourse of care and connectedness that a reconceptualization of relationships can take place. We are caught up in public and private worlds. The decision not to participate in the public world must be made in light of the history of women's exclusion from this world, and the consequences thereof, as explained in chapter 2.

Generations of women have attempted to speak in public. Their voices have rarely been heard because they do not have to be heard. As Simone de Beauvoir explained, men define the world 'from their own point of view, which they confuse with absolute truth'.[2] Equality legislation, despite all its limitations, offers a small opening for the admission of women's points of view. As Kathy Ferguson states so clearly, women's experience in their private world is 'partial and incomplete. It has to be supplemented by an explicit commitment to a public discourse and practice of freedom and equality.'[3] If women are to affect existing conceptions of equality and justice they must participate in public discourse. Altering existing conceptions, structures, discourses and institutions involves the introduction of alternative perspectives, visions and discourses.

For those who do not understand this point about perspectives it can be illustrated by the points of view of women claimants who, although they suffered personal losses in going through an equality claim, nevertheless felt the exercise was worthwhile because it helped others. Seen in traditional legal, adversary, terms these applicants were either winners or losers. In law theirs was an isolated, individualistic experience. But in their language of connectedness with others, their victories, whilst extolling a personal cost, made ways for other women.

Entry into the public realm is necessary for any voice of opposition to the dominant perspective that wishes to speak. There are risks in this strategy, and this path is inherently and seriously limited. But in feminist discourse 'freedom . . . is to be found in relations with others . . . The caretaking values that inform feminist discourse, when not distorted by subordination or rendered partial by a too-great fear of loss, entail caring for others by caring for their freedom.'[4]

Notes

1 *Turner* v. *Labour Party*, [1987] IRLR 101 (CA) at p. 104.
2 de Beauvoir, S., *The Second Sex* (New York, A. A. Knopf, 1952) p. 133.
3 Ferguson, K., *The Feminist Case Against Bureaucracy* (Philadelphia, Temple University Press, 1984) p. 170.
4 Ibid., p. 197.

List of Cases

Ainsworth v. *Glass Tubes and Components Ltd*, [1977] ICR 347; [1977] IRLR 74.
Airfix Footwear Ltd v. *Cope*, [1978] ICR 1210; [1978] IRLR 396; (1978) 13 ITR 513.
Albermarle Paper Co. v. *Moody*, 422 US 404 (1975).
Albion Shipping Agency v. *Arnold*, [1982] ICR 22; 240, [1981] IRLR 525.
Allen v. *Flood*, [1898] AC 1.
Amin v. *Entry Clearance Officer, Bombay*, [1983] 2 AC 818; [1983] 3 WLR 258; [1983] 2 All ER 864.

Barber v. *Guardian Royal Exchange Assurance Group*, [1983] ICR 521; 191 [1983] IRLR 240.
Barker v. *National Coal Board*, [1987] IRLR 451.
Barnes v. *Costle*, 561 F 2d 983 (1977).
Bebb v. *Law Society*, [1914] 1 Ch 286.
Beets-Proper v. *F. Van Lanschot Bankiers NV*, Case 262/84, [1986] ICR 706.
Bhaduria v. *The Governors of Seneca College*, [1980] 105 DLR (3d) 707; [1980] 124 DLR (3d) 203 (on appeal).
Bick v. *Royal West of England Residential School of the Deaf*, [1976] IRLR 326.
Bilka-Kaufhaus GmbH v. *Weber von Hartz*, Case 170/84, [1986] 2 CMLR 701.
Borrie-Clarke v. *Chief Adjudication Officer*, Case 384/85, [1987] 3 CMLR 277.
Boyd Line Ltd v. *Pitts*, [1986] ICR 244; (1986) 83 LS Gaz. 117.
Brennan v. *Dewhurst*, [1984] ICR 52; 137 [1983] IRLR 357.
Brennan v. *Victoria Bank and Trust Company*, 493 F. 2d. 896 (1974).
Bromley and Others v. *H. and J. Quick Ltd*, *The Independent Law Report*, 13 April 1988.
Brown v. *Knowsley Borough Council*, [1986] IRLR 102.
Brown v. *Stockton-on-Tees Borough Council*, [1987] IRLR 230.
Brown and Royle v. *Cearns & Brown Ltd*, 6 *Equal Opportunities Review*, 27 (1986).
Bundy v. *Jackson*, 24 FEP Cases 1155 (1981).
Burton v. *British Railways Board*, Case 19/81, [1982] 2 ECR 555; 367 [1982] QB 1080; [1982] 3 WLR 387; (1982) 126 SJ 480; [1982] 3 All ER 537; [1982] 2 CMLR 136; 241 [1982] IRLR 116.

Capper Pass Ltd v. *Allan*, [1980] ICR 194; [1980] IRLR 236.
Capper Pass Ltd v. *Lawton*, [1977] QB 852; [1977] ICR 83; [1977] 2 WLR 26; [1977] 2 All ER 11.

Chorlton v. *Lings*, (1868) LR 4, CP 374.
City of Los Angeles Dept. of Water and Power v. *Manhart*, 435 US 702 (1978).
Clarke and Powell v. *Eley (IMI Kynoch)*, [1983] ICR 165; [1982] IRLR 482.
Clay Cross (Quarry Services) Ltd v. *Fletcher*, [1979] ICR 1; [1978] 1 WLR 1429.
Commission for Racial Equality v. *Amari Plastics Ltd*, [1982] 1 QB 1194; 424
  [1982] ICR 304; [1982] 2 WLR 972; (1982) 126 SJ 227; [1982] 2 All ER 499.
Conway v. *Queen's University of Belfast*, [1981] IRLR 137.
Corbett v. *Corbett*, [1971] P 83; [1970] 2 WLR 1306.
Cornelius v. *University College of Swansea*, [1987] IRLR 141.
Corning Glass Works v. *Brennan*, 417 US 188 (1974).
Corton House Ltd v. *Skipper*, [1981] ICR 307; [1981] IRLR 78.
County of Washington v. *Gunther*, 25 FEP Cases 1521 (1981).
Coyne v. *Export Credits Guarantee Department*, [1981] IRLR 51.
Craig v. *Boren*, 429 US 190 (1976).
Creagh v. *Speedway Sign Service Ltd*, (1983) unreported.
Cullen v. *Creasey Hotels (Limbury) Ltd*, [1980] IRLR 59; [1980] ICR 236.

Defrenne v. *Belgian State*, Case 80/70, [1974] ECR 445.
Defrenne v. *Sabena SA* (No. 2), Case 43/75, [1976] ECR 455; 259, 382 [1981] 1
  All ER 122.
Defrenne v. *Sabena SA* (No. 3), Case 149/77, [1978] ECR 1365; 378 [1978] 3
  CMLR 312.
Department of the Environment v. *Fox*, [1979] ICR 736; 175 (1979) 123 SJ 404;
  [1980] 1 All ER 58.
De Santis v. *Pacific Telephone and Telegraph Co.*, 608 F. 2d. 325 (1978).
De Souza v. *Automobile Association*, [1986] ICR 514; 149 (1986) 130 SJ 110;
  [1986] IRLR 103.
Dothart v. *Rawlinson*, 433 US 321 (1977).
Dowuona v. *John Lewis plc*, [1987] IRLR 310.
Drake v. *Chief Adjudication Officer*, Case 150/85, [1986] 3 WLR 1005; (1986)
  130 SJ 923; [1986] 3 All ER 65; [1986] 3 CMLR 43.
Dugdale v. *Kraft Foods*, [1977] ICR 48; 304, 308 [1977] 1 WLR 1288; [1977] 1 All
  ER 454.

Eaton Ltd v. *Nuttall*, [1977] ICR 272; 304 [1977] IRLR 71; [1977] 1 WLR 549;
  [1977] 3 All ER 1131.
EC Commission v. *Denmark*, Case 143/83, [1986] 1 CMLR 44.
EC Commission v. *Germany*, Case 248/83, [1982] 2 CMLR 588.
EC Commission v. *United Kingdom*, Case 61/81, [1982] ECR 2061; [1982]
  IRLR 333.
EC Commission v. *United Kingdom*, Case 165/82, [1983] ECR 3431; 382 [1984]
  ICR 192; [1984] IRLR 29; [1984] 1 All ER 353; [1984] 1 CMLR 44.
Electrolux Ltd v. *Hutchinson*, [1977] ICR 252.
England v. *Bromley London Borough Council*, [1978] ICR 1.
Equal Opportunities Commission v. *C. M. Robertson and others*, [1980] IRLR
  44.

Fernando Roberto Gimenez Zaera v. *Instituto Nacional de la Seguridad Social*,
  Case 126/86, unreported, European Court.

Meeks v. *National Union of Agricultural and Allied Workers*, [1976] IRLR 198.
Meritor Savings Bank FSB v. *Vinson* 106, Supreme Court 2399 (1986).
Miller v. *Strathclyde Regional Council*, (1986) unreported.
Ministry of Defence v. *Jeremiah*, [1980] ICR 13; [1980] QB 87; 136 [1979] 3 WLR 857; [1979] 3 All ER 833.
Moberly v. *Commonwealth Hall*, [1977] ICR 791; [1977] IRLR 176.
Muller v. *Oregon*, 208 US 412 (1908).
Murphy and Others v. *Bord Telecom Eireann*, Case 157/86, [1987] 1 CMLR 559.

Nairn v. *University of St Andrews*, [1909] AC 147.
National Coal Board v. *Sherwin*, [1978] ICR 700; 304 [1978] IRLR 122.
Nethermere (St Neots) Ltd v. *Taverna and Gardiner*, [1984] ICR 612; [1984] IRLR 240.
Newstead v. *Department of Transport and HM Treasury*, Case 192/85, [1988] 1 CMLR 219.
Noble v. *David Gold & Sons Ltd* [1980] ICR 543; [1980] IRLR 253.
North East Midlands Co-operative Society v. *Allen*, [1977] IRLR 212.

O'Brien v. *Sim-Chem Ltd*, [1980] ICR 573; 304 [1980] 1 WLR 1011; [1980] 3 All ER 132; [1980] IRLR 373.
Ojutiku v. *Manpower Services Commission*, [1982] ICR 661; [1982] IRLR 418.
O'Kelly v. *Trusthouse Forte plc*, [1984] QB 90; [1983] ICR 728; [1983] 3 WLR 605; [1983] 3 All ER 456; [1983] IRLR 369.
Oliver v. *Malnick* (No. 2), [1984] ICR 458.
Oxford v. *DHSS*, [1977] IRLR 225.

Page v. *Freight Hire (Tank Haulage) Ltd*, [1981] IRLR 13; [1981] ICR 299.
Peake v. *Automotive Products Ltd*, [1978] QB 233; [1977] 3 WLR 853; 134 [1977] ICR 968; [1978] 1 All ER 106.
Perera v. *Civil Service Commission* (No. 2), [1983] ICR 350; [1983] IRLR 166.
Performing Rights Society Ltd v. *Mitchell and Booker Ltd*, [1924] 1 KB 762.
Phillips v. *Martin-Marietta Corporation,* 400 US 542 (1971).
Pickstone and others v. *Freemans plc*, [1987] IRLR 218.
Pinder v. *Friends Provident*, (1985) unreported.
Piva v. *Xerox Corporation*, 654 F. 2d. 591 (1981).
Porcelli v. *Strathclyde Regional Council*, [1986] ICR 564; 244; affirming, [1985] ICR 177; 141 [1984] IRLR 467.
Prestcold Ltd v. *Irvine*, [1981] ICR 777; 425 [1980] ICR 610; [1980] IRLR 267.
Price v. *Civil Service Commission* (No. 2), [1978] IRLR 3.

Quinn v. *Williams Furniture Ltd*, [1981] ICR 328.

R. v. *Central Arbitration Committee, ex parte Hy-Mac*, [1979] IRLR 461.
R. v. *Secretary of State for Education, ex parte Schaffter*, [1987] IRLR 53.
Rainey v. *Greater Glasgow Health Authority*, [1987] IRLR 26.
Raval v. *Department of Health and Social Security*, [1985] ICR 685; [1985] IRLR 370.
Razzouk and Beydoun v. *EC Commission*, Cases 75/82 and 117/82, [1984] 3 CMLR 470.

List of Statutes and Statutory Instruments

Civil Rights Act 1964 (US).
Employment Act 1980.
Employment Act 1982.
Employment Equality Act 1977 (Ireland).
Employment Protection (Consolidation) Act 1978.
Equal Pay Act 1963 (US).
Equal Pay Act 1970.
European Community Council Directives:
   75/117/EEC (Equal Pay)
   76/207/EEC (Equal Treatment)
   79/7/EEC (Social Security)
   86/378/EEC (Occupational Social Security)
   86/613/EEC (Equal Treatment for the Self-employed)

Health and Social Security Act 1984.
Married Women's Property Act 1870.
Pregnancy Discrimination Act 1978 (US).
Race Relations Act 1968.
Race Relations Act 1976.
Representation of the People Act 1867.
Sex Discrimination Act 1975.
Sex Discrimination Act 1986.
Sex Discrimination (Northern Ireland) Order 1976.
Sex Disqualification (Removal) Act 1919.
Social Security Act 1975.
Social Security Benefits Act 1975.
Social Security Act 1980.
Social Security and Housing Benefits Act 1982.
Social Security Act 1986.
Statutory Instruments:
   1975/492
   1978/1340
   1983/1002
   1983/1004
   1983/1794
   1983/1807
   1984/1303
   1986/1960

Supplementary Benefit Act 1976.
Treaty of Rome 1957.
United States Executive Order 11.
Wages Act 1986.

Index